Brandeis
of Boston

Brandeis of Boston

Allon Gal

Harvard University Press
Cambridge, Massachusetts
and London, England 1980

Library of Congress Cataloging in Publication Data

Gal, Allon.
   Brandeis of Boston.

   Bibliography: p.
   Includes index.
   1.   Brandeis, Louis Dembitz, 1856-1941.
2.   Judges — United States — Biography.   I.   Title.
KF8745.B67G33   347'.73'2634 [B]   79-15501
ISBN 0-674-08043-2

To Ben Halpern and Morton Keller—
scholars, teachers, and friends

Preface

LOUIS D. BRANDEIS is hardly a neglected figure. His public
career has been thoroughly covered by Alfred Lief's
comprehensive volume, *Brandeis: The Personal History of an
American Ideal* (1936, 1964), and Alpheus T. Mason's massive
Brandeis: A Free Man's Life (1946). More recently, Melvin
Urofsky's *A Mind of One Piece: Brandeis and American Reform* (1971) and the annotated four volumes of Brandeis's letters (Melvin I. Urofsky and David W. Levy, eds., *Letters of
Louis D. Brandeis*, 1971-1975) have thrown additional light on
Brandeis's personality and public career. Yet the man himself
remains something of an enigma.

Despite his career as a businessman's lawyer, Brandeis became a leader in the movement that sought to shift the empha-
sis of law from individual rights to social realities, a movement
that advocated adaptation of the law to changing social needs.
A milestone in this aspect of his legal career was his *Muller* v.
Oregon brief (1908), which argued convincingly that long
working hours are detrimental to the health and morals of
women. His point of view began a whole new trend in legal
thought.

During the early years of his political life Brandeis was a
typical nineteenth-century liberal. The core of his political
and economic beliefs until the late 1890s was the preservation
of open competition. Free trade, an honest civil service, and a

stable currency seemed to him sufficient to ensure the success of democracy and the maintenance of a free economy. Gradually Brandeis became aware that social and economic justice were not necessarily served by these principles alone, and he turned to Progressivism. Always vigorous in implementing his ideas, he rapidly emerged as a Progressive civic leader—first in Boston, then more broadly in Massachusetts, then nationally. He became a close associate to Robert La Follette and was influential in shaping Woodrow Wilson's economic thinking. He was the source of many of the strategies and slogans that were decisive in electing Wilson to the presidency.

Brandeis's career poses the interesting question of why a successful businessman's lawyer would turn Progressive. Non-Protestant, the son of immigrants, and middle-aged when he joined the Progressive movement, he in no way resembled the stereotype of a Progressive. Nevertheless, he was the only public figure of consequence in Massachusetts to endorse the midwestern Progressive movement.

In explaining Brandeis's political choices, historians have attributed too much to the influence of his family. It is true that he absorbed fundamental values as he was growing up, and individualism and reforming zeal were part of his inheritance. Yet to interpret his growth as merely the result of these family characteristics is to blur the two political phases—the liberal and the Progressive—through which he passed.

Brandeis's ethnic awakening is intriguing also. Not until November 1905—when he was almost fifty years old—did he speak publicly on the subject of Judaism and Jewishness. In 1912-13 he joined the American Zionist movement; before that he had demonstrated virtually no concern for the Jewish community. In 1914, by accepting the chairmanship of the Provisional Executive Committee on Zionist Affairs, he in effect became the leader of American Zionism. His renown as a Zionist later became worldwide.

Why did Brandeis become heavily involved with Jewish affairs so late in life? Why did he associate himself with the most nationalistic expression of his ethnic group? Had he by 1914 developed a coherent concept of Judaism and Zionism that prepared him for this role? The answers to these questions, and the explanation of why Brandeis became a La Follette Progressive, are at the center of this biography. The Progressive and the Zionist in him are closely interwoven. When Brandeis joined the Progressives, he did so partly in reaction to Boston's bitter ethnic cleavages; when he made Zionism his credo, he was already a committed Progressive.

Brandeis was not a person to be moved by abstract theories. The realities of his Boston setting were an essential stimulus to his thinking, and this book examines many of the organizations and persons with whom he associated. Furthermore, since Brandeis was extremely rigid in his beliefs and controlled in his emotions, this biography explores in detail his patterns of behavior and his style of writing. The minutiae are significant. They allow us to penetrate the mask of a taciturn figure and thereby understand his metamorphoses. At the same time they illuminate for us the political and ethnic factors at work in American society during that era.

My interest in Brandeis originally stemmed from a broader concern with the relationship between nationalism and social forces, particularly with the social background of American Zionism. Early discussions with Professor Ben Halpern of Brandeis University led me to reassess the career of Louis Brandeis and suggested new lines of research. Professor Morton Keller, also of Brandeis, was another invaluable guide in my study, as was, in a later stage, Professor Arthur A. Goren of the Hebrew University, Jerusalem.

The cooperation of Lewis N. Dembitz, Charles F. Dunbar, Mrs. Elizabeth Brandeis Raushenbush, Mrs. Charles G. Tachau, and Samuel D. Warren contributed significantly to the development of my research. Insights into the Jewish and Protestant communities of Brandeis's time were provided by Richard Ehrlich, Samuel Markell, Eliott Perkins, Mrs. Abraham E. Pinanski, Lothrop Wakefield, and John M. Whitcomb.

I thank especially the persons interviewed who are mentioned in my list of sources. Others who shared their information with me are Dr. Sidney M. Bergman, Alexander Brin, Mrs. Minna Kirstein Curtiss, Mrs. Herbert Ehrman, Phillip Eisemann, Estelle S. Frankfurter, Mrs. Nathan H. Gordon, the late Louis Gottschalk, Frank L. Kozol, Phillip W. Lown, Mike (Max) Mitchell, Sam Seegal, Samuel L. Slosberg, Richard L. Sloss, Peter W. Solomon, David M. Watchmaker, Mrs. Neiman Whitman, Alexander W. Williams, and Judge Charles E. Wyzansky, Jr. The following scholars have my gratitude for answering more specific questions: Richard M. Abrams, Marjory R. Fenerty, Samuel Haber, Oscar Handlin, Sarah Landau, Arthur Mann, Alpheus T. Mason, Morton Rubin, Nathan C. Shiverick, Barbara M. Solomon, and Melvin I. Urofsky.

Mr. Leonard Kaplan provided access to the archives of Brandeis's law firm, now Nutter, McClennen & Fish of Boston; I should like to thank him and other members of the firm, especially Dennis Baker, Michael Bohnen, George Davis, and Sandy Mank, for their generous help and cooperation.

I am also grateful for the assistance of Edward Baker, in charge of the deposit of the Combined Jewish Philanthropies, Boston; Irit Bar and Yoram Ephrati of the Aaronsohn House Archives, Zikhron Ya'aqov, Israel; Mrs. May Cochrane and Mrs. Muriel Peters of the Dedham Historical Society; Robert Lovett of the Harvard Business School Archives; Darlene Roby of the Louisville Free Public Library, Kentucky Division; and the late Mrs. Pearl W. Von Allman of the University of Louisville Law School Library.

The State University of New York Press has given me permission to quote from the *Letters of Louis D. Brandeis* (ed. Melvin I. Urofsky and David W. Levy, © 1971, 1972, 1973, 1975 by the State University of New York). Part of Chapter 5 was included in my article on Brandeis ("In Search of a New Zion") published in *American Jewish History*, 68, no. 1 (September 1978).

I am indebted to Bonnie Fetterman, Lee Goldstein, and Myrna Pollak for their valuable editorial assistance during various stages of my work.

Financial support for this study came from the Israel Foundation for Cultural Relations with World Jewry (Jerusalem), the Irving and Rose Crown Fellowship Fund, Brandeis University, and the World Zionist Organization through the Zionist History Project. To all these I offer my thanks.

My wife, Snunit, and our children, Shahaf, Peleg, and Keren—each in his own way—have made the completion of this book possible.

Contents

Brandeis
of Boston

1

Brandeis the Liberal

Early Influences

LOUIS DEMBITZ BRANDEIS was born in 1856 to Jewish parents who had immigrated from Bohemia to America in the wake of the 1848 revolution. His father, of an established Prague family, eventually became a prosperous grain merchant in Louisville, Kentucky, where Louis was born. Both Adolph Brandeis and his wife, Frederika Dembitz Brandeis, had been much affected by the 1848 revolution with its demands for political democracy and national liberation, and Louis was no doubt influenced by its spirit as well. He also inherited a strong tradition of family loyalty, and he both admired and loved his parents. (Louis's own wife, Alice Goldmark, was his second cousin, whom he chose to marry on his older brother's birthday).[1]

Brandeis chose the profession practiced by his revered uncle Lewis N. Dembitz, his mother's brother, and even adopted his uncle's surname as his middle name (which was originally David) as a sign of his regard. His Uncle Lewis was to be a major influence in shaping Brandeis's liberal viewpoint. A knowledgeable Louisvillian did not exaggerate when he remarked that "no biography of Brandeis could be complete without a study of this incredible man."[2]

A major figure in Louisville intellectual and political life, Dembitz was the author of several legal works, an authority on Judaism, and a student of philology, mathematics, and astronomy. He was known as a lawyer of strict and uncompromising morality, so strict and uncompromising that it kept not a few clients away from his door. Brandeis much admired his integrity and his wide-ranging intellectual interests. Much later Brandeis was to write, upon the occasion of the presentation of the Dembitz Collection on Palestine and Hebraica to the University of Louisville: "With him, life was unending intellectual ferment . . . He grappled eagerly with the most difficult problems in mathematics and the sciences, in economics, government and politics. In the diversity of his intellectual interests, in his longing to discover truths, in his pleasure in argumentation and the process of thinking, he reminded one of the Athenians."[3]

Louis remained in touch with his uncle even after he left Louisville for Harvard in 1875. Visits by Brandeis to Louisville and by his family and friends to Boston were frequent, and the correspondence between Brandeis and the family was extensive. The extant correspondence between uncle and nephew, covering the years 1881 to 1905, embraced personal matters, common business interests, problems of legal theory, and historical questions. Politics were often discussed, especially when the two men met. Dembitz, a generation older, was more patriarch than equal; his tone remained both authoritarian and somewhat paternalistic to the very end.[4]

Dembitz was one of the few citizens of Louisville to join the Republican party when it was formed in 1856 and to vote for John Charles Fremont, its first presidential candidate. Soon an active Republican, he was a delegate to the National Republican Convention in 1860, enthusiastically supporting the nomination of Abraham Lincoln for the presidency and working hard for his election (he named his second son after Lincoln). He remained a strong political force among Kentucky Republicans until 1884, when he left the party to join the followers of Grover Cleveland in support of free trade, civil service reform, and the gold standard. In that year and in the two subsequent presidential elections, Dembitz voted for Democrats. But by the summer of 1896, the free-silver faction was in control of the Democratic party, and he returned to the Republican fold. Between the two evils of Republican high tariffs and Democratic cheap money, the choice was clear. In his later years, though politically less active, Dembitz did not abandon his principles of the 1890s. Until his death in 1907, Dembitz expounded his political and social views in pages of the *Nation* — then, aside from the *New York Evening Post*, the most conspicuous proponent of civil reform, sound currency, low tariffs, and antiimperialism.[5]

From 1884 to 1888 Dembitz served as assistant city attorney of Louisville, establishing a new city tax-collecting system and authorizing the first Australian ballot law in the United States, a reform that passed, despite bitter opposition, on February 18, 1888. His achievement was duly reported to the readers of the *Nation* and helped Massachusetts reformers to establish the first state Australian ballot in the United States.[6]

The Louisville of the 1870s boasted a thriving intellectual circle, in which the Brandeises participated and Lewis N. Dembitz was a leading figure. Abraham Flexner (who was later important in American medical education) was an active member of this group. In his autobiography he tells of his liberal views and of his "interest in the *Nation*, edited by Edwin A. Godkin, a weekly that . . . [he] continued to regard as gospel as long as Mr. Godkin lived." And he adds: "My enduring interest in politics I ascribe to Mr. Cleveland . . . I rate Cleveland high in the list of our American Presidents . . . No President from that day to this [1940] has been his equal in point of character." Flexner, though ten years younger than Brandeis and politically less sophisticated, may have somewhat buttressed Brandeis's growing liberal convictions. On occasion the Flexners visited the Brandeises, and when Brandeis came to Louisville he sometimes saw them. Brandeis thought very highly of Flexner's educational enterprises, and at times helped him to advance his cause.[7]

Abraham's brother Bernard Flexner, a Louisville lawyer, shared the basic liberal views held by Abraham. When in

Louisville, Brandeis often discussed political issues with his fellow lawyer, and Bernard Flexner came to play a role in forming Brandeis's liberalism.[8]

Brandeis's association with the Taussig family also helped bring him into the ranks of the liberals. William Taussig (1862-1913) was a childhood friend of Adolph Brandeis in Prague, and when Taussig came to America he settled in St. Louis, Missouri, close enough to Louisville for the two to remain close friends. Taussig was a noted physician of Jewish origins, a very capable businessman, and a devoted civic leader. A Republican, he served the cause of the Union during the Civil War; in 1865 Lincoln appointed him a collector of internal revenue. He was active in politics, especially during the 1870s, when he joined with Carl Schurz and others in promoting the Missouri Liberal Republican movement. William Taussig's influence on Brandeis may have been substantial. Brandeis's brother married William Taussig's daughter in 1884, and Louis and Taussig remained on intimate terms thereafter. Visits and correspondence between the two continued until Taussig's death.[9]

The Goldmarks, a Jewish family related to the Brandeises who also immigrated to the United States after the 1848 revolution, were another liberal influence on Brandeis. Joseph Goldmark had been very active in the revolution in Vienna, and, like many of the forty-eighters, was a follower of Carl Schurz in America. In 1891 Brandeis married Alice, the daughter of Joseph and Regina Wehle Goldmark. Alice undoubtedly sustained her husband, but it is doubtful that she influenced his politics—Brandeis continued to oppose women's suffrage until June of 1911. The marriage with Alice brought Brandeis into association with her sister's husband, Felix Adler. Founder of the Ethical Cultural Society, Adler was loosely associated with the liberal trend in American politics. An admirer of Carl Schurz, he at times was active in New York's affairs together with the leading Mugwump, George H. Putnam.[10]

At the Brandeis home in Louisville, the cultural atmosphere

was strongly German. The music, art, and literature enjoyed
were all German, and German was spoken in the home — a cultural loyalty that was especially easy to encourage in Louisville,
where nearly three-fifths of the foreign-born population were
German-speaking. Steeped in this atmosphere, young Brandeis studied the German language and the achievement of German civilization.[11]

After graduating from the German and English Academy of
Louisville in 1872, Louis intended to continue his schooling at
a gymnasium in Vienna, but he failed the entrance examina-
tions. In the end he went anyway and spent the winter taking
private lessons, attending lectures at the university, and enjoy-
ing music and the theater. In the fall of 1873 Louis took ex-
aminations, this time successfully, to enter the Annen-Real-
schule in Dresden, where he later claimed he "learned to
think" and to exercise his mind analytically. Though Brandeis
disliked the authoritarian aspects of German education, his
overall attitude toward his Dresden education remained positive, and he himself remained strongly German in his cultural
orientation. His letters were peppered with German expressions; he was sympathetic to, if not always an admirer of, German contributions to world civilization and to American life,
and he occasionally praised the social and economic achievements of Germany.[12]

When Brandeis entered Harvard Law School in September
1875, he had no ties in Boston; most of his friends were thus
transplanted Kentuckians and men of German background.
Long after he had finished law school, the German connections remained. He joined the German Club and the Turn-
verein, an athletic and social club composed largely of German-Americans, and was for some time a contributor to the
Deutscher Hilfsverein, a German philanthropic organization.
In April 1901 he helped form an organization to found a Germanic museum in Boston, became a life member of the museum association in November 1901, and joined the association's board of directors shortly thereafter. The Germanic
Museum (later renamed the Busch-Reisinger Museum after its
two most prominent patrons) was opened at Harvard in No-

vember 1903; it was intended to be "the center of a systematic and comprehensive study of German artistic and spiritual achievements." Kuno Francke was its curator, Carl Schurz its president.[13]

Brandeis's involvement with the Germanic Museum Association, which extended from its inception until mid-1912, while never intense, was nonetheless a commitment that was not without political and social implications. German-Americans in the nineteenth-century United States had distinctive political views. They were abolitionists, and they were in favor of civil service and party reform, sound money, peace congresses, personal liberty, and independent voting. German-Americans in Boston had more or less adopted all these liberal tenets. Though Ephraim Emerton, who had introduced Brandeis into German circles, did not hold any official position in the Germanic Museum, he was typical of those who were associated with the project. Emerton, a member of the New England Free Trade League, was a characteristic nineteenth-century liberal. His association with Francke, whom he had brought from Germany to Boston, also had its liberal aspect: Francke admired Germans of the school of Henry Villard (the French name was assumed) and Carl Schurz; of the Harvard people he revered William James and Charles Eliot as democrats and antiimperialists. He was closely affiliated with Frank Taussig, a vice president, along with his father, William, of the Germanic Museum Association. Though not all the leading members of the association were of German stock, they shared some basic political views. Henry H. Putnam, the chairman of the Germanic Museum Association's board of directors, was a municipal reformer and a free-trade advocate who vehemently defended (in 1882) Frank Taussig's right to teach economics at Harvard along free-trade principles.[14]

Of the German-American group's spokesmen, Brandeis particularly admired Carl Schurz and the economist Jacob Schoenhof. Schurz—who according to a biographer had by 1870 already "won recognition as the out-standing spokesman of the German-American population of America"—had an early and deep influence on Brandeis's thinking. In a letter to his fiancée in October 1890, Brandeis wrote about this liberal leader: "I am on my way home from the Mass. Reform Club before whom Schurz has spoken on the tariff. And spoken greatly. He affected me, as many times before, and as no other moral teacher ever has."[15]

Jacob Schoenhof, an articulate liberal economist who emigrated from Germany to the United States in 1861, was the economic analyst for the *New York Evening Post*, the nationally known Mugwump newspaper. Brandeis had undoubtedly learned about him in the early 1880s, probably through Frank Taussig, who published work in the same George Putnam series ("Questions of the Day") to which Schoenhof contributed. Brandeis read Schoenhof's publications with care and found them both stimulating and convincing. The two actually considered meeting (in 1902) in Boston, where Carl Schoenhof, Jacob's brother, was a well-known bookseller and importer and an old client of Brandeis; but there is no record that they did meet.[16]

The Harvard Milieu

The Harvard milieu sustained Brandeis's liberal leanings. The university was a seminal source for ideas favoring free trade and sound currency, and opposing jingoism and imperialism. Brandeis's close relations with some of the university's leading educators ensured Harvard's influence upon his thought. Brandeis, who graduated first in his class, remained close to his law school teachers. Of Professor James B. Thayer he wrote in 1890: "He was my best friend among the instructors at the Law School and we have been quite intimate ever since." (Ezra R. Thayer, James's son, was to become a partner of the Brandeis firm in 1896, where he remained until 1900.) James Thayer was an honest and involved citizen. A tariff revisionist, he was later to associate himself with some Boston and national Mugwump publications, and when the contest over James Blaine's nomination broke out in 1884, he joined the bolting Republicans and assumed a leading position among them.[17]

Brandeis was also impressed by Professor James B. Ames.

While a first-year student at Harvard Law School, Brandeis described Ames as a rising light, "a man of the most eminent abilities as instructor, possessing an infallibly logical mind and a thorough knowledge of the Common Law . . . 'He'll make his mark.' " His high opinion did not lessen in later years. Indeed, Brandeis, as founder of the Harvard Law School Association, member of the Committee of the Overseers to visit the Law School, and trustee of the *Harvard Law Review*, worked closely with Ames, who was dean of the Law School from 1895 until his death in 1910.[18]

Though not active in politics, Ames held some strong convictions that associated him intellectually as well as organizationally with Boston's genteel reformers; he joined the anti-Blaine camp in 1884, and from that time on was a loyal member of the pro-Mugwump Massachusetts Reform Club. He unequivocally sided with the low-tariff advocates and was a member of the New England Free Trade League. During the Philippine war Ames was active in opposing McKinley's policies; he headed the antiimperialist "Committee of Fifteen" and undoubtedly encouraged Brandeis to participate. In a letter to Charles Nagel, who married his sister, Fanny, Brandeis wrote that "Prof. Ames, Dean of the Harvard Law School, telephones me that he has written you asking you to become a member of the Committee . . . I think the work which is being done is a very important one, and that you should become a member, as I am . . . Ames has probably written you who the other members are — first rate people all."[19]

Harvard's spirit left its mark on Brandeis through others besides legal scholars. Also on intimate terms with Brandeis was Nathaniel S. Shaler, the eminent professor of geology. He, too, was born in Kentucky and had a sympathy for students who were strangers to exclusive New England. Shaler admired and was attracted to Jews, whom he regarded as talented people persistently striving for self-realization. As a student Brandeis had frequently visited the Shaler home; when he was contemplating the direction his career should take after graduating from law school, Shaler was among those he consulted. Brandeis was both stimulated and impressed by Shaler's ideas, and his notebooks refer to him and occasionally quote him admiringly. Even after he became a Supreme Court justice, he continued to mention Shaler; to Brandeis, Shaler represented the ideal teacher.[20]

In addition to geology, Shaler had competence in other fields, including geography, anthropology, and ethnology, and was a prolific writer on many subjects, such as social and moral philosophy. In an article for the *Dictionary of American Biography*, William James called him a "myriad-minded and multiple-personalitied embodiment of academic and extra-academic matters." From Shaler Brandeis acquired much of his veneration for individualism. Shaler was a lonely Democrat on the Harvard faculty but remained totally detached from the party's organization. It was Cleveland's Democratism, as represented in Massachusetts by Governor William F. Russell, that Shaler approved. In the years following Russell's death in 1896 (of a heart attack) — after trying in vain to halt the ascendancy of Bryan's forces in the Chicago convention — the imperialist issue came to the nation's attention; and Shaler unequivocally opposed policies leading toward annexation of foreign territories.[21]

Frank W. Taussig, the son of William and Adele, enrolled in Harvard College the same year that Brandeis entered law school, and he never left it. Under the sympathetic eye of Charles Franklin Dunbar, who headed the political economy department, he became by 1882 an instructor, in 1886 an assistant professor, and in 1892 a professor. He gained an international reputation as a teacher and scholar, especially in the areas of commercial policy and international trade, and he was a prominent advocate of the gold standard and free trade (except for infant industries). During their years at Harvard, Louis and Frank developed an enduring friendship. In September 1884 Alfred, Louis's brother, married Jennie, Frank's younger sister, and for Louis, kinship with Frank Taussig had important intellectual and ideological implications: Taussig was an important influence in the formation of Brandeis's commitment to free trade and sound money.[22]

The influence Glendower Evans had on Brandeis's political

thought is unknown. That friendship lasted just a few years, from February 1883 to Evans's untimely death in March 1886; but it was intimate while it lasted, and Glendower Evans was a person of deep liberal convictions. During his college years at Harvard, Evans had developed close ties with two giants of liberal Boston: Charles Eliot Norton and William James. He was especially close to James, and the bond endured after Evans finished Harvard Law School. The tie between the young reformer and the Mugwump philosopher was transmitted to Evans's widow; after her husband's death, Elizabeth Evans's relations with William James and his wife remained warm and substantial. Mrs. Evans shared with the Jameses a stern antiimperialism, and together they were active in the Philippine Information Society, with which Brandeis was also associated. In fact it was Mrs. Evans who, having become since her husband's death the closest friend of the Brandeises, had recruited Louis to the movement. Thus thanks to her, Brandeis moved in the circle whose inspiring leader was William James.[23]

The role of Charles W. Eliot in Brandeis's political life was marked. When Ephraim Emerton married in the spring of 1877, Eliot appointed Brandeis as proctor in Harvard College in Emerton's place. Later in that year Brandeis graduated from law school and was chosen by his class to be the commencement orator. According to university rules, a student under twenty-one could not get his degree, and Brandeis was still under that age. Brandeis thus had cause to meet Harvard's president, and Eliot's response — a friendly and explanatory refusal — left Brandeis full of admiration for his efficiency and decency. Five years later Brandeis was to have tangible proof of Eliot's generosity. In 1881 Professor Thayer of the law school was due to go on leave, and at his suggestion Brandeis was invited to give his course on evidence. The leave was postponed, but in March of 1882 Eliot invited Brandeis to give the course in the following year at a high salary. This was a complimentary and generous offer, and Brandeis, not yet twenty-five, accepted it.[24]

Charles Eliot was one of the early leaders of the civil service

reform movement in Massachusetts. He was an active partici-
pant in the political events of 1884 and, as the temporary
chairman of Boston Mugwumps' Committee of One Hundred,
drafted a political platform: according to one account, "It
showed him a confirmed Liberal, distinctly of the Mugwump
stripe . . . It comprised a list of principles . . . these included
integrity in office-holders, merit civil service, lower tariffs and
other taxes, no currency depreciation," and in foreign affairs
"sobriety and candor." For the next two decades, Eliot was
rightly labeled the "king of the Mugwumps."[25]

In the 1880s and the 1890s Eliot and Brandeis were of one
mind on political issues, and there is no doubt who functioned
as the mentor. Correspondence between the two also touched
on some legal questions. They disagreed on trade unionism,
but this did not breach their relations or Brandeis's reverence
for Eliot. Eliot always embodied for him "morals," "good citizenship," and "high ideals."[26]

The Law Firm of Mr. Brandeis

The veteran partners of Brandeis's law firm — the cofounder
as well as the trio associated with Brandeis in the eighties and
after — were men of strong convictions. Brandeis was the head
of the firm, but he also absorbed the values subscribed to by
his earnest colleagues.

Brandeis's original partner was Samuel D. Warren, a friend
from his law school days. The partnership, formed in 1879,
lasted ten years. Warren left the firm in 1889 to enter the
paper-manufacturing business previously run by his father,
who had died the year before. Warren hoped that Brandeis
would enter public life. In a letter in 1891 he praised Brandeis's qualifications and suggested that he consider "whether
or not you will direct your course towards public life. I think
you are fitted for it. This would not mean to seek office or
place, but to command the leisure for public service as opportunity presents."[27]

A self-described independent Democrat, Warren associated
himself on the local level with some of Brandeis's efforts to
achieve honest and effective government. He was a member of

the Massachusetts Civil Service Reform Association and the Massachusetts Reform Club throughout his life. Among those listed in the *Boston Advertiser* as opposing the Blaine-Logan ticket of 1884, we find the name of Brandeis immediately after that of Warren. Together with Brandeis Warren was also a member of the New England Free Trade League. Free trade was an enthusiasm shared by many in the Reform Club; for Samuel Warren, however, it also was connected with the fortunes of the family. The Warrens' paper-manufacturing interests led them to oppose what they considered as artificial obstacles on imports. When in January 1883 young Warren married the daughter of three-term Democratic Senator Thomas F. Bayard of Delaware, a typical nineteenth-century liberal and Grover Cleveland's future secretary of state, the commitment of the paper men to free trade acquired a family dimension as well.[28]

Warren and Brandeis acted as counsel for S. D. Warren and Company from the law firm's beginnings, and after 1889 the two firms shared the same address. The closeness between the firms was also manifested after the elder Warren's death, when Brandeis advised the Warren family on the reorganization of the business. In 1886 Brandeis vehemently fought to exempt raw materials imported for the Warrens' factories from certain duties; and in 1908 he lobbied in Washington on tariff matters on behalf of that family's paper interests.[29]

Fiske Warren, Samuel's younger brother, entered the paper business in 1884 and was a partner in S. D. Warren and Company after his father's death. Like Sam, Fiske was a member of the New England Free Trade League. He was interested in the single-tax movement, and he helped to found several single-tax communities across the country. But most of all, Fiske Warren was a force in the antiimperialist movement: from 1900 to 1918 he served on the executive committee of the Anti-Imperialist League, and from 1903 to 1911 he was director of the American Peace Society. He also helped bring Brandeis to oppose the American policy in the Philippine question. Though it was Elizabeth Evans who recruited Brandeis for the antiimperialist movement, Fiske Warren also played a role.[30]

William H. Dunbar became a member of the firm in 1887, and in 1897 became a partner. Both through his personal characteristics and through his connections, Dunbar had a part in Brandeis's political development. Charles Franklin Dunbar, William's father, headed Harvard's political economy department for about thirty years. Though as a lecturer and a writer (he edited and contributed to the *Quarterly Journal of Economics* and was president of the American Economic Association) Professor Dunbar avoided discussion of current questions, the political implications of his adherence to the English liberal school were evident.[31]

At Harvard, Charles Dunbar—dean of the college faculty from 1876 to 1882 and of the faculty of arts and sciences from 1890 to 1895—assisted Eliot in his educational reforms. In a letter to Mrs. William James written after Dunbar's death, Eliot spoke of the loss to Harvard and to himself: "I was sure of his quality in 1869, and as soon as I became President urged him to take a professorship . . . Ever since 1871 he has been a priceless advisor and friend . . . He was just like a brother to me all through the past twenty-eight years." The son of Brandeis's partner William Dunbar reports that Eliot's friendship included his father as well. "Mr. Eliot was very fond of my father as he had been of my grandfather. The latter was one of his closest friends and one of the few who habitually called him by his first name . . . the family friendship has now reached the fourth generation."[32]

William Dunbar had deep-seated political convictions. By character and belief he was a genteel reformer, and he infused a certain political atmosphere into the law firm. The opportunities to influence Brandeis were numerous since the association between the two was professionally as well as personally close.[33]

A couple of years after William Dunbar joined the firm, his cousin George Read Nutter came on board. Nutter's name first appeared—after about a decade of work with the firm—in 1897 when the partnership officially became Brandeis, Dunbar and Nutter, but in fact from the beginning he was a force second only to Brandeis himself. In a letter to his fiancée on

October 13, 1890, Brandeis observed: "Nutter is very able and is my first lieutenant." Nutter was a graduate of Harvard College and had his law degree from Harvard Law School. One of the top students in the class of 1885, he took a very active role in its affairs. He was one of the original editors of the *Harvard Law Review* and for a while its editor-in-chief. He originated the trust fund for the *Review* and served (for a long time together with Brandeis) as one of its trustees until his death. Nutter was involved in civil service reform and occasionally cooperated with President Eliot, whom he had served as a secretary from 1885 to 1886, in this endeavor. But he much preferred the aloof moral style that the Good Government Association had adopted.[34]

In the spring of 1903, a group of professional and business organizations formed the Good Government Association. Its stated objectives were "first, to arouse in the citizens of Boston a sense of political duty; and second, to aid the voters in a practical way to secure the election of aggressively honest and capable men." Though considered idealistic by many, the organization became a force in Boston's public life. Louis Brandeis supported the GGA from its inception, but both officially and in practical matters Nutter came to be regarded as its leading light. He joined the executive committee in 1904, where he remained for thirty years of energetic service in the cause of rectitude in civic affairs. When this puritanical bachelor (several of whose ancestors were known by the name of Hate-Evil Nutter) joined the law firm, he brought with him a stern attitude toward public morality.[35]

David Blakely Hoar, one year older than Brandeis, joined the firm at about the same time as Nutter and Dunbar, but his name was never included in the firm's title. He was also active in the New England Free Trade League during the 1890s and on its executive committee by 1899. When in 1902 the league went national, changing its name to the American Free Trade League, Hoar continued to serve in the same important position. Probably it was the cause of free trade that led Hoar to help found the Young Men's Democratic Club at the beginning of 1888. The club took stands on many issues, including the maintenance of the civil service laws, and Brandeis joined it in the early nineties. Thus David Hoar may have contributed something to Brandeis's adherence to the principles of Cleveland Democracy.[36]

Brandeis remained aloof from the whims or narrow interests of his clients. Though a corporation lawyer, he differed from the stereotype in two significant ways: "First, he dealt only with the heads of corporations as his personal clients, and never acted as a mere legal employee of a corporation itself . . . In the second place, he treated corporate practice in its broader business context, not merely in terms of legal issues," according to his biographer, Mason.[37] This style allowed Brandeis to work with his clients as an equal on the broader needs and the social consequences of their businesses, and on this two-way street Brandeis was both influencer and influenced.

Brandeis's clientele, despite its variety, had some distinct characteristics and, it seems, certain political tendencies as well. Many of his clients were akin to the Mugwumps, who were, by and large, "the old gentry, the merchants of long standing, the small manufacturers, the established professional men, the civic leaders of an earlier era," according to the historian Richard Hofstadter. "As a rule [they] did not go much beyond tariff reform and sound money—both principles more easily acceptable to a group whose wealth was based more upon mercantile activities and the professions than upon manufacturing and new enterprises."[38]

Businesses of medium and small size predominated among the clients of Brandeis, Dunbar and Nutter. The big clients of course provided much more business than their numbers alone would indicate, but they did not entirely overshadow the medium-sized firms that constituted the bulk of the office's clientele. Brandeis's firm had no business among the industry that dominated the state's economy: the textile business, whose average factory employed more than three hundred wage earners. This was about four times larger than the number employed in the average factory in the boot and shoe industry, which gave to the law firm its largest manufacturing clientele.

In second place among the firm's manufacturing clients was the paper industry. The average paper factory employed not even half the number of people in an average textile factory. Some of the shoe and paper manufacturers who worked with Brandeis, Dunbar and Nutter did have larger concerns, but they were outnumbered by owners of medium-sized and small ones and probably provided less business.[39]

Paper manufacturers were an early and solid clientele. After the mid-nineties the shoe industry dominated. But both were soon matched by the merchants, and it was the merchants that Brandeis himself was closely associated with from the founding of the firm.[40]

Brandeis's association with Boston mercantile circles began when Brandeis came to study at Harvard. Jacob H. Hecht, an established Boston merchant of Hecht Brothers and Company, put up surety for his tuition, and the letter of recommendation that opened the doors of Hecht Brothers to young Brandeis was probably written by Louis's brother, Alfred, who subsidized his studies and was a prominent grain merchant in Kentucky. Financial help was needed because Louis's father's grain business had suffered heavy losses in the postwar depression of the early 1870s; and between the years 1875 and 1878, when he attended Harvard Law School, his father hardly managed to pay his debts.[41]

Immigrants from Germany, the Hechts were noted wholesale dealers in boots and shoes. As a leader of the Boston Jewish community (in 1876 he had become president of the United Hebrew Benevolent Association), Jacob Hecht was a likely recipient for the credentials of the promising Jewish youth from Louisville.[42] The relations between the two were sufficiently close to form the basis of the later business ties between Hecht and Brandeis.

Brandeis had at first been reluctant to enter a partnership with Samuel Warren, because Warren would be able to come to that partnership with a large and solid clientele through his business and social connections. When Brandeis finally did make up his mind to ally himself with Warren, he was determined to collect his own clients as quickly as possible. A Harvard connection, Professor Charles S. Bradley, whose son Brandeis had tutored, was helpful in referring some clients. But far more important was the connection with Hecht; it proved to be the first link in his long and impressive chain of merchant clients. The first case argued by Brandeis before the Massachusetts Supreme Judicial Court was on Hecht's behalf. Hecht's circle included Germans and philo-German Yankees as well as the Jewish community. Jacob Hecht was a member of a great many of those German clubs that Brandeis also so purposefully attended in the eighties; about a decade later Hecht and Brandeis were together on the board of directors of the Germanic Museum Association. Hecht's German-American ties paved the way for Brandeis to recruit more businessmen as clients. Connections with the Jewish community proved to be perhaps even more lucrative, for the German Jews—who dominated it throughout the nineteenth century—were a closely knit group, and a great number of Jewish merchants came to consult Brandeis's firm. Indeed, merchants accounted for about one-third of the firm's clientele.[43]

The firm also belonged to the influential Boston Merchants Association, which until it merged with the Boston Chamber of Commerce in 1909 was the firm's only such business affiliation. Some of Brandeis's early and important merchant clients were active in the organization. When it merged with the Chamber of Commerce, the resulting group remained dominated by merchants during its early years. Of these merchants, Edward A. Filene was closest to Brandeis. When Filene in 1909 became the chairman of the Industrial Relations Committee of the new Chamber of Commerce (and also a member of its executive committee), Brandeis was his right-hand man. George R. Nutter represented the law firm on the membership committee of the Boston Merchants Association; a number of years later he became the president of the new Chamber of Commerce.[44]

The role of Boston's mercantile elements in crystallizing the Mugwumps' advocacy of low tariffs was crucial, and the course

17

favored by these circles included other features of Mugwump-ery as well. No one represented this political mood better than Charles Sumner Hamlin. His father and brother were numbered among Boston's most prominent merchants and were affiliated with the Merchants Association, as was Hamlin himself. His record included the vice presidency of the New England Free Trade League, the presidency of the Massachusetts Reform Club, active membership in the Massachusetts Civil Service Reform Association and the Civil Service League, and membership on the executive committee of the Young Men's Democratic Club of Massachusetts. An avowed Cleveland Democrat, he served in Cleveland's second administration as an assistant secretary of the treasury. Frank W. Taussig also belonged to the association, representing it at monetary conventions and serving on its committee on banking and currency. Both he and Hamlin reflected the twin interest of the mercantile constituency in free trade and the gold standard.[45]

Of the three major groups of Brandeis, Dunbar and Nutter's clientele—manufacturers of paper, manufacturers of shoes, and the merchants—the political climate provided by the last reflected most closely Brandeis's own views as a liberal. The merchant Isaac Kaffenburgh was one of Brandeis's oldest clients, and since I. Kaffenburgh and Sons imported leaf tobacco from abroad, the participation of the company's head in the Free Trade League was natural. Sydney S. Conrad, also a Free Trade League member, was another old client. D. Conrad and Company, which specialized in women's wear, was very successful, and Sydney Conrad consulted Brandeis on every facet and venture of the business.[46]

The wife of William Filene, the founder of his family's retail business in America, was a relative of the Conrads, and Edward A. Filene stood beside Sydney in the camp of the Free Trade League. The presence in this group of three such important clients could only have intensified Brandeis's own opposition to protectionism. Years later, during Wilson's first administration, Brandeis helped try to revise the textile tariffs; in this he relied on the opinion of one M. J. Fox and commended him to the secretary of commerce for his connection with R. H. White Company, "one of our largest department stores," and for his having been "formerly associated with the Filenes." The secretary, an avowed free trader, did indeed rely on Fox's opinion for shaping the administration's revisionist tariff policy.[47]

The law firm's connection with mercantile elements had implications in other areas as well, particularly city government. It was as the representative of the Boston Merchants Association that George Nutter served on the executive committee of the Good Government Association. The role of the BMA in good government affairs was not incidental; the merchant class of Boston lobbied for clean city government. In his history of the GGA, Nutter says that the initiative for its creation came from the then president of the Boston Chamber of Commerce, William H. Lincoln. This public-spirited figure, a prominent Boston shipping merchant, was also a member of the New England Free Trade League. The chairman of the Good Government Association was Laurence Minot of the Real Estate Exchange; Lincoln was the vice chairman. Brandeis's as well as Nutter's activities on behalf of good government were favorably reported in the pages of the Merchants Association's *Bulletin*.[48]

Although the city's merchants had some liberal characteristics, it is doubtful that the paper manufacturers as a group had any definable political stand besides their advocacy of freer trade. But the association of Brandeis with leather and shoe manufacturing clients did contribute in some ways to his liberal beliefs. None of Brandeis's civic-minded leather and shoe clients—such as Charles P. Hall, Charles H. Jones, and William H. McElwain—was active in the Massachusetts Reform Club. Jones associated himself with the club for a few years in a late stage of the club's history but did not belong to any other organization associated with Boston's Mugwumpery. Hall, the leather manufacturer of the trio, was a member of the Massachusetts Civil Service Reform Association. McElwain was the treasurer of the Philippine Information Society but only for part of the short life span of this moderate antiimperialist organization. In two fields, however, shoe manufacturers were in disagreement with standpat forces. The New England Shoe and Leather Association was the only manufacturing organization to belong to the Good Government Association, and in the nineties the Shoe and Leather Association joined some of the New England industries that had begun to demand tariff revision, particularly the free importation of raw materials. In 1897 — despite Brandeis's opposition before the U.S. House of Representatives Committee on Ways and Means — a duty of 15 percent was put on hides. For the New England Shoe and Leather Association, that year marked, according to the industry's trade journal, the beginning of its most "important, far-reaching, persistent and expensive trade campaign," run by Charles H. Jones, who served as its Washington lobbyist. After hides had been put on the free list by the tariff act of 1909, Brandeis congratulated him: "I have been hoping for some days to get a chance to see you and tell you how great an achievement I consider your free hide victory to be. It is about the only 'soul that was saved from the burning.' "[49]

The activities and affiliations of Brandeis's clientele can be evaluated by contrasting them with those of the New England textile industrialists. On the eve of the 1884 election, the Arkwright Club — the political arm of the powerful New England Cotton Manufacturers' Association — issued a militant defense of the cause of protection; to this was attached a pamphlet entitled "How Shall I Vote?" which commended the Republican Blaine-Logan ticket. This protariff stand characterized the political course of the New England textile industrialists for decades to come. The editorials of Boston's *Textile World* (later *Textile World Record*), which reported in detail on political developments and campaigns, consistently supported the policies that Blaine, and later McKinley, advocated.[50]

Another protectionist organization was the Home Market Club, established in 1887 by George Draper, a textile-machine manufacturer of Hopedale, Massachusetts, and an influential member of the New England Cotton Manufacturers' Association, and some of his business acquaintances. The club, together with its monthly *Bulletin* (later called *The Protectionist*), was a staunch advocate of protection, attacking the Boston Merchants Association for its opposition to the Dingley tariff in 1897 — the bill that Brandeis, representing the New England Free Trade League, had strongly opposed before the House Ways and Means Committee. The Boston Chamber of Commerce also was a frequent target. University economists were suspect in the eyes of the *Protectionist*'s sponsors; Harvard's sympathy with free-trade ideas especially annoyed them, and Charles Eliot and Frank Taussig came under attack.[51]

The Home Market Club and mercantile circles disagreed on foreign policy as well. Mercantile elements opposed the Spanish-American War and the annexation of the Philippines; the *Boston Journal*, controlled by the textile manufacturer Eben S. Draper, supported both. This son of the founder of the Home Market Club continued the family textile business with his brothers; all the Drapers remained loyal protectionists. Eben eventually entered politics (he was the governor of Massachusetts from 1909 to 1911); his two brothers served in turn as presidents of the Home Market Club.[52]

Yet another measure of the distance that separated Brandeis from the forces behind the Home Market Club is their stands on monetary policy. Like Brandeis the textile people supported sound money against the cheap money of William Jennings Bryan, as did most Massachusetts businessmen. But the new and small manufacturers (in all industries), while seeking tariff protection, were also looking for a broadening of the money market; and for a time in the nineties the Home Market Club favored bimetallism.[53]

A major segment of the Massachusetts textile industry dealt with the manufacture of woolens and worsteds, and the *Textile World* and the Home Market Club spoke for it as well as for the cotton manufacturers. The *Bulletin* of the National Association of Wool Manufacturers, a quarterly published in Boston, supported Blaine-McKinley's course through the entire period discussed in this book. Brandeis had some legal contacts in the early nineties with the prominent wool and cotton manufacturer William Whitman, but in their discussions they steered shy of politics. Whitman — influential in the National Association of Cotton Manufacturers and especially in the National Association of Wool Manufacturers, of which he was president for many years — explained some years later why: "I do not believe [political discussion] would be possible. Mr. Brandeis and I are on opposite sides of economic questions . . . The manufacturers and mills were what might be called protectionists. I have never known Mr. Brandeis to be such . . . I know very well what Brandeis' views were, because at one time he said to me . . . 'Oh, you could run your factory without any tariff.' That was sufficient to me that he was not sound on the tariff." Whitman was right; Brandeis came out in opposition to the protectionism of the woolen industry. In 1911 and 1912 Brandeis's ally Senator Robert La Follette led the resistance to the wool tariff. He seemed to have won a great victory when in July 1912 he induced Congress to reduce duties on wool and wool manufactures, though President Taft was to veto the measure a few days later. Brandeis, however, wrote to La Follette that he was "delighted to see of your victory on the Wool bill and to know of you again at the old legislative stand."[54]

Brandeis as Mugwump

Brandeis had always been concerned about the problems of corruption in government. He shifted his party alignment to support Grover Cleveland in 1884 principally because he thought government would be corrupt under James Blaine. Cleveland was a hero of sorts for Brandeis; explaining his vote for Taft in 1908, he wrote: "Taft is admirably qualified for the position and doubtless will — if he lives — prove a fine President, rather of the Cleveland type." In later years Cleveland was among the chief executives that Brandeis most highly esteemed (the others were Jefferson, Wilson, and Franklin Roosevelt); Cleveland, he said, was "an honest man, when honest men were rare in American politics."[55]

Brandeis's first struggle for clean government came when he was ten years old. He leveled against the treasurer of a debating society to which he belonged the charge of inaccurate accounting; the amount involved was forty cents. Only after an explanatory interview given by the treasurer did Louis agree to drop the investigation. Brandeis's earliest and keenest political feelings continued to be attuned to efforts to achieve honest and efficient government. In Boston he was active in reform movements in the early 1880s and was elected in 1884 to the executive committee of the Civil Service Reform Association of the Fifth Congressional District. In 1887 he joined the Boston Citizenship Committee, and from at least 1891 on he was a member of the Massachusetts Society for Promoting Good Citizenship. He was a subscriber to the work of the quintessentially Mugwump Massachusetts Civil Service Reform Association and was also a member of the executive committee of the Election Laws League. He also helped to organize the Good Government Association. For years his name was associated with the public drives of the Good Government Association, the major organization in Boston pursuing honest and effective local government.[56]

In 1890 Brandeis donated his legal services to the fight against corrupt lobbying by railroad and liquor interests. His later struggles in Boston had more of a social character but were often substantially involved with the cause of pure and public-spirited government (as, for example, in the struggle against the Boston Elevated Railway Company from 1897 to 1902). In numerous instances Brandeis took an active role in efforts to reform the corrupt conduct of the city's business. The Ballinger affair (1910), the case that was to make Brandeis a national figure, involved a major effort to restore "clean" national government. Brandeis's commitment to the cause of honest and efficient government was the most important aspect of his involvement with Boston Mugwumpery.[57]

In a letter to his father written in 1889, Brandeis praised Henry George. Unfortunately there is no indication of what facet of George's teachings attracted Brandeis. Henry George was, however, an avowed and articulate free trader who in some manner advocated free trade in all his writings. In the next year, following an address by Carl Schurz on the merits of free trade, Brandeis, in a letter to his fiancée, expressed his agreement with it, the first explicit evidence we have of his commitment to the principle. By 1895 at the latest he had joined the New England Free Trade League. Addressing a league meeting, he said:

> This asking for help from the government for everything should be deprecated. It destroys the old and worthy, sturdy principle of American life which existed in the beginning when men succeeded by their own efforts. That is what has led to the evils of the protective tariff and other laws to that end, by which men seek to protect themselves from competition. Never before did I realize the rightfulness of the movement we stand for and to which all must flock if they will save themselves and save American civilization.[58]

After the late 1890s Brandeis became much less vocal on tariff matters, as domestic reform began to absorb his time and energy. He chose to concentrate on defeating the "father" of the trusts — by which he probably meant the large banks — rather than their notorious "mother" — the tariff. Consequently his earlier rather dogmatic rhetoric on behalf of free trade somewhat mellowed during the first decade of the new century, though his attitude remained fundamentally the same. He continued to pay annual dues to the Free Trade League until 1914, when he wrote to its officers: "Now that the League has had part in a great success of tariff reduction, I tender my resignation to take effect at the close of the year."[59]

Concern for lowering tariffs was responsible for the first contact between Brandeis and Woodrow Wilson. It came in the form of a letter Brandeis wrote on August 1, 1912, supporting the Democratic candidate's tariff policies. On the same day Brandeis also wrote an encouraging letter to Wilson's future secretary of commerce, William Cox Redfield, who had gained attention as an ardent advocate of tariff reduction, in which he stated that there was a direct line of descent from his own appearance before the Dingley Committee in 1897 to his present advocacy of Woodrow Wilson's policies.[60]

Brandeis's other favorite cause was sound money. On July 31, 1896, the Gold Democrats issued a manifesto proclaiming their dedication to the preservation of sound money, limited government, and the liberty of the individual — and decrying the Democratic party's abandonment of these principles. Among the signers of this statement was Brandeis, who frequently spoke for the Gold Democrats during the next months of the campaign. He frequently cited as the major authority in the subject Frank Taussig, whose "Silver Situation in the United States" Brandeis considered "a very clear statement of the problems involved" with abandoning the gold standard.[61]

Brandeis continued to oppose Bryan as an advocate of cheap money even after 1896. In 1904, when Bryan lost the Democratic nomination to Alton Parker—a gold advocate—Brandeis supported Parker's campaign. In the next election, when Bryan once again was the candidate, Brandeis gave his vote to Taft.[62]

Brandeis doubted that improved monetary mechanisms would avoid economic recessions. In June 1913, in a two-page letter to President Wilson on the proposed currency legislation he considered in some detail the question of bankers' control and the money trust but devoted only a few lines to currency: "The effect which the enactment of an improved currency law would have in preventing or allaying financial disturbances has, I believe, been greatly exaggerated. The beneficent effect of the best conceivable currency bill will be relatively slight, unless we are able to curb the money trust." Indeed, so deep was Brandeis's faith in the gold standard that he continued to adhere to it even in the face of Keynes's arguments and during depressions; he opposed Franklin D. Roosevelt when he took the country off the gold standard in 1933.[63]

It may be that Brandeis's Mugwump economic views, particularly his strong commitment to gold, led him to prefer conservative bond over speculative stock investments. In 1903 he suggested that his brother not invest in stocks, elaborating on the subject in his typical way: "It seems to me that when men having a business as you and father have are intending to make investment outside of the business, the investments should be gilt-edged, and that safety . . . should be the first consideration." A year later Brandeis strongly argued to his brother: "Father also talked to me about your stock purchases . . . I feel very sure that *unser eins* [people like us] ought not to buy and sell stocks. We don't know much about the business — and beware of people who think they do. Prices of stock[s] are made. — They don't grow; and their fluctuations are not due to natural causes . . . And when you buy, buy the thing which you think is safe — and will give you fair return." Brandeis himself invested his substantial savings solely in railroad, utility, municipal, or government bonds, according to his secretary and to the available documents. When he lent money against notes, he preferred the safest way: mortgages.[64]

Around 1910 nationalism and internationalism began to crop up as matters of profound interest in Brandeis's letters and public statements. Even early in life he had demonstrated an interest in small nations and an admiration for their achievements. On March 20, 1886, he wrote to his brother: "I send by mail De Amicis' 'Holland & Its People' which I thought might refresh the memories of 1873 [when they visited Holland], for you. Doubtless Pa will enjoy the book." In July 1905 he wrote to his father: "There were many, many years of failure before the Dutch were [missing words] for the war of independence." Years later Brandeis spoke in a similar vein — showing great respect for the determination to survive and hardy achievements of Palestine and Denmark.[65]

When in 1899 the United States decided to annex the Philippines, Brandeis had strong reservations; and in the spring of 1900, when he heard Taft's defense of the McKinley administration's course, his opposition crystallized. He became active on behalf of an organization informally called the Committee of Fifteen, which, while claiming not to be "antiimperialist," was distinctly opposed to American policy in the Pacific. The committee was dissolved in favor of the newly formed Philippine Information Society, which undertook to provide reliable information about the islands to the American people. Like the Committee of Fifteen, the Information Society, though not formally antiimperialist, certainly leaned in that direction.[66]

In order to remain nonpartisan, the Information Society dissociated itself from more militant antiimperialist groups. Brandeis for his part turned down an invitation to become a vice president of the New England Anti-Imperialist League. He did, however, subscribe to the journal of the league, and his law firm assisted the representative of the Filipino insurrection movement in the United States.[67]

In December 1903 Erving Winslow, the secretary of the New England Anti-Imperialist League, asked Brandeis to take part in a meeting of protest against the revolt, backed by Theodore Roosevelt, that was to give the United States control of the Panama Canal Zone. Brandeis declined, but his attitude toward Roosevelt's policies was nonetheless critical: "I have been much disappointed in the action of the President in the Panama matters." In July 1905, in a letter to his father, Brandeis once more denounced Roosevelt's actions regarding the Panama question.[68]

Brandeis was an admirer of the Chinese nationalist movement. In a protest against exclusion of the Chinese from the United States, a Chinese boycott of American-made goods was called in 1905. Though the boycott had little effect, Brandeis saw it as a manifestation of the "Eastern mind" and an example of the determination of China to act in its own interest as a nation. It indicated that the Chinese nationalist movement was a persistent one. In a letter to his brother Brandeis emphasized the depth and strength of the movement.[69]

When the Russo-Japanese war broke out in 1904, Brandeis sided with the Japanese because he thought they would help topple Russia's decaying empire. He was so sympathetic to Japan that he had a luncheon with Baron Jutaro Komura, the chief negotiator at the Portsmouth peace treaty conference after Russia's defeat in 1905, during which he promised to visit Japan. Brandeis seemed also to look favorably on the Russian Revolution of 1905, which broke out after Japan's victory. Apparently Brandeis hoped the revolt was the beginning of an independence movement by nations under the yoke of the Russian czar, which he equated with the Netherlands' long-term struggle to gain independence from the Spanish kings.[70]

Typical of Brandeis's attitude to antiimperialistic efforts was his response when asked to join the American Peace Society in April 1909. The invitation was issued by the group's president, the Boston antiimperialist leader Robert T. Paine. Brandeis declined, explaining that he was already fully committed to other public ventures, but offered his "best wishes for the success of your Society's efforts."[71] In his characteristic fashion, Brandeis declined to participate actively in antiimperialist organizations or to take overt political action; but intellectually he consistently upheld the right of nations to achieve their independence, and he detested imperialism and the power politics associated with it. In this, as in most other areas, he was a true Mugwump.

Mugwumpery's tenents were most conspicuously represented in 1904 by Judge Alton B. Parker, who in that year won the Democratic nomination for president. Brandeis devotedly helped him by providing a list of the Massachusetts Reform Club members as the appropriate addressees for a message of wholehearted support to be delivered by Carl Schurz. The Reform Club was surely the most obvious collection of Massachusetts Mugwumps, and Brandeis had associated himself with it from its earliest days, retaining his membership until 1904.[72]

2

From Mugwump
to Progressive

City Divided

BRANDEIS'S political beliefs as well as his legal business
developed in a city deeply divided along ethnic lines. By
the time the Warren and Brandeis firm was founded, the immigrant population of Boston was already in the majority, and
it continued steadily to increase. It represented 64 percent of
the city's population by 1880, 68 percent by 1890, 72 percent
by 1900, and 74 percent by 1910. Many of these immigrants
were, of course, gradually assimilated into American society.
Others, though eventually acculturated, clung tenaciously to
their ethnic roots.[1]

Historians of this period and of this region appropriately
take ethnic politics for granted. The observations of Robert
Woods, the head of the South End House from 1891 until his
death in 1925, and of his settlement-worker associates provide
us with a clear picture of the city's ethnic divisions. By the end
of the nineteenth century, with the introduction of the urban
streetcar, an increasing number of people had moved to the
city's suburbs, immigrants among them. Success or lack of it
largely determined where they lived, but it did not eliminate
ethnic divisions. When Woods and his associate Albert Kennedy of the South End House studied immigrants who had
moved to the suburbs for their book *Zone of Emergence*, which
focused on Roxbury, South Boston, Dorchester, and several
towns across the Charles River, they found that despite Ameri-

canization, ethnic groups that joined the middle class did not necessarily assimilate. They were also impressed by the successful growth of the more ethnically organized communities.[2]

Most of the largest immigrant group, the Irish, arrived in Boston in a relatively short period and consequently found assimilation particularly difficult. Centuries of bitter conflict with the English had strengthened their national feelings, and they retained strong ties with the homeland. "The coherence and isolation of Irish ideas facilitated political organization," writes Oscar Handlin, and he concludes: "Though the Irish acquired [by 1880] a secure place in the community, they remained distinct as a group . . . They never merged with the other elements in the city and consistently retained the characteristics originally segregating them from other Bostonians."[3]

The cohesion of the Irish group and its massive, concentrated arrival in Boston were not the only things that set it apart. The nature of the population it found there also contributed to ethnic division. The term "Yankee" stood for a distinct character and culture that encouraged homogeneity, selfsufficiency and hostility to strangers. The Irish "invasion" only sharpened the insularity of the native Bostonians. As the newcomers managed to take over the city's political machine, the upper class Yankees closed ranks as the financial elite. The enormous number of clubs and institutions they founded at the end of the century represented to some extent an erection of barriers against the newcomers. A historian of the period writes that "the multiplication of charities, of schools, and of other cultural institutions during those decades [1870s and 1880s] was a shrewd and successful rearguard action to substitute financial for political power . . . Boston's clubs [were] the caucus rooms of the city's financial and charitable leaders."[4]

Family connections loomed large in the business practices of the Boston elite. Marriage alliances and business arrangements were closely related; kinship rather than merit emerged as the criterion for commercial success. Brahmin fortunes were increasingly tied up in family trusts, which have been described as devices designed "to protect status continuity over the generations by prohibiting heirs from touching the principal of their legacy. The management of family fortunes was given to trusted, blueblood lawyers and bankers." Thus the natural conservatism of Massachusetts capitalists was encouraged by the changes in the city's racial and political balance; the upper class of Boston was transformed into a business aristocracy.[5]

Whereas the social and financial reorganization of the Boston Yankees had its antiimmigrant motive, the founding of the Immigration Restriction League of Boston had no other. The league, established in 1894, began modestly enough, alerting people to the dangers of unrestricted immigration but admitting that immigrants of suitable morals and character posed no threat. In its next dozen years, however, the league deepened the ethnic cleavage in Boston with the racial overtones of its polemics.[6]

The strife between Boston's Yankees and its Irish affected other groups within the city. "No man," writes Oscar Handlin, could now "think of his place in society simply in terms of occupation or income level. It was necessary also ever to consider ethnic affiliation." This reality led the local Jewish community to develop unity and to assume increased responsibility for solving its own problems. In 1895 the first Jewish federation in the history of American Jewry, the Federation of Jewish Charities, was founded in Boston.[7]

The existence of anti-Semitism in Boston only partially encouraged this trend toward self-sufficiency. In New England contradictory elements contributed to the image of the Jew: on the one hand, there was the traditional Puritan veneration of the Bible and the "chosen people" of the Bible; on the other was the attitude of the Boston Brahmins, who felt themselves threatened by new fortunes and immigrant hordes. By 1912, but generally not earlier, the anti-Jewish influences had won. But even much before this time, the social reorganization of Boston had affected the Jews' place in Boston society. The barrier of Brahmin social facilities, completed during the 1880s and erected mainly against the Irish, served also to exclude the Jews; *en passant*, they, too, became outsiders.[8]

Although the elite of Boston's Jewry, largely of German origin, were eager to be Americanized, for most of them this in no sense meant assimilation. It is true that they went far in rejecting traditional customs and in diluting the Jewish nationalist component of their beliefs, as well as being by and large Reform-oriented. They did not, however, regard these changes as a means to assimilation, but mainly as a way of adjusting Jewish traditions to life in America. German Jews shared interests and communal responsibilities and moved in the same circles, a social cohesion soon institutionalized in the Elysium Club, a Jewish answer to Brahmin exclusivity. Here Jews could be themselves, gossip, and talk business. Like the Brahmins, the bulk of the Boston German-Jewish families were related through marriage, and these ties added to the unity of the closely knit subcommunity.[9]

Although the German Jews dominated the Boston Jewish community, they by no means monopolized it. The East European element had an early and growing role in community affairs. In other parts of the country (notably New York and Philadelphia), the East Europeans, who had arrived en masse since the early 1880s, constituted — vis-à-vis the older German element — a separate and inferior subcommunity, but the case of Boston was different. Immigrants from East Europe had begun arriving in Boston as early as the 1840s (roughly when the German "pioneers" arrived), and they also had had their successes in business and the professions. Many had contributed to the United Hebrew Benevolent Association, a predecessor of the Federation of Jewish Charities. When the federation itself was formed in 1895, one of its five first constituents was an East European immigrant agency. The growing voice of the East Europeans in community policies was again heard in 1908 with the reorganization of the federation under the new name of Federated Jewish Charities. An East European, Max Mitchell, played a central role from 1899 on in the work of the federation and its successor. Socially, the Germans and the East Europeans achieved some rapprochement. Acquaintances, friendships, and marriages between them were not unknown, although to be sure the two groups were never fully integrated. Nevertheless cooperation increased, no doubt stimulated by the realities both outside and within the Jewish community: ethnic barriers, and the East Europeans' early and constant progress up the socioeconomic ladder. The histories of the New Century Club and of the Mt. Sinai Dispensary (later Beth Israel Hospital) reflect this trend. [10]

On January 1, 1900, thirteen men met in a little restaurant in Boston at the behest of Jacob J. Silverman, a newly minted lawyer from Boston University. The meeting was attended by former members of a law club at the Boston University Law School called The Century, together with about half a dozen physicians and several miscellaneous quasi-professionals. By the evening's end the New Century Club was born. It was first of all a *Jewish* club; its raison d'être was the desire of Boston Jewish professionals to share a social life and talk about Jewish subjects. "One god, one race, one victory / From fate; this is our unity," was how William M. Blatt, poet and cofounder of the club, would soon phrase it. [11]

The emergence of a social club for Jewish professionals reflected an ethnic division within Boston to which lawyers were especially sensitive. Their very livelihood depended upon a trusting clientele that expected understanding of its special problems. Attorneys were thus largely confined within ethnic barriers. The average Jewish lawyer relied mainly on coreligionists for his business. The idea of forming a club for Jewish lawyers was consequently a favorite topic of conversation in Jewish legal circles in the city. It is small wonder that we find Silverman and Blatt establishing a framework within which their ethnic identity, social bent, and common concerns could be expressed. [12]

The New Century Club was also indicative of the early and impressive progress of the East Europeans in Boston. Jacob Silverman was the son of a Russian Jew; William Blatt was only one generation removed from Eastern Europe. The New Century Club soon also included increasing numbers of German-Jewish professionals and gradually became a tiny Jewish melting pot. Its main impetus, however, continued to be the rising East Europeans. [13]

Most of the doctors among the original founders of the New Century Club were also associated with the establishment of a Jewish hospital in Boston, as were some of the lawyers, including Jacob Silverman. Mt. Sinai Hospital was founded in 1901 and opened the following year; its leadership was instrumental in the establishment of Beth Israel Hospital a little over a decade later. The Federation of Jewish Charities supported the effort and also served to unite the new immigrants with the established Jewish community. But the main force behind this endeavor was and continued to be the East Europeans.[14]

"An Outsider, Successful, and a Jew"

Brandeis's career at Harvard was first supported by Jacob H. Hecht, the president of the United Hebrew Benevolent Association, a major philanthropic and communal Jewish institution in Boston, run by German Jews. The young Jewish student from Louisville was often seen at the Sunday open house that Jacob and Lina Hecht held at their home on Commonwealth Avenue, a salon run by Mrs. Hecht for intellectuals and artists. Devout, high-minded, and childless, she ran a proper Jewish household, which meant inviting mostly Jewish guests to her home. These weekly gatherings no doubt extended Brandeis's circle of acquaintances in the Jewish community and perhaps also increased his sense of Jewishness.[15]

Brandeis's upbringing made it possible for him to blend into Boston's Jewish establishment, but it was the Hechts who firmly ensconced him in the proper Jewish circles. This connection with the Jewish establishment was to extend into Brandeis's later life. When he came back to Boston in 1879, he undoubtedly subscribed to the United Hebrew Benevolent Association. He was among the charter subscribers when the Federation of Jewish Charities was founded in 1895, and he continued to pay annual dues without interruption.[16]

While he was still a student at Harvard Law School, Brandeis's friendships were formed primarily with fellow Kentuckians (Nathaniel S. Shaler was prominent among them) and with Bostonian enthusiasts of German culture (the Emertons, for example). None of these associations helped him to make inroads into Boston society. Nor did his friendship with Lorin F. Deland and his wife, Margaret, outlanders from Pennsylvania, or with his former classmate Walter Bond Douglas, a Missourian, with whom he roomed at 13 Avon Street (and who later started a practice in St. Louis).[17]

One friend who might have helped was Samuel D. Warren, an assured member of Boston society. A Harvard graduate, he had belonged to the Hasty Pudding Club and the Institute of 1770, the prestigious Porcellian Club, and the prominent St. Paul's Society; combined with his background, these achievements gave Warren entrée in Boston. Brandeis, a Southerner and a Jew, lacked even that most basic requirement of membership in the city's establishment — graduation from Harvard College. Because social connections were apt to be a precondition for success as a lawyer, Brandeis thus possessed a genuine handicap. (At the point of graduating from law school, Brandeis was probably loath to use his connection with Warren to establish himself in Boston.) That was why he at first decided to seek his fortune elsewhere.[18]

When he graduated from Harvard Law School, Brandeis left Boston and in the summer of 1877 read law in the Louisville office of his prospective brother-in-law, Otto Wehle, leaving his friend Samuel Warren behind to read law in the Boston firm of Shattuck, Holmes and Munroe. That summer Brandeis no doubt discussed the issue of his future with his parents, his brother Alfred, his sister Amy (who married Otto Wehle in August of that year), and his uncle Lewis Dembitz, without any clear results. In any case, he returned to Cambridge in the fall but passed the year 1877-78 aimlessly. He began graduate study at Harvard but did not work at it very seriously. Instead he concentrated on improving his finances. As a proctor and tutor at Harvard College, he earned enough to repay some money he owned his brother and to save over a thousand dollars, but the work involved was neither scholarly nor good practical experience for a would-be lawyer, and it could not result in any offers of a job. Again he looked south.[19]

His attention was attracted to St. Louis, where the Taussigs and his brother-in-law Charles Nagel lived. In July 1878 there was an opening in the office of James Taussig, and Brandeis decided to accept it. He may have chosen this course under the influence of his friend and classmate Walter Bond, who had been practicing in St. Louis since February, but the depressed business situation in St. Louis, of which Brandeis was aware, suggests the case was more one of his being unsuccessful in Boston than of his being attracted by St. Louis.[20]

Brandeis arrived in St. Louis in November. By April 1879 he was already confirming that indeed "litigation and legal business is very much depressed here. Everybody complains and most with reason. Even in our office business is poor. A host of old cases, dating from better times, alone serves to keep us occupied."[21]

When Brandeis returned to Boston it was in response to Samuel Warren's call to found a partnership; his connections with Boston Yankee society were and remained fragile. Warren did introduce his friend to Oliver Wendell Holmes, Jr., but this meeting did not develop into a social relationship. Invitations from the Holmeses to Brandeis occurred rarely and were limited to his early years in Boston. He was also once invited to a Fourth of July gathering on Lake Champion as a guest of Henry Lee Higginson. None of these occasions represented acceptance into Brahmin society. Brandeis was, of course, close to the Warren family itself, but even this relationship had its bounds and cooled after Samuel Warren's marriage in 1883: Brandeis was not among the hundred guests invited to the wedding. Since in those days the lady of the house tended to dictate social relations as the guardian of the family's reputation and its pedigree, his absence from the list was ominous. Indeed Warren's wife, Mabel, the daughter of Senator Thomas Bayard, Sr., did not look favorably upon the friendship of her husband with Brandeis and tried to discourage it by omitting him from her guest list whenever she could.[22]

When Brandeis himself married, the ceremony took place in New York as a strictly family affair. Some calls and presents did arrive from leading families in Boston. But the fact that

Brandeis had married a Jewish woman with a conspicuously Jewish name did not help him socially. Brandeis's wife never exchanged visiting cards with his prominent Yankee clients. His clients and friends among the Brahmins did not invite his family to social gatherings. Asked about the Yankee friends of the family in Boston, Brandeis's daughter Elizabeth gives a very short account:

> The closest friend was Mrs. Elizabeth Glendower Evans for whom I was named. Her husband had died very young. She lived at 12 Otis Place. We moved to 6 Otis Place in about 1900. She was at our house a great deal. Other good friends were Lorin and Margaret Deland. She was a writer of novels. He was in some kind of business. A friend with a small cruising yacht was Herbert H. White. Before he was married, my father went camping and cruising with Mr. White. Later my parents may both have gone cruising with him.[23]

Actually none of this circle served to buttress Brandeis's place in society. Mrs. Evans, indeed a Proper Bostonian, had however led a tragic life. Her architect father died when she was young, and she and her mother lived for some years as the paternal grandparents' unfortunate relatives, until with the help of an inheritance she established an independent life. She married a Philadelphian like her mother, but he died when she was thirty. These "irregularities" in Mrs. Evans's life made her own place in Boston society rather uncertain. The Delands, strangers in Boston and rejecters of normative Christianity, were by no means in a position to bolster Brandeis's social status. Nor was Herbert White, a client and playboy about fifteen years younger than Brandeis.[24]

Sponsored by Samuel Warren, Brandeis was admitted to the socially prominent Dedham Polo Club in 1887 and, again following Warren, bought a country house in Dedham in 1900. But neither his country house nor his membership in the Polo Club contributed much to his social standing. His daughter Elizabeth reports: "Sam Warren had a place in Dedham. I don't know of any other special Dedham friends. What I chiefly remember about Dedham were our family activities there — the walks my sister and I took with my father and our frequent canoeing on the Charles River. These doings were on Sunday." The picture drawn by Susan, Brandeis's oldest daughter, also suggests the lack of any real involvement in society: "The social life of my parents in Dedham, I am ashamed to say, I remember little about . . . Weekends (Saturday evenings and Sunday mornings) were spent at this house [of the family] a great deal from 1905 and 1912, for the whole winter." The memories of senior citizens of Dedham corroborate those of the daughters of Brandeis: they recall hardly any intercourse between the Brandeis family and anyone from the town. Brandeis was on very good terms with the charming Mrs. Elizabeth A. Wakefield and the genial Herbert Maynard, but it is doubtful that the relationship included any of the families. Knowledgeable Dedham people readily explain the social isolation of the Brandeises: the town was small and the Yankee community close-knit; outsiders, any outsiders, were unwelcome, but the Brandeis family, Southern and non-Christian, were particularly so (even Alice Brandeis's accent worked against her). As the only Jewish family of consequence in Dedham, the Brandeises were respected by some as the descendants of the "people of the Book." But others, perhaps the majority, saw them as intruders. Virtually none of Yankee Dedham would consider them as candidates for friendship, not to mention marriage.[25]

Brandeis's membership in the Dedham Polo Club did not help, although there was no apparent reason why it should not have. Samuel Warren was the club's founder and president, and Brandeis loved to ride; but Brandeis seems not to have participated in club affairs, and as time passed the situation became more, not less, acute. Brandeis's family had little to do with the club. His daughter Susan (born in February 1893), remembers "Karlstein [the club's field] as we of course went there from time to time," but Elizabeth, the younger daughter (born in April 1896), recalls neither the club nor riding in

Dedham. John Torrey Morse, a well-connected and well-informed Brahmin, wrote in 1916: "I knew him some twenty-five years ago, when the influence of Sam Warren got him into the Dedham Polo Club. It was a club of gentlemen, and Brandeis was soon conspicuously left to 'flock by himself,' with the result that he ceased to frequent the club and his absence was not regretted."[26]

The Brandeises' social isolation in Dedham is revealed in some details of their life there, none of which in itself is important but all of which taken together tell us a good deal about the life of a Jewish family in a Yankee town. Brandeis, left to "flock by himself" at the Polo Club, took up solitary pursuits such as walking and canoeing and apparently also sought the company of children in a way that his natural disposition would not have suggested. People who cannot recall their parents' ever dining with his family do remember Brandeis speaking to them as children about their play, what they were reading, and their opinions on various topics. The daughter of the milkman who supplied the Brandeis household can today provide more information than anyone else in Dedham about the Brandeis family's life there, for it was she who was the frequent companion of the girls in the spring and fall seasons. Brandeis had moved to Dedham because visiting his friend Samuel Warren there and riding horses at the Polo Club, he had become attracted to the place. In 1889 he had written to his brother: "Dedham is a spring of eternal youth for me. I feel new-made and ready to deny the existence of these grey hairs to which Percy Lowell called attention last evening." But once having moved there, Brandeis and his family found that neither Percy Lowell nor anyone else made them welcome.[27]

The Brandeises shared in their neighbors' life in only a superficial way: living in Dedham in the spring and autumn, wintering in Boston, and summering on Cape Cod, they followed a typical routine for most Dedham residents in their economic bracket. But though most Dedham residents participated in town affairs, shaped its development, voted for and served on its municipal committees, Brandeis did not. For some time he did hold membership in the Dedham Historical Society, but the society ignored him and kept no record of his activities, if there were any. The official record of the town's history does not mention his name at all. The Brandeises did not send their girls to Dedham schools, but to the socially acceptable Winsor School in Boston, where the daughters remember the teachers always asking which of the students came from the "old" families. For the family was isolated in Boston as well; in matters of society, Dedham was in many ways an extension of the city.[28]

New England gave birth to the country-club movement; Yankees established clubs outside Boston where they could relax and play games, mainly polo. Wives and children gradually joined in, and the importance of the country club in upper class social life became paramount. The Brookline Country Club, the first in the United States, was founded in 1882 and remained the most prestigious in New England. Needless to say, Brandeis was not invited to join, although all the other members of the Dedham Polo Club were either members of the country club or had close relatives who were.[29]

Brandeis came to Boston just in time — before Brahmin Boston set up its exclusive social system — still to be included at least nominally in its society; his name was listed in the *Blue Book of Boston* in 1886 and five years later in the *Social Register*. Thanks to his distinguished record as a student at Harvard Law School and his contributions to the Harvard Law School Association and the *Harvard Law Review*, he was appointed in 1890 to the Overseers Committee to Visit the Harvard Law School, an appointment with important social implications. Nonetheless his social position in Boston by no means reflected either his intellectual eminence or his accumulating wealth.[30]

All three of his social-club memberships in Boston were acquired thanks to the sponsorship of the Warrens. This fact, combined with his exclusion from other clubs, put him in an inferior position vis-à-vis his law partner: he was a member of the Dedham Polo Club but was excluded from the country club, a member of the Union Boat Club but excluded from the Athletic Club, and a member of the Union Club but excluded from the Somerset. His other club affiliations (the Boston Art Club and the Exchange Club) scarcely affected his place on the social ladder. Years later Brandeis wrote (from Detroit) regarding his exclusion from some of Boston's fancier clubs: "Anti-Semitism seems to have reached its American pinnacle here. New Athletic Club with *5000* members and no Jews need apply . . . But, as Percy Lowell said of our athletic club: 'It is the most inclusive club in Boston.' "[31]

Brandeis did not carry his associations with his colleagues in law beyond the office, with one conspicuous exception — Melvin O. Adams. Adams came from a small town outside Boston and, like Brandeis, was not a graduate of Harvard College. Adams belonged to the Curtis Club from January 1881, a club organized a year earlier by a group of recent graduates from the Boston University School of Law. In 1882 Brandeis joined the Curtis. He ought to have fit in well there, for the members were his age and also just beginning their careers, but he never did; in January 1912 he resigned.[32]

Brandeis himself admitted that his contact with Boston lawyers began to diminish after 1893. In a letter to Edward McClennen in 1916 he summarized his legal engagements and then added that since "1910 I have of course been very little in Boston, and had almost nothing to do with the Boston bar, but in the ten years preceding that, my contact with the Boston bar, other than in public matters, was very slight." According to the city's older lawyers, Brandeis was ostracized from his first years in Boston. Edward W. Hutchins testified in 1916 before the Senate committee considering Brandeis's nomination to the Supreme Court. Hutchins's testimony was based on about forty years of companionship with him at the bar, both being practicing lawyers. Opposing Brandeis's nomination, he tried to convey a sense of the atmosphere of distrust that had surrounded Brandeis for those many years. Boston lawyers "do not regard him as straight-forward . . . I think that the general opinion is that he is not straight-forward. I can find no better way to express it." The committee's members repeatedly pressed the witness: "Are we to understand from what you say that you speak of the reputation that Mr. Brandeis had at the

bar prior to 1892?" "I should say that his reputation was what I
have stated it to be back of that time," responded Hutchins.[33]

In somewhat different words, the pioneering civil-rights
lawyer Moorfield Storey, who censured Brandeis as an ambitious and aggressive lawyer, confirmed the atmosphere of
hostility that surrounded Brandeis from the very beginning of
his practice in Boston. Brandeis's reputation was of one "not to
be trusted," emphasized Storey, and to the committee's request
to clarify this statement he elaborated: "I mean to say there is a
radical lack of confidence in him among a representative class
of men in the community in which I live, and which has existed
for a good while . . . the members of the bar I think have never
had any other opinion." Both Hutchins and Storey (who also
opposed the nomination) were honest enough to admit that
Brandeis's public stance worsened his private position among
his colleagues in Boston but did not cause it. They were perfectly correct when they argued that Brandeis's antagonism
toward the vested interests in Boston only served to intensify
the atmosphere of suspicion that already surrounded him.
Their testimony was corroborated by Sherman L. Whipple,
who had practiced as a lawyer in Boston for thirty years:

> I think if they, when they discovered things which they criticize,
> had gone to Mr. Brandeis and said, "I want to talk this over with
> you; this is a matter of common interest to us; the way our profes-
> sion is looked upon is important to every member of the bar; let us
> discuss it," they would have gotten a totally different view with
> regard to Mr. Brandeis. On the other hand, I think that the same
> duty was laid upon Mr. Brandeis. Instead of wrapping himself in a
> sort of self-sufficiency of his own conscience and carrying out his
> own ideal, if he had said, " . . . You are friends of mine, and we
> are mutually interested" — they would not have impugned his good
> faith.[34]

It is clear that Brandeis was thought to be self-sufficient and
aloof and that the Protestant lawyers excluded him socially.
His membership in a few clubs was no defense against this exclusion. But perhaps the real reason for his unpopularity was,
as an established local lawyer knowledgeably assessing Bran-

deis's place in the city concluded, that he was "an outsider, successful, and a Jew."[35]

Brandeis perceived the Jewish community's potential as a clientele. When Brandeis accepted, after much hesitation, Warren's invitation to establish a law partnership in Boston, he intended the partnership with his Yankee friend to be an equal one, but the latter's superior social position meant that clients would come chiefly because of Warren's social and business connections. Therefore, before giving Warren his final approval Brandeis had visited Boston in the summer of 1879 and renewed his connections with Lina and Jacob Hecht. When he became convinced, through these contacts, that the city could provide him with a clientele that would allow him "to become known as a practicing lawyer," he agreed to join Warren.[36]

To build up his clientele, Brandeis activated his old school connections: Harvard Law School people, Germans and philo-German Yankees, and German Jews. Among the last the Hechts were, of course, the most important. On his above-mentioned visit to Boston Brandeis found the situation promising despite the presence of an able lawyer already serving many of the German Jews in the city: the office of Godfrey Morse included among its clients a substantial number of German Jews. It could not, however, possibly provide all the legal services demanded by Boston's German Jews. Sometime between the summer of 1879 and the winter of 1880-81, Brandeis began to act on behalf of Hecht Brothers and Company and thus established a solid foothold in the German-Jewish community.[37]

Hecht Brothers and Company had been in the wholesale boot and shoe business for more than fifteen years. Run by the father and his five sons, the family business was national in scope. Three of the partners lived in San Francisco; Louis, the head of the family, Jacob, and Louis junior lived in Boston. In the mid-eighties the firm shifted to wool marketing, Boston at that time being the center of the wool trade. Brandeis handled the abundance of Hecht Brothers legal matters that came his way, with an effectiveness that strengthened his ties with the family. About 1883 Jacob Hecht asked Brandeis to draw up his will, and when he died on February 24, 1903, Brandeis, Dunbar and Nutter was in charge of his estate.[38]

Following Jacob Hecht, other members of this family came into the firm's orbit, along with the Liebmanns, the Frank family, and the Vorenbergs. These prominent families and their enterprises made up the core of the Brandeis law firm's clientele in the German-Jewish community. More purely business clients included Isaac Kaffenburgh and Sons (whose first contact with Brandeis was in 1881), Lehman Pickert and Company, William Filene's Sons Company, Charles Weil and Company, Jacob Dreyfus and Sons, and Conrad and Company. Family connections that the owners of these enterprises had with other prominent Boston Jews led to further business for the law firm. The three daughters of Charles and Carrie Weil were married off to leading German-Jewish businessmen: Theresa to A. Lincoln Filene, Edna to Sidney Dreyfus, and Selma to Ludwig Eisemann. The Eisemanns were, along with the Hechts and Liebmanns, the leading wool merchants among Boston's Jewry. The Eisemann brothers, Nathan, Julius, and Ludwig, had the Brandeis firm draw up their wills, as did Louis Baer, an intimate of the Eisemann family and a partner of the Eisemann Brothers from the nineties, who later became the president of the Federated Jewish Charities.[39]

Except for the Filenes, virtually all Brandeis's German-Jewish clients were active in the Jewish community, and some were its leaders. In 1876 Jacob Hecht became president of the United Hebrew Benevolent Association. When the Federation of Jewish Charities was founded in 1895, he served as its president (until 1901). From 1904 to 1908 Lehman Pickert, an early and steady client of Brandeis, was president (the lawyer Godfrey Morse had served for the previous two years). Other clients and their wives were equally active in the Federation as well as in various communal institutions. Charles Weil, who was considered second only to Jacob Hecht in influence in the Jewish community, was a trustee of his temple and an active member of the Federation of Jewish Charities, the Leopold

Morse Home, and the Elysium Club. His wife, Carrie, who was also a temple trustee and active in the federation, had been vice president of the Hebrew Women's Sewing Society since 1880 and, like Lina Hecht, had a central role in mobilizing Boston women for communal efforts. Almost all these clients contributed heavily to the major Jewish philanthropic organizations; their wills continued those commitments after their deaths.[40]

Because of the ethnic divisions in Boston and the relative cohesion of the local Jewish community, the Brandeis firm's Jewish clientele soon extended beyond the rich German Jews to include a broader group. The membership of the Federation of Jewish Charities can be used to examine this trend. In 1895 approximately one-fifth of those who donated between twenty-five and forty-nine dollars to the federation employed the services of Brandeis's firm; more than one-third of the subscribers who donated fifty to ninety-nine dollars were in that category, as were almost half of those who gave one hundred dollars or more. Between 1895 and 1905, of those who subscribed twenty-five dollars or more to the federation, about a third were clients or had consulted Brandeis, Dunbar and Nutter. From the standpoint of the Jewish community, Brandeis's firm was "Jewish"; it certainly served a significant component of the community's leadership. Thus even though the majority of the firm's clients were non-Jews, the Jewish clientele were in numbers and significance an important part of the law firm's business. Furthermore the number of Jewish clients continued to increase.[41]

It was, of course, Brandeis who managed the contacts with the Jewish clientele. The technical aspects of many cases were handled by William Dunbar, but always under Brandeis's direction. The pressures of Brandeis's public responsibilities in the 1890s and his steadily increasing Jewish clientele induced the firm to take in another Jewish lawyer. David A. Ellis, a graduate of Harvard Law School, entered the law firm in 1896. During his four years there he dealt largely with Jewish clients, some of whom he had brought to the firm through his own connections. Ellis was an active member of the Jewish

community, notably in the Young Men's Hebrew Association
and Mt. Sinai Hospital. Although a Democrat, he was not
associated with the corrupt local machine and pursued a liberal and at times Progressive political course. Ellis left the firm
at the end of 1900 to establish his own practice, but his relations with Brandeis remained amicable.[42]

Ellis's departure left vacant a position for a Jewish lawyer to
work as Brandeis's right-hand man with the firm's Jewish
clients. When at the end of 1903 Walter S. Heilborn was
brought into the firm, he was probably intended to fill this
position. Jacob Heilborn, Walter's father, a businessman and a
loyal client of Brandeis's, was a conspicuous figure in the Jewish community. Brandeis trusted both son and father completely and had followed Walter's progress. Thus he readily
admitted him to the firm. Walter Heilborn moved to New
York City in 1906 and his place was taken in 1910 by Jacob J.
Kaplan, who like Heilborn was active in the Jewish community.[43]

By 1905 Brandeis was on his way to becoming a millionaire.
His German-Jewish clientele was partly responsible, with the
Yankee paper and shoe manufacturers also helping the firm to
thrive. For the latter, Warren and, later, Dunbar and Nutter
were the attractions. But Brandeis was known for his shrewd-
ness, ambition, and integrity, and many Protestant businessmen ignored ethnic barriers to consult him. Nonetheless there
were rather obvious limits to the scope of the firm's practice.
Considering the size of its Yankee clientele, for example, it received few family trusts. Nor did it succeed in penetrating the
bastions of big capital invested in banking, railroads, and textiles. Social reality decreed that a Jewish lawyer's firm could
play only a marginal role in Brahmin Boston.[44]

Antagonists of Carriers

Brandeis's relation to the vested interests in Boston was to be
further defined by his stand on transportation issues. This
same stand was later to make him criticize a fellow liberal, the
politician and merchant Charles S. Hamlin, who Brandeis felt

had been induced to support the railroads at the public expense. Thus in March 1913 Brandeis expressed the opinion that Hamlin "tries to be on good terms with all elements of his party. Long had general retainers from railroads; [may] not have now. Eminently respectable but spineless, and could never be induced to take part in any of the fights to protect the people." Apparently this was a strange political opinion for Brandeis to hold. Hamlin and he belonged to the same party; the former was elevated by the same new Wilsonian administration that sought to appoint Brandeis to the Supreme Court and finally succeeded; both were ardent believers in the same liberal tenets and in fact had sat together in a number of Mugwump clubs; and both were intimately connected with liberal-mercantile circles in Boston. Yet there was a difference: Charles Sumner Hamlin remained throughout his political career within the ideological framework of classic liberalism. Brandeis developed toward Progressivism, the movement that strove, among other things, to promote general welfare and social justice and censured unlimited private property rights particularly in the form of monopolies and corporate finance.[45]

Perhaps Brandeis's reference to Hamlin's "general retainers from railroads" was unfair; still, his connection with vested transportation interests was a major factor keeping Hamlin a steadfast Cleveland Democrat, and he was not alone. Most traditional Yankee Democrats comfortably managed a peaceful coexistence with those substantial transportation interests that wielded power in the Democratic party. The Bay State's Mugwumps also had their railroad patrons. Foremost among them was the tycoon John Murray Forbes; other eminent Boston Mugwumps—including Charles Francis Adams, Jr., and Moorfield Storey—were closely connected with railroads as well.[46]

Brandeis, perforce detached from the big concentrations of capital, had no meaningful connections with the railroad interests. When Edward F. McClennen, a member of the firm of Brandeis, Dunbar and Nutter from 1896 on, wrote his article "Louis D. Brandeis as a Lawyer," he did not mention railroads in the firm's range of clientele. The firm's archives yield the same result: railroads and transportation interests were almost completely absent. The firm was in fact heavily involved with a business community whose paramount interests were diametrically opposed to those of the railroads. Most of Brandeis's clients — manufacturers and merchants alike — shared shippers' concerns. His responsiveness to shippers' needs was what eventually led Brandeis to Progressivism.[47]

As it happened, Brandeis's family also contributed to this transformation. Alfred, Louis's older brother, was already an important representative of shipping interests when Louis had his first skirmishes with transportation interests in Boston. Except perhaps for Uncle Lewis Dembitz, Alfred held the most central place in Louis's life. Alfred's daughter speaks of

> the warmth and depth of the relations between those two brothers . . . Louis revered his brother — two and half years the elder — and he believed . . . that Alfred's integrity was beyond any he would ever find . . . He, also, was very active in civic and national affairs. He spent many active years in connection with shipping rates and "rebates" before the Interstate Commerce Commission and was well known in Washington in the early years of the century as was Louis . . . They certainly needed each other . . . This kind of closeness . . . was not of a sentimental nature; it was a matter of meeting of minds and mutual respect.[48]

Alfred belonged to a firm of "receivers and shippers of grain," and for a few years served on the Grain Committee of the Louisville Board of Trade to which his father had belonged before him. In 1894 he joined the local Transportation Committee and remained on it — at times as its chairman and always as an active member. In 1899 the Louisville Board of Trade created a new committee specifically designed to deal with shipping matters, and Alfred became a member of that as well. He was also a member of the Transportation Club, where he and his fellow grain shippers used to meet to design ways of improving and lowering the cost of transportation. In 1904 midwestern shippers under the leadership of the powerful Illinois Manufacturers' Association founded the American Shippers' Association to combat proposed increases of railroad freight rates; it was quite active for some years and Alfred Brandeis was Kentucky's representative on its executive committee. Later Alfred became a leader of the Southwestern Freight Association, another shippers' organization.[49]

Brandeis was considerably influenced by Alfred toward taking up the cause of shippers. Correspondence between the brothers from July 1906 on often deals with railroads, especially their practices and rates. The brothers made similar criticisms, and they worked in similar ways to advance shippers' interests in their common effort to strengthen the Interstate Commerce Commission.[50]

Brandeis's antirailroad stance, combined with his commitment to Mugwump tenets, caused him to develop a special political course in Boston, as his falling out with the Democratic reformer-lawyer George Fred Williams demonstrates. Before 1896 the public careers of the two men were entwined, but when Williams, a delegate to the 1896 Democratic National Convention, announced his conversion to free silver and led the state's Bryan forces in the election, Brandeis, strongly committed to the gold standard, dropped out of the Bryan-Williams camp. For the next decade, the antirailroad forces among the Massachusetts Democrats had Bryanite leadership. His association with Williams broken, and the Democratic machine too corrupt and opportunistic for his taste, Brandeis ended his active role in the Democratic party.[51]

When the newly organized Boston Elevated Railway Company secured grants of permanent franchises from the 1897 legislature to build a subway under many of the city's principal streets, Brandeis as a gold Democratic bolter could summon no opposition to Boston Elevated among the ranks of the Democratic party. Instead, the opposition, led by Edward A. Filene and Brandeis, took the form of the Public Franchise League, which planned a nonpartisan mobilization of mass opinion against private control of the city's streets. The secretary of the PFL was another gold Democrat and Brandeis friend, Morton H. Prince. In this subway fight, Brandeis's first great public battle, Prince was the lawyer's right-hand man.

On December 9, 1902, the voters of Boston overwhelmingly approved the construction of the subway according to the PFL plan — a triumph, especially for Brandeis.[52]

In this first political endeavor some of Brandeis's clients played crucial roles. One such client was the merchant Edward A. Filene, who as owner of the biggest retail business in Boston was concerned about the existence of cheap and convenient transportation in the service of consumers. He turned to one lawyer after another in quest of a man unafraid to challenge the powerful transportation interests. It did not occur to him at first to ask Brandeis, although he had served the store in a legal capacity since 1891. When Filene finally did approach Brandeis, he was pleasantly surprised to find the attorney already angered by Boston Elevated's plan. They agreed to work together to prevent the city from surrendering control of its transportation facilities to what they regarded as a usurping clique. Filene helped organize the PFL, subsidized it heavily, was in charge of its financial affairs, and gained the support of the city's newspapers. Although the accepted version of the struggle having Brandeis as the chief-of-staff and Prince as his aide-de-camp is probably correct, without Filene Brandeis would probably have had neither staff nor army.[53]

Not all the city's merchants were as sensitive as Filene to Boston Elevated's encroachment upon the public domain. The Boston Merchants Association, though it took a stand, did not play an important role in mobilizing opposition. Much more militant in favor of a publicly owned subway was the Boston Associated Board of Trade, which communicated with Brandeis as early as March 1900 and whose backing was a major factor in Brandeis's success. A great many manufacturers affiliated with the Associated Board of Trade, especially producers of consumer goods, had an interest, just as merchants like Filene did, in opening the commercial center of Boston to shoppers via cheap and convenient public transportation. These supporters of Brandeis's movement were not necessarily concerned with larger transportation issues. James R. Carter, a manufacturer of paper and stationery, president of the trade board, and Brandeis's client, was, like Filene, not interested in the national debate over lower freight rates. Nevertheless the urban-transportation and the more general railroad battles had something inherently in common, and this was their opposition to inordinate profits in the transportation business. Through public pressure and demands for the regulation of the transportation industry, these businessmen of Boston were, willy-nilly, supporting the Progressive cause.[54]

Brandeis, however, emerged from this struggle a genuine Progressive. Before the fight against Boston Elevated he had certainly read the antimonopoly writings of Henry George and Henry Demarest Lloyd. Thus he had a broader view of the struggle and did not single out monopoly in transportation as the only culprit.[55] What for many in the Merchants Association and in the Board of Trade was simply a matter of self-interest soon became for Brandeis part of a broader Progressive view: from free trade he had arrived at free *domestic* trade. But despite this developing concern, we know that abstract theories and distant events did not move him. The major reason for his conversion to Progressivism must be sought in his experiences as a Boston lawyer, particularly the social isolation he was subjected to and the fact that his law firm had no stake in the transportation industries (the latter being an expression of the former). The combination made Brandeis only too happy to lead his troops against the particular vested interests and to conduct his campaign along democratic and militant — Progressive — lines, as only an outsider would have done.

Brandeis next became involved in a struggle to check the privileged power represented by the gas combine. In 1903 the eight firms that supplied gas to Boston merged into the Boston Consolidated Gas Company. Two issues were involved: fair valuation of the new company's stock and the price of gas to the consumers. Brandeis suggested a plan along the lines of the city of London's municipal "sliding scale" utility rates. In this scheme, as the dividend to stockholders rose, the selling price of gas to the consumer fell. After protracted negotiations a sliding scale was signed into law in May 1906.[56]

In the fight against the gas combine, Brandeis worked in concert with the Massachusetts State Board of Trade, which he represented as unpaid counsel. This organization, founded in 1890, was intended "to concentrate the power and usefulness of the various boards of trade and other business associations of the State in one corporate organization, in order to secure prompt consideration of questions pertaining to the financial, commercial, industrial and of all the material interests of the State at large." The State Board of Trade's constituency comprised, in addition to local boards of trade, a number of trade associations which included the Shoe and Leather Association but not the textile industry. Both in number and in influence, the mercantile organizations involved were important: they included the Boston Merchants Association, the Boston Druggists Association, the Boston Fruit and Produce Exchange, the Boston Wholesale Grocers Association, and the Real Estate Exchange. A prosperous merchant, Charles Elisha Adams, was founder and president for many years of the State Board of Trade.[57]

The Public Franchise League, which came to Brandeis's aid in the gas fight, had among its members many clients, chiefly mercantile men, of Brandeis, Dunbar and Nutter. Morton Prince, a stable and generous contributor, was not a client but most large contributors were; they included E. A. Filene, James Carter, and Brandeis's shoe and leather clients, especially Charles H. Jones, W. H. McElwain, and C. P. Hall.[58]

The fact that banking interests were involved in both the reorganization of Boston Elevated and the consolidation of the gas companies did not decrease the militancy of Brandeis and his allies: the firm of Brandeis, Dunbar and Nutter was totally detached from the banking world. It had only a few small brokers among its clients and apparently stood to lose nothing from a confrontation with major financial interests. But the reality proved much more complicated.[59]

Actually Brandeis did not challenge his own city's financial community until about 1905. Indeed, according to rumor, he may even have served it, albeit somewhat accidentally, in the Boston Elevated affair.[60]

The organization of the Boston Elevated Railway Company

in 1897, which resulted in the acquiring of a charter from the city, was conducted by the rivals of Boston's bankers: a group of New York capitalists backed by J. Pierpont Morgan who took control of the Boston Elevated Railway and arranged with the West End Street Railway for a ninety-nine-year lease of the latter's lines. The deal, made through Kidder, Peabody and Company, placed surface, elevated, and underground transportation under the control of the New York group. Though the headquarters of Kidder, Peabody and Company were located in Boston, the House of Morgan was its close associate for almost a half century (1880s-1930), and the two firms had participated regularly in each other's syndicates; the partners were on friendly terms as well. Kidder, Peabody and Company had an archrival in Boston in the form of Lee, Higginson and Company, which, having no share in the deal, was pleased by Brandeis's opposition to the reorganization of Boston Elevated. The persistent rumor that Brandeis was retained by Lee, Higginson was refuted by Brandeis, and he wrote a special letter about this to the counsel of Boston Elevated. Brandeis was, strictly speaking, correct when he claimed not to have been retained by the Higginsons' interests. He did not have to be "retained," however, to share the concerns of the Higginsons in blocking the Boston Elevated effort.[61]

In March 1900 Brandeis wrote to J. Richard Carter regarding the beginning of his representation of the Boston Associated Board of Trade against Boston Elevated: "I have had a talk with Laurence Minot, who takes our view, and who has very clear ideas on the subject, and he has promised to come up." Minot was a well-connected financier in Boston, and Brandeis was right to count on his help. Both were members of the Massachusetts Civil Service Reform Association, the New England Free Trade League, and the Massachusetts Reform Club, which were some of the city's political clubs. By the spring of 1900 their relations were close enough for Brandeis to ask Minot to draft the bills opposing Boston Elevated. Minot did so, and in a few days Brandeis sent over a complete version of the bill, which stated that if Boston Elevated refused to operate the subway under certain restrictive terms, the city could lease the project to other businessmen. The leader of this group — Boston's businessmen and bankers who challenged Morgan's encroachment — was Francis Lee Higginson, the brother of Morgan's rival. When Brandeis sent the transit bill to the Committee on Metropolitan Affairs, he delivered a copy of the bill and an explanatory letter to Henry Lee Higginson, on the suggestion of Minot, a close friend of Higginson.[62]

Minot contributed a great deal to the defeat of Boston Elevated and its New York backers. His influence was felt in a quarter Brandeis could not have penetrated without him, demonstrated when the Brahmin *Boston Transcript* published an editorial favorable to their cause. In June 1902 the legislature approved the Washington Street subway bill embodying Brandeis's proposals. In the wake of this victory, Brandeis wrote to Henry Lee Higginson: "I hope you are satisfied with the subway bill. You have been so much interested in the work of the Franchise League that I venture to tell you that the expense of the campaign has been quite large, and to ask whether you care to make a contribution." The fact that Brandeis did not get an answer to this request meant that his understanding with the financial pillars of Boston was to remain tacit.[63]

From 1903 to 1906, when the gas issue was at its height, nothing happened to impair the discreet relationship between Brandeis and the financial circle of the Higginsons and the Lees. This was so since after the consolidation of gas companies in 1903, the two leading gas executives were Henry M. Whitney, whose traditional financial backer was Kidder, Peabody and Company, and James L. Richards, whom the same investment house selected to head its gas interests. Thus when the Public Franchise League and Brandeis worked to restrict the power of the new gas company in Boston, they did not disturb the rest of State Street; an olive branch had been quietly extended from those bankers to the offices of the Franchise League. Even without being a client of Brandeis, Dunbar and Nutter, as were most of the contributors to the Public Franchise League, Joseph Lee made a gift to the PFL outdone only by that of Filene. Though the money did not come directly from the coffers of Lee, Higginson and Company, it originated not far from that source. Joseph was the son of Henry Lee, who had been a senior partner of the investment banking house, and the nephew of Henry Lee Higginson himself.[64]

More than ties of business and blood connected Henry and Joseph Lee; ideologically the two were much akin. Both were liberals of the old school, the same tradition from which Brandeis himself had emerged. The political posture adopted by the firm of Lee and Higginson was characteristic of a considerable part of the financial community, although liberals were in greater abundance among the city's merchants. In addition to Joseph Lee and Henry Lee Higginson, who were at the very heart of Boston's financial power, other State Street figures were also leaders and financial backers of a variety of Mugwump causes.[65]

But Brandeis's relationship with liberal banking circles—despite points of ideological accord—was mostly a collaboration between two different interests. Boston's bankers were undoubtedly dismayed by the populist vehemence with which the Jewish lawyer directed his struggles against their common adversaries. They perhaps had already asked themselves if they would always be able to ride this wild horse.

Learning Trade Unionism

Besides taking an antimonopoly and especially antirailroad stance, Brandeis developed a growing concern for the welfare of labor. The source of this interest cannot really be traced to his family: the labor issue did not greatly affect the Brandeis clan in Kentucky (or Missouri). Alfred Brandeis, usually a strong influence on Louis, was more occupied with his dealings in grain and with furthering shippers' interests. Though a prosperous businessman and a Republican in national politics, he was also, however, never "antilabor," showing none of the hostility to labor typical of the industrial barons of Illinois (with whom he shared shipping interests).[66]

Nor did Lewis Dembitz have any decisive effect on his nephew's growing sensitivity to labor distress. He was by no means, however, a Bourbon liberal, and his fights for liberal causes such as free trade and sound money characteristically took account of the wage earner's stake in sustaining them. In the same year that the American Federation of Labor was established, he publicly claimed the right of workers to unionize and strike, though he rejected the idea of a closed shop and had begun to formulate the approach that came to distinguish Brandeis's later years.[67] But concern with workers' rights and welfare never occupied a central place in Dembitz's world: he was inclined to see these issues as adjuncts to the greater questions of currency and tariffs.

As I have noted, Brandeis was deeply impressed as early as 1889 by a speech of Henry George; and in 1895 he was stirred by Henry Demarest Lloyd's *Wealth against Commonwealth*. It is doubtful, however, that these formulations deeply influenced him on the questions of social deprivation and labor rights. Mason believes that "probably more instructive to Brandeis than books and speeches was actual labor warfare such as he witnessed during the Homestead strike of 1892 and the acute labor troubles of his own industrial clients." Brandeis's memoirs corroborate this assessment: "I think it was the affair at Homestead . . . which first set me to thinking seriously about the labor problem . . . it took the shock of that battle, where organized capital hired a private army to shoot at organized labor for resisting an arbitrary cut in wages, to turn my mind definitely toward a searching study of the relations of labor to industry." It was undoubtedly because of the influence of Mary Kenney O'Sullivan, the first woman trade union organizer and a close friend and associate of Elizabeth Evans (who became part of the Brandeis family), that the event made such a great impression on him. Josephine Goldmark, a labor crusader and a sister-in-law of Brandeis, writes of her:

Mary Kenney had come to Boston from Chicago as a labor organizer. She had been at the Carnegie Steel Company at Homestead in 1892 and seen the preparations for the terrible strike when workers were shot down and killed by machine guns. She had been through the Haverhill shoe strike of 1894; she was active in all the textile strikes at Lawrence and Fall River. The workers' side on those struggles lost nothing in her telling, and in Mr. Brandeis she had found a deeply attentive listener.

The version given by Alfred Lief, the biographer who was close to Brandeis, also associates the lawyer's social conversion with the Irish labor leader: "His friend Kenney had gone down to Homestead before the company's agreement with the union expired; she saw walls being built around the mill grounds, with apertures for guns."[68]

Two years after the Homestead affair, Brandeis and Kenney had a public debate over the Haverhill shoe strike. While Mary Kenney—whose style it was to blend realism with compassion—spoke on the conditions of labor, Brandeis appraised the problem from a point of view closer to that of his shoe-manufacturer clients. After that, Brandeis began to reformulate his approach and to realize that trade unions were important to both labor and management.[69]

When Mary Kenney came to Boston she was welcomed, through the prompting of Samuel Gompers, by John F. O'Sullivan, president of the Boston Central Labor Union and a labor reporter for the *Boston Globe*. From that moment he worked closely with her, and in 1894 they were married. O'Sullivan shared Mary Kenney's crucial role in the development of Brandeis's labor views. The Kenney autobiography relates: "It was through Mrs. Evans that we first met Louis D. Brandeis . . . It was all joy for me when he and Jack O'Sullivan discussed one after the other the problems of industrial betterment. Mr. Brandeis had to be shown and it wasn't easy. He had been thinking on the other side so long. However, his mind was at all times open to conviction. If ever a man talked facts, it was Jack O'Sullivan. He was known for facts." A labor unionist who "talked facts," the language Brandeis understood best, was the sort who would gain Brandeis's ear. Jack O'Sullivan "enjoyed the confidence of both laboring men and men of wealth, who heeded his advice for they knew when he spoke upon a contested question, that his opinion was of an honest man."[70]

In August 1896, when Brandeis wanted to influence workers to reject Bryan's free-silver platform, he sought help from John O'Sullivan, and it was through this labor leader that he became aware of the viewpoint of the working class. He wrote to Mrs. Evans: "I want to take up this question with the working-men, through him," for, he said, the workingmen "are the people most interested — they will lose the ground gained in so many years [*sic*] struggle — if Bryan wins. I want, too, to discuss it with them because I look to the workingman's seriousness for our general political salvation. I want to talk only to them." After cooperating with O'Sullivan on the monetary issue, "many an evening [Brandeis] spent in [the O'Sullivans'] house on Carver Street, Jack doing most of the talking — on labor," as Lief says of this period. "Together, the O'Sullivans educated him in unionism."[71]

What Jack O'Sullivan could offer Brandeis was not just "unionism": he was a man with broad political interests and connections. He had a major role in organizing the Seamen's Union and was its representative at an international meeting in Glasgow, where he came into contact with European labor leaders. Among the O'Sullivans' visitors were noted Labor party leaders from England. O'Sullivan was also known in Boston as a social reformer. He was president of the Boston Central Labor Union, a sort of clearinghouse for the city's working class ideologies, where the remnants of the Knights of Labor, Single-Taxers, Fabian Socialists, and Populists gathered to talk. After O'Sullivan's death in 1902, Brandeis came to know another very active member of the Central Labor Union, Henry Abrahams, the president of the cigar-makers' union, and he continued to support Mary O'Sullivan's efforts on behalf of the working class and social reform in Massachusetts.[72]

The Irish community in general played a pivotal role in converting Brandeis to Progressivism, and this fact was a consequence of the lawyer's marginal position in the Boston establishment. Brandeis was naturally attracted to a circle that eschewed the haughtiness of the natives and demonstrated a moral fiber of its own. The affluent lawyer often ventured from Mt. Vernon Street to the heart of the working class quarter of downtown Boston, spending many evenings with Irish labor leaders to learn from them about "unionism."

At the same time, the family of Samuel Warren, Brandeis's only solid connection in Brahmin Boston, was also becoming involved in social welfare. Active in the development of a Boston settlement project, Denison House, was Cornelia Lyman Warren, Samuel's sister, who was the chairman of the governing committee from 1895 to 1910. On her estate in Waltham, Cornelia built a house for Helena S. Dudley, the chief force behind the Denison project from 1893 to 1912. Brandeis of course knew Cornelia Warren and helped her at times, giving public and legal assistance to Denison House. Others in Brandeis's life also lent aid to the project: D. Blakely Hoar of Brandeis's law firm was a member of the Denison Home Extension Committee and Brandeis's wife was a constant annual subscriber.[73]

Mary O'Sullivan had joined the settlement project soon after arriving in Boston. The founder of the house, Vida Dutton Scudder, asked her to organize women's trade unions, and after a short time Mary and John O'Sullivan became central to the workings of Denison House. Scudder relates:

> We foregathered with the best of the Boston labor leaders . . . Jack O'Sullivan, good to look at, his face stamped with refinement, but constantly heavy-lidded with fatigue. For he allowed himself scant sleep, and spent his nights, like many labor men, in the endless meetings, and it must be said, wranglings, that obtained in his organization. Jack O'Sullivan was our romance; he married Mary Kenney, a noble young woman on fire for her cause who came to us from Hull House—with which we early formed connections—to organize the women workers in the East. We rejoiced in the marriage, and in the O'Sullivan babies, one of whom was born at Denison House.

"These friends of ours were very perfect gentle knights; fighting in as worthwhile a battle as the world was ever seen," writes Vida Scudder. "As for us, we threw ourselves zealously into the movement to organize women, with Mary Kenney to guide. The Women's Trade Union League, still active, dates from that time."[74]

Elizabeth Evans was also close to the affairs of the Denison House and one of several Boston society women who sympathized with the labor cause. Kenney's meeting with her was memorable:

> One day Mrs. Glendower Evans came over. She wanted to have us at dinner with Mr. and Mrs. Brandeis that evening. As there was ironing to be done I told her I couldn't accept the invitation. She asked, "Where are the clothes?" "Some are folded and sprinkled and some are on the line." She said, "If you heat the irons, I will iron them." She brought in the clothes, sprinkled them and did the ironing. Here was a new experience in my life. A woman of wealth did my ironing![75]

Brandeis's connection with the Filenes also added to his involvement with the labor movement. In 1881 William Filene opened a store on Winter Street which soon grew to be the largest retail business in the city. In the eighties the store employed a relatively small number of employees, and Filene held informal meetings with them in which they were encouraged to express their ideas on all aspects of running the store. Those conferences evolved into the Filene Cooperative Association, organized in 1898; its first constitution was drawn up in 1903. In 1901 William had turned the store over to his sons, who carried on this extraordinary tradition in management-workers relations, and in fact further developed it along more rational and systematic lines. The Filene Cooperative Association strove, among other things, to give to the workers a voice in management and to sustain a just and equitable relation between employees and employers. It had the power to initiate, amend, or modify store rules regarding discipline, working conditions, and any other matter except business policies. One of its most vital concerns was working hours. The Filenes also encouraged the development of welfare projects to be managed by the workers; one of the first of them was providing insurance for members and their families in the event of sickness or death; as early as 1898 an insurance committee was established which later was known as the Filene Cooperative Association Benefit Society. In 1901 an arbitration board was organized as a representative institution of the FCA, and this acted as a final court of appeal in all cases of controversy between the company and an employee and between one employee and another.[76]

These and other Progressive aspects of the Filenes' store reflected a distinct philosophy of industrial relations, which though only gradually developed, was comprehensive as well as practical from its very beginning. It was associated with the notion of "industrial democracy," the two most important elements of which were workers' rights and labor's participation in management. Brandeis's connection with these efforts was not confined to legal matters. He was one of the speakers at the Filene Cooperative Association in 1898-99, as were Charles W. Eliot, William James, and Thomas W. Higginson at other times. He later acted as the FCA's adviser on general as well as legal affairs. In June 1906 he wrote to E. A. Filene an admiring letter suggesting that he bring "the results of the Filene experiment in cooperation and industrial democracy . . . to the attention of the nation."[77]

When this letter was written, Brandeis had already cooperated with the Filenes on the Industrial League project. The legal work involved in the founding and running of the league was carried out by Brandeis's law firm. The first available document (dated July 18, 1903) regarding the establishment of the league suggests both how decisively the Filenes influenced Brandeis in labor matters and how intensely the law firm was involved with the Filenes' aspirations. The Industrial League's goal was defined as "promoting the investigation and study of and providing instruction as to economic and industrial questions and aiding in improving the relations between employers and employees."[78]

During the early years of the organization, it was successful in raising the issues it had set out to address: at monthly meetings the subjects discussed included "the welfare and other work for employees carried on by [the participants in] several establishments," "profit sharing," "the system of educating apprentices," and "the nature of the relation between employer and employee." As eventual president of the league, Brandeis contributed suggestions for improving the lives of working people and for adding to understanding between labor and employers. He initiated the enlargement of labor's role in the Industrial League. It was characteristic of such an enterprise as the league represented that of the trio who comprised its core (which included Brandeis as a president), the secretary was a paper manufacturer and the treasurer was a merchant, A. Lincoln Filene. Thus "A. L." and "E. A."—the Filene brothers whose history was so intimately interwoven with that of Brandeis—were among those who led this venture in pursuit of "industrial democracy."[79]

During the decade following the establishment of the Filene Cooperative Association and the Industrial League, the Filenes expanded their social innovations and prospered as well, moving in September 1912 to a new building with more than nine acres of floor space. In the following month, Brandeis commemorated the occasion with his famous address "Business—A Profession," in which he commended the Filenes to the nation as businessmen par excellence by virtue of their material success and their pursuit of industrial democracy and social justice.[80]

Brandeis's thoughts on the value of trade unions for America's democracy and prosperity crystallized during the ten years following the Homestead strike of 1892. In addition to the part played by the O'Sullivans and Filenes in Brandeis's shift away from a conservative-Mugwump labor attitude, Henry Demarest Lloyd—whose *Wealth against Commonwealth* Brandeis had read—exerted an influence on the lawyer's development, and by 1902 the latter was ready to learn from Lloyd in labor matters as well. Lloyd was then in Boston, and the two men cooperated in the Pennsylvania anthracite-coal strike. This experience was an important milestone in Brandeis's growing responsiveness to workers' grievances and rights. When Lloyd died in 1903, Brandeis professed "great affection as well as admiration for him."[81]

Brandeis's position in capitalist Boston contrived to sustain his new ideas on labor. His most significant manufacturing clientele—the shoe and boot manufacturers—generally had good relations with their workers, in sharp contrast to the textile industry. Although the average annual wage in 1905 for a worker in the shoe industry was about $530, in the woolen goods industry it was only $430, and in cotton goods, the biggest industry of all, $360. Part of the reason for this discrepancy was that the cotton and woolen industries employed a much higher percentage of women than did the shoe industry and about four times as many children. Shoe manufacturing required skilled labor and owners complied with their workers' basic demands in order to keep them. The textile industry, on the other hand, could draw from an enormous pool of relatively unskilled workers and could afford to be militantly anti-labor. Their political arm, the Arkwright Club, founded around 1880, was established mainly to combat labor legislation. The militancy of the New England textile men and their fellows elsewhere in the country was effective: between 1881 and 1905 only 18 percent of the strikes in this industry resulted in total victories for the workers, and 30 percent were partial victories, as compared with figures of 48 percent and 15 percent for all other industries. Brandeis was pessimistic about the outcome of the 1904 Fall River textile strike: "I am disposed to think that, with the exception of the highly skilled help, the cotton manufacturing business is a very undesirable one for any class of persons in Massachusetts who have reached a higher standard of living."[82]

In 1902 the shoe manufacturer William H. McElwain asked for Brandeis's help to defeat his striking workers. The lawyer discovered that the workers were fairly paid when they worked but that employment was erratic. Rather than take sides against labor, Brandeis solved the problem at issue by convincing McElwain to organize his factories in a way that would ensure steadier work. At the same time he established good

relations with the workers' spokesman, John F. Tobin, the
president of the Boot and Shoe Workers Union (A. F. of L.).
Like Jack O'Sullivan, Tobin was an Irishman and was well informed on labor matters. Brandeis found all his arguments
"perfectly right" and was willing to follow his advice. In March
1905, when Tobin agreed to permit "employers the right to
discharge for good and sufficient reasons," Brandeis commented: "Your policy in this, as in so many other respects, appears to me to be eminently wise and one which will greatly
conduce to the success of your Union."[83]

But Brandeis's growing sympathy with labor's demands did
not alienate him from capitalist Boston: his shoe-manufacturer clients were ready to accept his views in a great many
instances, and some merchants even helped him. Nor did the
new course sever his understanding with liberal State Street.
The Higginson-Lee circle resembled some other financial and
corporation leaders in the country (but was unlike the National Association of Manufacturers) in tending toward a
reconciliatory course in the labor question. Brandeis and that
circle did not share identical views on labor, but a peaceful
coexistence prevailed between them throughout the period.[84]

It was only incidentally that the immigration policies of Boston's Mugwumps and reformers were in the interests of organized labor. Motivated by a concern for the democratic process
and fear of control by ward bosses, as well as by their nativist
tendencies, the former opposed mass immigration that would
produce concentrations in the city of poor and uneducated
citizens. In 1894 they established the Immigration Restriction
League; many of its founders (including among their number
Charles Warren) and early leaders were men schooled at Harvard College and belonging to the Mugwump-Democrat-free
trade element of the community. Immigrants were specifically
excluded from membership. It was the manufacturers and
protectionists in Boston who at first did not oppose immigration: many of them were dependent upon a steady flow of
cheap labor, which also helped to undermine the trade unions.
Brandeis himself felt that large infusions of helpless and naive

immigrants would hinder good government and reform politics. In 1904 he wrote to one of the league's leaders: "I should be entirely ready to adopt the educational test [as a criterion for admission to the country] but for the apprehension which I feel that such a step would be followed by other legislation induced by baser motives." Nevertheless Brandeis must have felt the ethnic bias underlying the opinions voiced in the Immigration Restriction League, and the elitist atmosphere in the reform clubs to which he belonged made him feel equally uncomfortable.[85]

The nativist attitude of the Massachusetts Reform Club helped move Brandeis into a more radical camp. By the spring of 1905, he had resigned and joined the Economic Club of Boston. Established at the turn of the century, this club shared the fundamental liberal principles of the Reform Club but not its nativist spirit. Its stated purpose was "to assist in bringing about a more harmonious relationship between labor and capital and to foster broad and independent economic thought." It concentrated on domestic problems and initiated discussions of social grievances and urban ills. Through the efforts of the Economic Club of Boston, a National Economic League was established in 1908. Brandeis was the sole representative of Massachusetts on the National Committee of the League, and a member of its National Council and Executive Council.[86]

3

The Claims of Ethnicity

Ethical Judaism

LIKE Brandeis's bent toward liberalism and reform, the nature of his bond with Judaism had its source within the family. In a letter to her son, Frederika Dembitz alludes to the spiritual values and religious ideas that must also have guided him in his childhood:

> I do not believe that sins can be expatiated by going to divine service and observing this or that formula; I believe that only goodness and truth and conduct that is humane and self-sacrificing towards those who need us can bring God nearer to us, and that our errors can only be atoned for by our acting in a more kindly spirit. Love, virtue and truth are the foundation upon which the education of the child must be based. They endure forever . . . God is the consummation of all virtue, truth and nobility. To strive for these should be our aim wherever life leads us . . . And this is my justification for bringing up my children without any definite religious belief: I wanted to give them something that neither could be argued away nor would have to be given up as untenable, namely a pure spirit and the highest ideals as to morals and love. God has blessed my endeavors — may his blessing be with you always!"

Despite its eschewal of religious observance and belief, in general moral tone this attitude was linked with Jewish tradition. Furthermore when Frederika educated her children in "virtue, truth and nobility," she did not merely instill abstract ethical ideals: elements of Jewish history and religion were subtly interwoven in that moral framework.[1]

Brandeis's ancestors had been followers of the eighteenth-century independent Sabbatian Jacob Frank. One of them, Jonas Wehle, was the spiritual leader of the Frankists in early nineteenth century Prague, from which the Frankist-Sabbatian tradition was carried by emigrants to the United States. Gottlieb Wehle, Jonas's nephew and the great-uncle of Louis Brandeis, who came to America in 1849, reveals in his will composed in the 1860s his great pride in the sect's heritage. Josephine Goldmark, a cousin and sister-in-law of Brandeis, voiced similar sentiments. Brandeis's mother was well aware of the family's affiliation with the Bohemian Sabbatian movement, and Louis himself knew about it, at least after 1881 when his mother wrote to him, at his request, a letter about the Frankist Messianic tradition of the family. Her position was complicated. On the one hand, she criticized the belief of her forebears in the coming of the true Messiah as superstition; on the other, like Gottlieb Wehle and Josephine Goldmark, she took pride in the family heritage. Her ancestors, she believed, had finally rejected formalities and rigidities and were successfully striving toward genuinely important spiritual values:

> I mentioned earlier the religious sect to which my parents belonged. I do not know what they believed and what Jewish doctrines they discarded, but I do know that they believed in goodness for its own sake and they had a lofty conception of morality with which they imbued us and which I developed further for myself . . . I saw that my parents were good Jews, and yet did not associate with Jews and were different from them and so there developed in me more affection for our race as a whole than for individuals.[2]

Frederika Dembitz believed that although a great moral principle was at the heart of both Judaism and Christianity, the former was closer to the truth of things: "That the Christian Messiah had not brought salvation to the world became clear to me in spite of my reverence for him . . . a religion which in the name of its God perpetuated the most cruel and the lowest acts of infamy could not be the longed-for gospel."

The Frankist underground did indeed pursue as its goal ultimate goodness, and Frederika felt that this had been attained by her parents who were at the same time "good Jews." The pattern set for Louis to follow was one of antitraditionalist Jewish deviation.[3]

The religious philosophy of Brandeis's mother was, in some respects, characteristic of Frankism (as distinguished from classical Sabbatianism). Jacob Frank and his followers emphasized the Diaspora and the Jewish mission among other nations rather than the renaissance centered in the Land of Israel; they held that Jews were expelled from their homeland not because they had sinned, but in order to bring about the world's redemption. To accomplish this mission they must join, though not assimilate with, other nations. Its approach to religion made Frankism, especially as cultivated in Prague, responsive to Enlightenment currents; it thus synthesized rationalism and a radical sense of worldwide mission.[4]

Rationalism and commitments to world redemption were not forces likely to preserve Judaism as a tradition, for they opened the door to non-Jewish practices. Christmas, though secularized, was probably part of the Brandeises' life, but pseudo-Christianity was not otherwise a part of family practices. Louis Brandeis probably spoke accurately when he said (in December 1910): "My early training was not Jewish in a religious sense, nor was it Christian." A dim sense of a Jewish mission, tinged with Jewish dissent and family pride, was Louis's spiritual heritage.[5]

Lewis Dembitz, in contrast to Frederika, was a devout Jew and ardent Zionist and was closely associated with the beginnings of Conservative Judaism in America. A creative scholar of Judaism, he actively helped in the founding of the Jewish Theological Seminary, which became the center of this branch of Judaism and most of whose members were fervent Zionists. He contributed not only to the *American Hebrew*, a publication begun by rightwing Reform and liberal Orthodox Jews, but also to the *Maccabaean*, the journal of the Federation of American Zionists. When Jacob De Haas, secretary of the federation, toured the Border States in the early twentieth century, he visited Lewis Dembitz and was deeply impressed by this high-minded Zionist. De Haas stayed with the Dembitzes long enough for one of Lewis's daughters to fall in love with the urbane, witty raconteur. De Haas married someone else, but he treasured the image of the dignified head of this family. As it turned out, the marital union of the families was only delayed; in 1937 Dembitz's grandson married Jacob De Haas's daughter.[6]

On the surface, the conduct of Lewis Dembitz's life was sharply different from the one commended by Frederika in her letters to Louis. In fact Lewis did share some of his sister's moral and religious beliefs. Though in general an observant Jew, he disregarded some important Jewish practices. He did not accept at face value the body of Jewish law, but rather felt that it was intended to further moral values and to "better men and women," a philosophy that placed Lewis outside of Orthodox Judaism. After the Jewish Theological Seminary conferred upon him the degree of Doctor of Hebrew Literature in the spring of 1904, an editorial in the *American Hebrew* emphasized three characteristics of the man: his secular learning, his interest in the affairs of his home state, and his tolerance of diverse trends in Judaism. Although the degree had been awarded mainly for his book on Jewish religious services, Dembitz did not want to see American Jewry become a separate social group (he waged a constant and bitter war against the use of Yiddish by American Jews) and wanted neither his Jewishness nor his Zionism to imply any disharmony with the larger American society. Devoted Zionist though he was, he was equally enthusiastically involved in American politics.[7]

Brandeis was very much aware of Dembitz's place in the Jewish community, and the two even discussed specifically Jewish topics, such as the role of the Jews in American politics, when they aroused Brandeis's curiosity. He happened across some previously unknown correspondence by Judah P. Benjamin of Louisiana (1811-1884), the first Jewish United States senator, and sent one of the letters to his uncle, asking for comments.[8]

Most of Lewis's children were also involved in Judaism and

Zionism. His son, Arthur Aaron Dembitz, became a significant Jewish scholar and may also have served to strengthen Brandeis's relation to the Jewish people. He did at least try to do so. In September 1905 Brandeis wrote to Arthur: "I thank you very much for the volume *Leading Cases in the Bible,* which has just reached me. I look forward with great pleasure to reading it." The book (written by an important Jewish lawyer) analyzed legal cases in the Bible and underlined the Bible's contribution to the modern ethical system.[9]

The "Judaizing" influence of Uncle Lewis was countered by Brandeis's older brother Alfred, who was rather indifferent to Judaism. Alfred's daughter records that he had very little association with Jews socially or in public affairs, that the family did not belong to a synagogue or to any conspicuously Jewish organization, and that her father was sought after by clergymen of all denominations to take part in their conversation clubs. He had only the vaguest contacts with the Jewish life in the city, contributing to Jewish charities, but also to non-Jewish ones, and belonging to a Jewish club, but not actively. He was, however, popular among Jewish businessmen, and he himself admired the Jewish shipping merchant and noted communal leader Judah Touro. Occasionally the local community might make mention of Alfred as one of its members, but on the whole he lived on its periphery. He was married to a Gentile.[10]

Brandeis's family also included the founder of the Society for Ethical Culture, Felix Adler. At the time of Louis's engagement to Alice Goldmark in 1890, her sister Helen had been married to Adler for ten years. Louis and Alice were married in a civil ceremony performed by Adler at the Goldmark's house in New York. Since the ceremony was carefully planned, Adler's officiating no doubt reflected Brandeis's regard for the man. Son of the rabbi of the famous Temple Emanu-El in New York City, Adler himself was critical of the Jewish religion and of traditional religions in general. He preached a creed of moral action that would transcend the theologies of the various religions. The motto of the Society for Ethical Culture, "Deed not creed," reflected a religious society that was intended to be practical as well as spiritual and remain unhampered by sectarian dogma. The philosophy had its appeal for Brandeis, since it harmonized well with the maternal teachings of his youth.[11]

When Brandeis became his brother-in-law, Adler was generally regarded as a Jew devoted to moral Judaism. He had some interest in the Jewish contribution to ethics, and the Jewish community for its part tolerated him, especially since his efforts on behalf of social reform had benefited the lot of poor Jews. In addition many Jews belonged to Adler's Society for Ethical Culture. (The leadership of the New York Society for Ethical Culture and the vast majority of its following was and still is Jewish.) The *New York Evening Post* spoke of Adler in 1905 as being a representative Jew in an essay on the two hundred and fiftieth anniversary of the arrival of the Jews in America: it referred to the "invaluable service our best Jews have performed in every campaign for municipal or national reforms . . . No man in America has stood for a higher moral standard than Felix Adler, or voiced a purer idealism . . . in and out of the orthodox church, . . . to such America owes a great debt."[12]

Brandeis respected Adler as a great moral leader. In a letter to his fiancée in 1891, he spoke of Adler's "general view of the divinity of man—to which I attribute largely his power as an ethical leader." The two men indeed shared some views on moral issues: in matters of justice and social welfare, Adler and Brandeis both took positions somewhere between the interests of the employer and those of the working man. It was not uncharacteristic of their relationship that in 1904 Adler asked Brandeis to send him a copy of his important address delivered at the annual banquet of the Boston Typothetae concerning the printers' union strike. Adler asked Brandeis to become Boston head of the Society for Ethical Culture; Brandeis declined. But in May 1905, he did address the Harvard Ethical Society (which was part of the Society for Ethical Culture) on "The Opportunity in the Law," and at that time discussed the role of lawyers in society.[13]

Brandeis admired Adler for his involvement in the New York movement for good government, for his efforts in social reform movements, and for his following a moderate prolabor course[14] (activities that Brandeis tended to associate with the Jewish tradition). But the relationship should not be exaggerated; while Adler developed his nonsectarian culture society, Brandeis remained, however peripherally, a Jew. Perhaps because his profession as well as his aspirations brought him into contact with the hard realities of society and politics, Brandeis could not afford to deny his ethnic roots.

Brandeis and the Boston Jewish Community

Throughout his life Brandeis remained loyal to the rationalist heritage of his mother. His daughter records: "Re: religion: the tone in the family was definitely agnostic . . . We children did have a Christmas tree, but it had no religious significance whatever." Furthermore Christmas was strictly a children's affair in the family. When Brandeis was active among Christian Germans and philo-Germans during his early years in Boston, he was invited by a friend for Christmas. As he wrote to his sister, he "was constrained" to excuse himself: Christmas for the busy lawyer was an opportunity to catch up on work or to relax. He certainly made no attempt to affiliate himself with any church and took pains to avoid the impression that he had done so. In a letter to his brother-in-law Otto Wehle, he mentioned going "to hear some very good music" at a church but added: "after Church hours."[15]

Brandeis did not speak in public on a Jewish subject until 1905, when he was almost fifty years old. By then events had contrived to encourage him to become an identifiable member of the Jewish community. Up to that time, he apparently considered himself a sharply dissenting Jew whose special obligations lay in upholding morality and improving civic life. While he and his wife paid membership dues to the United Hebrew Benevolent Association, from his first year as a lawyer in Boston (1879), he assumed no further responsibility in the Jewish community and took care that his donations reflected that inactivity. In December 1905 Harry Liebmann, an officer of the Benevolent Association and a Brandeis client, proposed to increase membership dues to fifty dollars. Brandeis, who had paid twenty-five dollars in previous years, refused: "In lieu of increasing my membership fee," he wrote, "I enclose herewith my check for $25 — as a special donation to the fund."[16]

When the Federation of Jewish Charities was founded in 1895, Brandeis was among the charter subscribers, and, again, his contributions were both regular and minimal. His annual income at that time was well over fifty thousand dollars. While Jacob Hecht contributed seven hundred and fifty, his wife Lina two hundred and fifty, and his brother Louis, Jr. three hundred and fifty dollars, Brandeis donated fifty dollars. Another lawyer of the German-Jewish community, Godfrey Morse, gave three hundred dollars. Brandeis kept this very low Jewish profile through the period under discussion. From 1902 to 1904, or probably 1905, he contributed sixty dollars annually; in 1906-7, seventy-five dollars.[17]

In the same years, however, many of Brandeis's professional activities were strengthening his affiliation with his ethnic group. In February 1880 he was asked by Jacob Hecht on behalf of the United Hebrew Benevolent Association to sue a member for back payment of his annual dues. Brandeis argued the case before the Massachusetts Supreme Judicial Court and won. It was one of his earliest cases, and his first before the state's high court. He remembered the success all his life.[18]

Several years later Brandeis again had an opportunity to give legal help to the Benevolent Association. In the winter of 1882-83, a wave of Jewish immigrants from Eastern Europe arrived in Boston, where they appealed in vain for help from the community's philanthropic institutions. Some of them sought refuge in the public poorhouse, the Commonwealth Alms House at Tewksbury. They were the first (and the last) Jews of this city ever to land in a poorhouse: Jacob Hecht and other leaders of the Jewish community made arrangements that all Jewish applicants for welfare be referred to the United Hebrew Benevolent Association. Following the crises Yankee charity workers regarded this Benevolent Association as the only organized body competent to deal with Jews from Eastern Europe. Many residents of the North End decided to join the now more prestigious United Hebrew Benevolent Association in preference to continuing the recently formed North End Benevolent Association. However in February 1883 a suit was brought against Jacob Hecht by some of the refugees, challenging his integrity in handling the matter, and Brandeis came to his defense. When the case was settled in his favor after two years, Hecht wrote to Brandeis: "The matter of $25 in suit of Rittenberg v. Hecht, I told you at the time that would be a labor of charity, as the Association would have to bear the expense. However if you think the society ought to pay the bill, please let me know, and I will lay it before the Directors, and they will no doubt pay. I know it is imposing on your goodness, but it is only the good who have to do the bulk of such things." Brandeis apparently capitulated, eliciting from Hecht "in the name of the U.H.B. Association" thanks for his kindness and generosity. This occasion was perhaps the first time that Brandeis, though perhaps not altogether voluntarily, donated his legal services.[19]

Brandeis's firm later served the legal needs of the Hebrew Industrial School, which had its roots in a project initiated in January 1890 by an instructor at the Young Men's Hebrew Association to teach sewing to Jewish girls. The undertaking was financed by Lina Hecht and supported by the Hebrew Ladies' Sewing Society. It developed into a major communal enterprise; thousands of children both learned a vocation and received an education in citizenship through a program of Americanization that was also designed to strengthen Jewish religious life. The school's legal needs were provided by Brandeis's law firm. Moreover Brandeis and his wife subscribed to the school and donated money annually. When the continuation of the school was threatened in 1903 because of other pressing needs of the community, Brandeis urged the school to "keep on"; the enterprise was finally saved. Brandeis's interest in educating people and providing them with skills led him to impress upon the director, Golde Bamber, the necessity of making the school better than the public schools.[20]

Brandeis's connection with the Jewish community was significantly intensified during October and November of 1902. Upon the request of his "old and valued friend," Jacob Hecht, he assisted in the effort made by American Jews to remove discrimination in Russia against the entry of American Jews into Russia. He helped in mobilizing support of non-Jews as well as in revising the Jewish appeal itself. The appeal stated that the time for negotiating a new commercial treaty with Russia had nearly arrived, that "the United States should insist — as an indispensable condition — of entering a new treaty that all discriminations by Russia against any portion of our citizens shall cease" and suggested that "such action would be American, and as Americans of the Jewish faith, we demand such action."[21]

Jacob Hecht's death (in 1903) did not loosen Brandeis's tie with the community. He was still besieged by constant calls for contributions — material, professional, and organizational. As a subscriber to philanthropic institutions and as a lawyer to many influential Jews, he was continually expected to give assistance to the Jewish community. Despite these pressures, however, Brandeis did not increase his activities in this area until the end of 1905; in the meantime the community received a minimum amount of his time and resources. He never flatly rejected a request but would simply evade it with the excuse of other engagements, calls out of town, and the like; he would generally finish by "wishing success" to the enterprise, which signified in his personal code that he supported the community in principle.[22]

The non-German-Jewish establishment also tried to elicit from Brandeis some participation in their affairs. The Russian-born Joseph Bergman, the spirited vice president of the Mt. Sinai Hospital Association and after 1903 its president, invited Brandeis to address the association at the formal opening of the new building of the Mount Sinai Hospital Society. Brandeis sent a characteristic response: "I regret that I shall not be able to attend at the formal opening of the new building. I enclose, however, my check for $25 — for the uses of the hospital. Wishing the society much success."[23]

The Jewish Nationalists also made the attempt in vain. In February 1905 Israel Zangwill, the Jewish Territorialist leader, visited Boston. Though not a Zionist, he was a nationalist dedicated to the creation of a Jewish autonomous territory in some country. Edward J. Bromberg, the secretary of the Mt. Sinai Association, asked Brandeis to come and meet Zangwill. But Brandeis avoided this occasion, saying that he expected "to be out of the city."[24]

It is interesting to consider how ordinary non-Jewish Bostonians saw Brandeis in terms of his ethnicity. Though Brandeis did not attend church, neither did he belong to a synagogue or observe the Jewish holidays. His name did not appear in the *Jewish Encyclopedia*, and as I noted, he did not address himself publicly on any Jewish subject until the end of 1905. Still, Jacob De Haas's assertion that Brandeis "was in 1910 neither regarded as a Jew locally nor nationally" is quite misleading.[25] Though not many in non-Jewish Boston were aware of Brandeis's being a lawyer with a substantial Jewish clientele nor of the Brahmins' anti-Semitic snubbing of him, the fact that he and his wife were early and loyal, if modest, members of the United Hebrew Benevolent Association was probably well known, as was his contributing regularly to the Federation of Jewish Charities. Brandeis's response to the plight of the Jews in Czarist Russia probably also marked him: in 1902 he was active in the campaign to abrogate the United States-Russia commercial treaty.

A year later Brandeis's concern for the Russian Jews was not so visible. After the Kishinev massacres in the spring of 1903, the Boston Jewish community established a Kishinev Relief Fund and staged public protest meetings. The Jewish Federation had the idea of asking Brandeis to address the meeting, perhaps because of his earlier involvement with the problem. He was approached by Lehman Pickert, an officer of the federation as well as a client. The usual response — revealing his desire to keep a low Jewish profile — was received: "Dear Mr. Pickert: I enclose herewith my check for $50 for the Kishineff sufferers. I think it best that I should not speak." Pickert thanked him for the check and added: "I regret very much that you could not see your way clear to speak at the meeting next Sunday P.M., but I fully understand your position and certainly will not urge the matter any further." Two years later, a new wave of persecutions occurred in the empire. A non-Jewish Bostonian who was moved by these events wrote to Brandeis: "Enclosed please find my mite for the poor sufferers of your race in barbarous Russia. May God, in His Infinite Love and Mercy, who does not willingly afflict, nor grieve, the children of men, in His own good time, relieve, and succor them." The sender wrote his letter by hand and enclosed one dollar; he clearly knew who Brandeis was. He may have heard something about Brandeis's efforts to abrogate the Russian-American commercial treaty, and anyway he knew enough to recognize him as an appropriate person to address. Brandeis sent the letter, the dollar, and his own check for fifty dollars to the fund.[26]

Brandeis had in common with the local Jewish community the German origins of its leaders. German Jews tended to cling to their German cultural roots. Much more assimilated in the old country than their East European counterparts, they often chose to spend their lives in a German-American milieu, in Boston as elsewhere. The Germanic Museum Association included on its board of directors, in addition to Brandeis, two distinguished Jews: Godfrey Morse and Jacob Hecht.[27]

Although there were some attractions in their milieu, Brandeis could not fully identify with the German Jews. For one thing, they tended to be conservatives. The standpat wing of the Republican party generally represented their views; they respected the established order and its money-making credo. That first-generation German Jews were preoccupied with accumulating fortunes and climbing the social ladder probably accounted for their conservatism. Years later Brandeis recalled these Boston Jews as being "crude materialistic [*sic*]" and depicted them as opposing any real "scope in education" or "broadly thoughtful view of life." It was certainly true that the atmosphere at the main social club of the city's German

Jews, the Elysium, was emphatically not conducive to intellectual discussion.[28]

On the other hand, German Jews were not generally found in the ranks of the imperialists, and a considerable number of them favored tariff revision. The Filenes, who were German Jews, were even well known as liberals and demonstrated, as we have seen, an abiding interest in social problems and some Progressive causes; but they were hardly integrated into the local Jewish community. Their names did not appear among the contributors to the Federation of Jewish Charities at its founding in 1895, even though social and family ties connected the Filene brothers to the German-Jewish group. (Edward Filene remained a bachelor, but Lincoln married the daughter of Charles Weil, a pillar of the German-Jewish community.) But as early Jewish liberals, they were atypical of their subgroup. On the whole, social respectability and economic ambition dominated Boston's German Jews and determined their political behavior. It remained for the second and the third generation to reshape that pattern.[29]

The politics of the East European Jews — albeit in a different way from those of their German brethren — were also determined by their being foreigners in the land. Insecure and unfamiliar with American politics, they let themselves fall into the hands of the Irish ward bosses. These ward rulers represented to the new immigrants not only an old and powerful political apparatus, but a source of aid in their distress. Many of the East European Jews therefore gladly gave their votes to the Democratic Irish machine.[30]

Like that of the German Jews, the East European subcommunity was not a homogeneous one. It included a leader of the cigar union and a radical trade unionist, Henry Abrahams, who was elected in 1888 to the presidency of the state branch of the American Federation of Labor. He was also an important figure in the Central Labor Union. But Abrahams, like the Filenes in the German-Jewish group, was not representative. Though he occasionally turned in an article to the local Jewish weekly, he did not have a close association with the Jewish community. That a prominent Jewish trade unionist did not influence the politics of his Boston coreligionists reflected the fact that they were not concentrated in a few trades nor did they have an esprit de corps as developed, for example, among Jewish workers in New York City.[31]

It was the East European professionals who later came to the forefront of the Jewish community's public life to extend its interests beyond private ambition to social compassion.[32] In the meantime the Jewish community was divided between conservative Republicans and followers of the Democratic machine. There was no strong constituency at the time that would lend its support to a liberal, not to mention a Progressive political course.

In Search of Identity

Not able to identify fully with Boston's German Jews, Brandeis could not identify with the German community either. It seems that this group was small in Boston and not cohesive enough to offer him a viable object for identification. Brandeis's connections with most of the various local German associations faded away by the beginning of the twentieth century. Although he was its director, it appears that Brandeis's actual involvement with the Germanic Museum Association was never intensive; there is indication that after 1906 he resigned from this directorship.[33]

Instead Brandeis was to become increasingly attracted to Boston's Irish community. His Irish associates — the O'Sullivans, John Tobin, and Mayor Patrick A. Collins (a prominent ally in some Progressive fights) — were quite a different lot from those who dominated the party machine in nineteenth-century Boston. The *Pilot*, their favorite and the leading Catholic weekly, crusaded against predatory capitalism and for government regulation: if the wage-earner could not hope to achieve utopia in this world, he was nevertheless encouraged to try; this theme was played by the weekly without variation throughout the 1890s. John Boyle O'Reilly and James Roche, the editors of the *Pilot*, also spoke out against anti-Semitism, combining the causes of social progress and ethnic tolerance. John J. Williams, the archbishop of the diocese from 1866 to 1907, encouraged the growth of Americanism in Catholic teaching and kept the more conservative Roman churchmen at bay. It was in part owing to him that the school of thought led by O'Reilly and Roche could flourish.[34]

But after the death of O'Reilly in 1890, the decline of the Irish liberal-Progressive trend began. In 1905 Mayor Collins died as well; 1907 brought an end to the regime of Williams and consequently to the lingering tradition of O'Reilly and Roche. Brandeis, already ambivalent, was probably repelled by what was left of Irish politics. In his crusade against corrupt city government, he could not ignore what every Bostonian knew—that the Irish were the ward bosses running the Democratic machine. He was also rather unsympathetic to Catholicism, nor did his law firm ever deal with Catholic Boston. His attitude is expressed in a letter to his fiancée in 1890 in which he wrote: "Politics—Congressional and State—are very active here, and I hope the very black Republicans will receive a blow. Their party organization is so disgustedly good—almost as good as that of the Catholic Church—and, at present, it serves no better purpose."[35]

Brandeis's Irish collaborators, however, as conscious and proud Irish nationalists, may well have left him to contemplate his own ethnic roots. Furthermore the fact that a Yankee, the newspaper editor Edwin Grozier, worked intimately with Brandeis in numerous struggles and spearheaded the Boston community's support for the Irish Nationalism cause, may have added to this effect. Occasionally Brandeis himself received invitations to support the Irish people in their fight against British domination. There was no way to escape the force of ethnicity in Boston politics.[36]

In Brandeis's developing identity, his relation to the traditions of New England played a pivotal role. Brandeis deeply admired native New Englanders and their heritage of individualism, hard work, excellence, reform, and tempered realism. He wrote to his sister: "the sense of being always under the necessity of preparedness to justify myself—is doubtless as wholesome as Puritan ancestry."[37]

Young Brandeis had identified easily with the community incorporating these values. He had been happy at Harvard Law School; he admired the case study method for its intellectual and spiritual foundations, revered the faculty, and even considered becoming a legal scholar. Later he was a loyal alumnus: in the years from 1880 to 1900, the law school was his chief interest outside of work. He founded the Harvard Law School Association and was its first secretary. In 1891 he was awarded an honorary A.M. degree in recognition of these services.[38]

As a student Brandeis came to love deeply New England's landscapes. And Boston's cultural and intellectual life totally absorbed him. It is in the context of his feelings about the region that his reverence for Emerson is understandable. "I have been indulging in 'Emerson,' " he wrote "and can conscientiously say, that my admiration for him is on the increase. I have read a few sentences of his which are alone enough to make a man immortal."[39]

These sentiments were to remain with Brandeis. In a speech given in November 1914, he claimed that the Puritans, through their attachment to democratic values and training in obedience, had brought American democracy to its fullest expression and commended them for their intellectual attainments. He continued to admire the New England educational system, which he saw as being exemplified by Harvard College.[40]

In his 1915 testimony before the New York State Factory Investigation Commission on the subject of the minimum wage law, Brandeis had occasion to express his feeling of the superiority of Massachusetts legal traditions. He was arguing that New York should adopt a law with compulsory or prohibitory powers; in Massachusetts, he added, that kind of legislation had not been needed until recently: "That fact that we in Massachusetts have adopted a law with recommendatory powers is to be explained rather on local grounds and historically. We in Massachusetts in the past have been a community differing radically from most of the communities in America." Recommendatory powers had been sufficient because the state had been small, possessing "the old puritanic sense," loyal to its tradition, and homogeneous. Brandeis felt that Massachusetts had a history of communal responsibility and a concomitant reform tradition.

You can see the difference between conditions in Massachusetts and New York or any other states by our experience with the franchise tax. Long before you here — we had a franchise tax upon our public service corporations . . . the amount of money that was held back by your corporations for that was about twenty millions of dollars. I made a study of this matter and found that the amount which our public service corporation had failed to pay in their franchise tax . . . was fifteen hundred dollars. In Massachusetts, I think we were the first in this country to introduce a public service commission or railroad commission as they then called it. For a generation our railroad commission had no power except the power of recommendations, because a recommendation that came from that commission was accepted as a rule of action on the other hand by the people . . . The same thing was true in a very great measure in regard to our factory laws.[41]

Brandeis's initiation of a course on the "Peculiarities of Massachusetts Law" is another example of his enthusiasm for the Massachusetts legal tradition. He proposed this course to the Harvard Law School just after his appointment (at the end of 1889) to its visiting committee. In his letter to the dean of the law school, in which he offered to teach the course himself, he said that it "might be justified through the honor which the Overseers have recently conferred upon me in appointing me to an office, whose duties I but imperfectly comprehend." Writing to President Eliot, he went on to explain:

The law of Massachusetts, while conforming in the main to the general law, has distinct individuality. Local customs, traditions and the peculiar habits of mind of its people, have resulted in a spirit which is its own. This is manifested partly in its statutes, but even more largely in what may be termed its common law. In my opinion the practitioner in Massachusetts should learn the Massachusetts law in this sense.

Brandeis showed great stubbornness in establishing this course at Harvard and later in sustaining it despite its initial failure. In the academic year 1895-96, the course was taken over by his junior law partner Ezra R. Thayer. Through Thayer's influence, courses on New York and Pennsylvania practice were also added; it was arranged that the course on Massachusetts law would be taught biennially, and it became a standard elective in the law school curriculum.[42]

Brandeis's fondness for New England ways was extremely strong, as his determination to institute the Massachusetts law course reflects. It may have been a case of the outsider's over-identifying with the insiders he admired. Samuel D. Warren once told him: "In many ways you are a better example of New England virtues than the natives." People who worked with Brandeis tell stories about his strictness, austerity, and frugality. Even his fantasies were borrowed from the Yankee world and reveal his idealization of its traditions: Paul Freund (who was for some years a law clerk to Justice Brandeis) recounts that Brandeis pointed to the cooperative ventures of the old New England seafarers as the essence of freedom, courage, and responsibility.[43]

As far as Brandeis's identity as a Jew was concerned, he may actually have been encouraged by the political atmosphere in Boston around the beginning of the twentieth century to demonstrate his bond with the Jewish community (he first publicly acknowledged his Jewishness in 1905). In any case he was generally known to be a Jew even before then, but in spite of this probably was not subjected to any upsetting incidents of anti-Semitism. On the contrary, the reformist movements alive at the time made Brandeis's ethnicity something of an asset, as he represented to some Bostonians the inheritor of a great moral tradition.

Of all the public struggles Brandeis engaged in until 1906, none generated more heat than his crusade for clean government. Brandeis repeatedly questioned the integrity of City Hall officials, exposing specific cases and boldly citing names.

His March 1903 speech before the Boot and Shoe Club was particularly aggressive. In the following month, he spoke before the Unitarian Club and this time attacked the Board of Aldermen for corruption. His sardonic tone coupled with a strong moral appeal gratified his Yankee supporters; furthermore, in his speeches for the cause of good government, he commended the ethics and dignity of the established business community. The Irish machine that dominated the Board of Aldermen was irritated by Brandeis's allegations, although Brandeis was careful to pay tribute to the integrity of Irish Mayor Patrick Collins (the board, however, did not resort to anti-Semitism).[44]

The man chosen to defend the board's integrity was Edward J. Bromberg, also a Jew and active in the Jewish community. The sharpest words he could muster to criticize Brandeis were that "his entire life . . . is colored by the greenish-gold light of finance." Obviously in no position to use anti-Semitism as a weapon, he instead tried to demonstrate that he himself was a better Jew than his "coreligionist."[45]

Because the philo-Semitic Puritan tradition was still alive in Boston, positive references to Brandeis's Jewishness were not infrequent. When the *Roxbury Gazette*, generally friendly toward Brandeis, found him complimenting Mayor Collins, they complained that Collins did not deserve his compliments. Brandeis himself must pursue the cause of good government, the article went on to say, because the lawyer had a great moral heritage, his ancestors and their immortal legacy deserving the admiration of all: "No, Mr. Louis D. Brandeis, . . . the blazing out of the path to good government did not await his [Collins's] advent to the mayoralty chair," stated the *Gazette*: "Thousands of years ago, on Mount Sinai, when Jehovah gave the commandments to Moses, the path to good government was blazed out in the words of that commandment which says 'Thou shalt not steal.' " The association of the Jews with the admired biblical tradition was probably a theme Brandeis got used to. His good friend Elizabeth Evans tells us that her reaction to learning that Brandeis was a Jew was that "it gave an aroma to his personality. 'A Jew! He belonged then to Isaiah and the Prophets.' "[46]

Ethnic Politics

On September 8, 1905, Brandeis got a telephone call from Max Mitchell, the superintendent of the Federation of Jewish Charities, concerning the problems of Robert Silverman, a Jewish law student and resident of the West End of Boston. Silverman had charged the district's educational system with corruption and had been accused of criminal libel. Brandeis promised to look over the material and see what he could do. In a few days he had received the following account of the situation from Silverman himself. The previous June, around the time the reappointment of the headmasters for the public schools was to be determined by the school board, a young teacher named Mildred Kallen had approached Silverman with evidence of mismanagement in the Washington School, one of the largest educational institutions in New England and one that also enrolled many Jewish children. Silverman investigated and found Miss Kallen's accusations well-founded, so he drew up and circulated a petition. "I presented the petition to the School Committee about the middle of June," he recounts. On September 6 a warrant had been sworn out against him and he appeared in Court on the seventh. The hearing was continued to the nineteenth of September. Appealing for Brandeis's help he wrote: "I knew how important it was to have the Public Schools clean and under honest and upright management in that part of the city where home influence and the environments of the school children were so bad. I knew that it was an outrage to find the same kind of men at the head of the schools that the little children were accustomed to see come out of the bar rooms and dives aside their very homes." Silverman gave Brandeis the names of two Jews who were well informed and capable of carrying on the battle: David Ellis, a member of the school board, and Max Mitchell, who was familiar with conditions in the West End. On September 14, under Brandeis's instructions, his law partner Edward McClennen consulted Ellis, a former partner in the firm.[47]

By representing Robert Silverman, Brandeis and his firm became caught up in the changes that were taking place in the local Jewish community. This transformation, exemplified by the founding of the New Century Club in 1900 and of the Mt. Sinai Hospital in 1901, involved the growing role of professionals among the Jews in Boston. The social worker Frederick Bushée, who wrote about the situation of the Jews in the West End in 1902, observed the background of this phenomenon: "Jewish children are among the brightest in the schools, and they study with a seriousness which is foreign to their Irish and Italian mates. High school and even college attracts a large number of those whose means permit." The historian Stephan Thernstrom has found that the percentage of white collar workers, including professionals, among East European Jews by 1910 was 25 percent of the occupational distribution of Jews (the parallel figures for Irish and Italians were drastically less).[48]

Late nineteenth-century immigration placed East European Jews in the majority within the local Jewish community before the turn of the century. From 1900 to 1910, the heavy influx of Jews from East Europe changed the demographic nature of Boston Jewry even more decisively. By 1910 there were more than forty thousand East European immigrants in Boston. Furthermore these newly arrived masses were not, like their predecessors, a demoralized and naive electorate. According to Jacob Neusner, who has closely studied the scene, from 1905-7 they began to free themselves from their dependence upon the ward bosses.[49]

The historian of the New Century Club and its president in 1905, William Blatt, wrote of the organization: "It is, indirectly and unofficially, but we think potently, behind every worthy movement for welfare and progress." Indeed though the club did not commit itself to any ideology of social progress, it did show a streak of militant idealism. According to a poem written by Blatt, the members were very much involved with social concerns: "To heal the sick, to help the weak, / For

Justice and the right to speak, / These, and a hundred other ends, / Each life its single journey wends." When these lines were written, in January 1905, the progressive Jewish professional had become a noticeable type and a strong force in Jewish Boston.[50]

By the first decade of the twentieth century, certain important trends had converged to make this new progressivism possible: the growing constituency of Jewish professionals, the East Europeans' emergence as a decisive majority, and the increasing political independence of the latter group. When they took up the case of Robert Silverman, Brandeis and his law firm came into contact with a very different Jewish community from the one they were used to. In the Kallen-Silverman affair, the firm, and Brandeis as an individual, were for the first time aligned with a Jewish progressive cause.

McClennen, the man in Brandeis's office best qualified for litigation, served as Silverman's counsel. The array of challengers to the school committee was formidable. One of these was James Storrow, an astute Brahmin leader in the field of education, accused by the school board of showing personal bias and creating disorder in censuring the Washington School authorities. McClennen brought to the stand, among others, Horace Kallen of Harvard University, Mildred's brother. Finally, when it was revealed that Martin Lomasney, the boss of Ward 8, backed the corrupt headmaster of the Washington School, the legal struggle to exonerate Robert Silverman developed into a political fight against the ward bosses. By mid-November the trial had caught the public's attention and was fully covered by the newspapers. "Speaking with suppressed emotion," recorded one journal, "Mrs. Duff [of the School Committee] . . . said that Robert Silverman, Mildred Kallen, Lawyer Brandeis and the other conspirators of the Public School Association had used her enemies against her."[51]

There were obvious ethnic overtones to the conflict. The West End was being vacated by the Irish, but those who remained behind still wielded tremendous political power and controlled the educational system. The Jews, who had become the majority in the West End, wanted schools that would serve

the educational ambitions they had for their children. In this
struggle the Jews gradually acquired significant Protestant
backing; this support represented a reaction to the school committee's bitter attack on James Storrow and the Yankee-domi-
nated Public School Association, who were trying to maintain
Boston's traditionally high educational standards.[52]

On September 29 the *Boston Advocate*, the city's most important Jewish newspaper, published a long editorial entitled
"Is Your Child in Danger?" and directed to hard working,
family-oriented Jews who wanted to give their children a "good
education . . . decent and uplifting." The *Advocate* dealt with
the dangers the Silverman affair was serving to uncover: "If
your boy at school is not in contact with men of the highest
character, you may be sure that before long he will be a
shadow in your life. If your boy is in daily contact with a vulgar
and depraved character, he will learn things that will make for
your own and his destruction . . . A teacher, and more particularly the master of a school, must be a model citizen. He must
embody the traits that make a gentleman. If he lacks these, the
boy will soon imitate the worst that he displays."[53]

The *Advocate*—itself not free of anti-Irish prejudice—then
called on its readers to reject the bosses and destroy their
hegemony. The coming election, it claimed, could well advance these ends:

> The book-loving race, whose passion for learning is one of their
> imperishable heritages, are in danger if they do not keep close
> touch with their children at school. At election time, you have an
> opportunity of voting for the men and women who select your
> teachers, directly or indirectly. They decide what the school policy
> shall be, and appoint the superintendent of the vast educational
> system. Do you inquire into the merits of the school candidates?
> Does a cheap ward politician tell you for whom to vote? If you
> have ever been approached by these parasites, you have been
> shamefully outraged, and should make up your mind what you
> will do if you are ever approached again . . . When the souls and
> the future of your children are part of the political spoils, are you
> not sinning against your own? Stand up for children! Destroy the

enemies who would sacrifice even them for their miserably selfish ends.

The *Advocate* told its readers that they were not in this struggle alone. "There is a sufficient number of good citizens in Boston who will take up your fight in the safe-guarding of your little ones. The entire city will rise against the enemies of childhood . . . Unless the voters of Boston stand up for the best service in the public schools, the fair traditions of the city, the educational treasures which make Boston so different from a Russian town will perish."[54]

For the Protestant allies of the *Boston Advocate* the struggle against the Irish bosses was by no means restricted to concern for the quality of education. With Mayor Collins's death in September 1905, they felt the decline of liberal Boston had begun. John Francis Fitzgerald, Collins's opponent, had moved swiftly to seize control of the Irish machine and represented to them its evils. When Fitzgerald won the nomination of his party to run for mayor in mid-November, the *Boston Transcript* violently attacked him; its favorite candidate was from the "better element" of Boston, Republican Louis Adams Frothingham. The *Transcript*'s editorial claimed that Fitzgerald was a real danger to "our high civic heritage" and that his victory would be "hardly less than a disaster, would be the creation of a municipal machine more unscrupulous, more tyrannous, more reckless than anything which Boston has ever experienced." Even more energetically than the *Transcript*, the Good Government Association worked to defeat Fitzgerald. Their choice, too, was Frothingham. For them, the mere possibility of Fitzgerald's coming to power seemed a catastrophe.[55]

Terrified by Fitzgerald's crowd, the *Transcript* and the Republican strategists sought to enlist the crucial Jewish vote on Frothingham's behalf. They were no doubt gratified to learn that a Hebrew Independent Club aimed at detaching Jewish voters from the machine had been founded in Ward 9 by the end of October. Several weeks later, the Republicans scored another victory: "Frothingham Their Guest: Hebrews'

Dinner to Republican Candidate," announced the *Transcript*, and informed their readers that Frothingham was the guest at a lunch "given in his honor by a number of the leading young Hebrews of the city."[56]

The Jewish community was perfectly and quite early aware of its pivotal role in the 1905 city election. By October 20 the *Boston Advocate* was already noting that there were about ten thousand Jewish voters in Boston and asking: "Do you know what it means to place the entire strength of this army of men in any one direction? The balance of power is held by the Jewish voters of this city." The *Advocate* lamented the misuse of Jewish voting power in the past and called for a new approach:

> Handed out here and there in small numbers to certain party bosses; was the Jewish vote for the good of the Jews? No, but for the good of the candidate selected by the bosses who will forget their promises nearly as soon as they are made. The Jews should not seek representation as Jews, but they should seek protection for themselves and families by honest legislation which can only be given by honest fearless men . . . Remember what our people have suffered through the influence of ward bosses . . . Above all be men now and evermore, and show by your sincerity, and truthfulness that you know your rights and will not under threat or promise, become a tool for any cause.

The article was a policy-making one, and from that point on the *Advocate* worked hard to mobilize the community along definite political lines. The establishment of decent and good education and the abolishment of machine politics were its themes.[57]

During the mayoral campaign, the law firm of Louis D. Brandeis had finally triumphed in the defense of Robert Silverman and Mildred Kallen. Furthermore the firm expressed its support for their cause, telling Silverman in January 1906: "We have concluded not to present any bill to you for the services rendered for you in the matter." Silverman wrote to Brandeis: "The City of Boston as well as my friends and I are greatly indebted to you for what is the most significant service the municipality has in the last year been rendered."[58]

When the struggle over the educational system in Boston broke out in the autumn of 1905, Brandeis had already been a member of the Public School Association for several years. He had joined this reform body under the influence of Charles Eliot and had been very active in it for some time. His involvement with the Good Government Association, with which the School Association cooperated, had also caused him to follow the latter's course with interest. Thus when Brandeis became engaged in the political campaign of 1905, it was only in part because of his concern for education; he was just as interested in the more general issue of good government.[59]

For Brandeis, as for the other leaders of the Good Government Association, the possible election of either John F. Fitzgerald or James Donovan, both aspiring to the Democratic nomination for mayor, represented an imminent danger to Yankee civilization. In October he signed a petition urging Louis A. Frothingham, the favorite of the GGA, to seek the Republican nomination. When asked for his reasons, Brandeis characteristically referred to Frothingham's loyalty to the values of old New England:

> If elected to the Mayoralty, he will come to the office absolutely without any pledges, and will administer the affairs of the City in the same fair, honest and impartial manner which has thus far characterized him in his career. He will have the courage to do what he believes to be for the best good of the citizens, without striving for any temporary popularity; he will administer the affairs of the office without any self-seeking, without any posing, in a simple and modest fashion, and in a way which must commend itself to the plain, sober, thinking people of the City.[60]

Though at times Brandeis commended Frothingham for his Progressive tendencies (mainly with respect to the Boston Elevated issue), he more often called him an upholder of the fundamental values of the Puritan tradition: it was chiefly the lack of these in Fitzgerald that had aroused Brandeis's hostility. In a letter to Edmund Billings, the secretary of both the GGA and the Public School Association, Brandeis asked: "Can you send me a memorandum of the reasons, besides his general reputation, why men should not vote for Fitzgerald? What facts have you in regard to his record?" When Billings replied that he had some information regarding graft and blackmail, but that the file was incomplete, Brandeis impatiently responded: "Men! Arms! Ammunition! We can't win without them." Brandeis knew enough by that time, however, to conclude that "Fitzgerald is one of the worst types of the Democratic Machine Man." Even when Fitzgerald won, Brandeis's animosity remained; and when he was defeated after two years, the lawyer speedily congratulated his successor.[61]

In 1905 Brandeis affiliated himself openly with a progressive Jewish organization. On October 26th he received an invitation to address the New Century Club of Boston. By that time he had become very active politically and was well known in the East, but he had not publicly addressed a Jewish group. Now he was ready to do so, and the New Century Club must have suited him well. The abiding interest of the club's membership was in good government, the democratic process, the merit system for selecting officials, honest administration, and reform. Club members William Blatt, Jacob Silverman, and Edward Bromberg were Republicans who abhorred the practices associated with names such as Donovan and Fitzgerald. In the campaign of 1905, these men headed Jewish organizations that actively worked to defeat the Democratic machine. The New Century Club would provide an audience to whom Brandeis could speak as a Jew and without undermining his liberal-Progressive image. Its members represented the "new" Eastern European Jew — idealistic, intellectual, and proud.[62]

Brandeis had been invited to speak in commemoration of the two hundred and fiftieth anniversary of the settlement of the Jews in the United States, but it was something outside the Jewish context that made him decide to address a Jewish organization for the first time in his life: the impending mayoral election. Brandeis considered the political situation in Boston to be at a critical point, with democracy and decent government threatened and the Puritan virtues in danger of extermination. He decided to descend to trying to convince the Jewish community to join forces with the Yankees.

Since his address (delivered on November 28) was designed to defeat Fitzgerald, Brandeis sought press coverage to ensure a wider audience. He entitled the talk "What Loyalty Demands," by which he said he meant "the obligation which this great privilege of American Citizenship involves—the obligation of loyalty to American Institutions and ideals." "In the first place," said Brandeis, taking aim at the Irish machine and the ethnic accent of "Honey Fitz's" campaign—"loyalty demands elimination . . . of class distinctions . . . There is no place for what President Roosevelt has called hyphenated Americans. There is room here . . . not for Protestant-Americans, or Catholic-Americans or Jewish-Americans, not for German-Americans, Irish-Americans or Russian-Americans," but merely for American citizens. Customs that tend to perpetuate differences in origin or religious beliefs are, he said, inconsistent with the American ideal of brotherhood, and are disloyal. Loyalty demands "people [who are] honest, courageous, intelligent and just." (Putting "honest" first was, of course, deliberate.) "Loyalty demands of every citizen active participation in Government . . . Nearly every male inhabitant holds by birth or naturalization the office of citizen, and as such has the right and the obligation to vote." He "must seek to distinguish between the good and the bad—between the genuine and the sham—between the demagogue and the statesman." The Jewish public could, through its vote, liberate itself from the reign of fear or favor of the Irish bosses by living up to the noble traditions of the Jewish race which meant showing "energy, perseverance, self-restraint and devotion . . . intelligence or genius . . . power . . . to hurl from its pedestal the Golden Calf," as well as "austerity."[63]

Lest his audience be misled into thinking that he was advocating Jewish separatism, Brandeis observed that Judaism was an all-embracing spiritual force. " 'Long after the Jewish state had fallen' their [the Jews'] religion became 'that of civilized humanity,' " quoted Brandeis. The laws of the ancient Jews regarding the treatment of strangers showed that the "demands of Jewish law 'knew no restrictions of race, so its privileges were open to all.' The recognition of those high ideals of the Jewish race its members found at least in America. Loyalty to them is loyalty to true democracy—loyalty to the American ideals of Liberty, Fraternity, Justice."[64]

Brandeis thus added his voice to that of the *Boston Advocate*, urging that a Jewish vote be cast on behalf of the noble American traditions. However the *Advocate* simply implied that Jewish values and American ideals were compatible and made its appeal instead to Jewish pride, "uniqueness," and interests. ("The Jews should not seek representation as Jews, but they should seek protection for themselves and families . . . 'self preservation is the first law of nature' and it is in such a movement that power can be brought to bear . . . There is no Jewish vote and there are not Jewish voters, but the Jews have a certain responsible position to fill during these important times and it is up to them to exercise this right.") Brandeis in his address before the New Century Club sought to show the connection between Jewish and American ideals and, by appealing to both, win the Jewish vote for his cause. Furthermore he claimed that the Jewish character made it especially qualified to defend these ideals to American society.[65]

Brandeis's address, though politically motivated, did make him feel more strongly his kinship with the Jewish people. A few days afterward he suddenly sent to his brother a "portrait of his old friend Judah Touro," and to his father, who was probably more conversant with Jewish matters than Alfred, he sent the manuscript of the speech and commented: "I am inclined to think there is more to hope for in Russian Jews than from the Bavarian & other Germans. The Russians have idealism & reverence" (that is, they were more Progressive).[66]

The German Jews by and large remained in the Republican camp and strongly opposed the Irish Democratic machine in the campaign of 1905. At the November 29, 1905, commemoration of the two hundred and fiftieth anniversary of the settlement of Jews in the United States held at Faneuil Hall, the acknowledged lawyer of Boston German Jewry Lee Friedman echoed Brandeis's concept of Judaism. He, too, felt that the ultimate responsibility of American Jews was to make a contribution to American society. But there was a difference: Friedman expressed the belief of German Jews that it was vital to preserve autonomous Jewish life and elements of Jewish religion for their own sake. For Brandeis in 1905 the only important aspect of Judaism was a set of social-moral values; by preserving them Jews could contribute most to the welfare of American society. A sense of mission and messianic redemption thoroughly determined Brandeis's first open expression of his Jewishness.[67]

When the election was over, the *Boston Transcript* lamented Frothingham's defeat; the community would now have to live under the mayoralty of John Francis Fitzgerald. The success of several Public School Association reform candidates was for the *Transcript* small compensation, but for the *Advocate* it represented "victory for the children" and the first successful attempt at mobilizing the Jewish vote. And out of these struggles came Brandeis's beginning perception that the Jewish community was a strong political force that could be enlisted to support the "right" causes.[68]

4

Daniel in the Lions' Den

Progressive Crusades

AT the same time that he was busy defending old New England values on the political front, Brandeis devoted himself to the preservation of what he considered traditional New England business ethics. In April 1905 some Brahmins who held policies of New York insurance firms became concerned by the financial scandals in the Equitable Life Insurance Society of New York, and they approached Brandeis to protect their interests. He responded by forming the New England Policy-Holders' Protective Committee, acting himself as unpaid counsel.[1]

On October 26 Brandeis criticized the conduct of New York life-insurance companies before the Boston Commercial Club and commended the practices of the Massachusetts savings banks. Conscientiousness, simplicity and efficiency, Brandeis said, characterized the management of this system. Against this model he exposed the frauds in the New York life-insurance industry, where extraordinarily high premiums were exacted for extremely low benefits. In the United States a movement proposing that the functions of savings banks be extended to include providing life insurance had been pioneered in Massachusetts during the 1870s by the insurance commissioner Elizur Wright, whose son, a well-known consulting actuary, now began to assist Brandeis in the New England Policy-Holders' Protective Committee. One result of their collaboration was the publication in the second half of 1906 of Brandeis's articles "Wage-Earner's Life Insurance," where he recommended that Massachusetts savings banks be authorized to sell life insurance, and "The Greatest Life Insurance Wrong." In the second article he wrote:

> Massachusetts laid the foundation of America's admirable system of savings banks by chartering, in 1810, Provident Institution for Savings in the Town of Boston. Massachusetts established for the world the scientific practice of life insurance by the work of its great insurance commissioner, Elizur Wright. It seems fitting that Massachusetts should lead in another great advance in the development through thrift of general prosperity by extending the functions of savings banks to the issuing of workingmen's life insurance.[2]

After reading the New York Armstrong Committee's findings on the affairs of the large insurance companies, Brandeis began to develop two new ideas: first, that finance capital was posing a special threat to free competition and, second, that bigness could lead to inefficiency. These notions, and especially his proposed remedies for the insurance industry, he thought to be in the tradition of Massachusetts business practices. Thus when opposition to his proposals arose on the part of the local businessmen whose New England virtues he so esteemed, Brandeis tried to explain it away as "a vague apprehension on the part of the savings bank men that confidence will be impaired in their banks." When he discovered in November 1907 that Boston's savings banks had illegally invested in the securities of the New Haven Railroad, he characteristically preferred to believe "that most of the officers of the savings banks and members of the investment committees are not aware of the facts . . . as to the right of the banks to invest in [those] securities." To convince the bankers that the public would have confidence in savings-bank insurance, Brandeis began to mobilize the public in support of the plan. The Massachusetts Savings Bank Insurance League, established in November 1906, represented this mobilization and tried to

pressure the banks into expanding their functions by developing insurance departments.[3]

Only gradually, within certain bounds, and in private, did
Brandeis begin to criticize the opposition of the savings banks,
which had originated in an alliance with other of the state's
financial interests, to his plan. In addition to his expectations
of support from Massachusetts bankers, the fact that among
those opposing him were men with whom he had been allied in
the recent campaign against John Fitzgerald gave rise to his
caution. The candidate of the good-government forces, Louis
Adams Frothingham, in whose campaign for the city's mayoralty Brandeis had invested so much, was the president of the
Blackstone Savings Bank and active in stalling the savings-bank
life-insurance plan. Frothingham supported another plan,
which was also the choice of the banker Henry Lee Higginson.
Higginson not only was a banker of the good-government
movement, but, like Frothingham, had given Brandeis substantial though quiet support in the subway and gas controversies. When Frothingham and Higginson unveiled their
"over-the-counter" plan in 1906, Brandeis was at first optimistic.[4]

The system called for the incorporation of an insurance society in which the stockholders would get a limited, fixed interest. Agents would not be used; instead the insurance would be
sold in law and trade union offices, factories, stores, and other
places similarly accessible to the public. A year later Brandeis
had reversed his attitude to Higginson's plan when he discovered that it would do much to improve the situation for
policies of over one thousand dollars in amount but would not
include an old age annuity provision or serve the working people's needs as cheaply and effectively as the savings-bank insurance plan. His conclusion was: "The Higginson 'Over-the-
Counter' bill not only fails to meet the industrial insurance
need, but I have reason to believe that for five months the
industrial insurance companies have been working to secure
the passage of that bill with a view to intrenching themselves in
their present position."[5]

In the meantime Brandeis's savings-bank insurance idea had been favorably covered by the Boston newspapers, and the Savings Bank Insurance League had become popular, allowing Brandeis to expand his connections with trade unions in the state, although among Boston's capitalists his allies remained largely his traditional ones. Since its leaders did not support the savings-bank insurance movement, the Policy-Holders' Protection Committee had not helped much. The textile owners were hostile to him, and Brandeis wrote to the president of the United Textile Workers of America that "the opponents of our savings bank insurance and annuity are making a great display at Lowell and Lawrence." The secretary of the Savings Bank Insurance League complained that its agents "are having a terrible experience" in Lowell and Lawrence and "I do not believe they can even get into the factories there without a campaign of some magnitude." The shoe manufacturers, on the other hand, did not disappoint Brandeis. William Douglas and shoe clients William McElwain, Charles Hall, and especially Charles Jones, played a vital role in the movement. The mercantile men were less influential, but maintained more intimate relations with Brandeis. On New Year's Day, 1907, when the hearings and discussions in the Massachusetts Assembly and Senate on the proposition to establish savings-bank insurance were about to begin, Brandeis wrote in his diary: "Drafted vote for Merchants Assn." It was printed in the *Bulletin* of the Boston Merchants Association for January-February as recommending "that the State Legislature take up the plans now being advanced for a system of Savings-banks Insurance." An item in the same issue congratulated Brandeis for his plan and for the successful drive "which aims to give insurance to the people of moderate means at a moderate cost."[6]

The other arm of the city's mercantile community, the Boston Chamber of Commerce, also supported the insurance plan. Brandeis was in constant touch with Bernard Rothwell, already a leader of the organization and soon to become its president. Rothwell helped Brandeis to increase his support; when the Chamber of Commerce and the Merchants Association merged in 1909, they included in their joint report a special item detailing their effort "to propagate the savings bank insurance system."[7]

The German Jews were also generally favorable to his savings-bank insurance plan. Edward Filene cooperated with Brandeis and later set up the Wage Earners' Committee on Insurance of the Boston Chamber of Commerce. His brother Lincoln brought Brandeis into contact with the New York Jewish financier Henry Morgenthau. Brandeis asked Morgenthau to get the liberal-Progressive *New York World* to agitate for his idea, expecting Morgenthau to mobilize Jewish support in like manner to "Mr. Thomas B. Fitzpatrick, whom we know of as the leading Irish Catholic businessman in the State, and president of the Union Institution for Savings [and who] is heartily in favor of the plan."[8]

But the main arena of the struggle was in Boston, and there Brandeis found supporters in the form of Lehman Pickert, the president of the Federation of Jewish Charities and a long-time merchant client of his (who became a member in the Committee of One Hundred, a special public body supportive of the Savings Bank Insurance League), a generally conservative German-Jewish constituency that was probably attracted by the informative rather than belligerent tone of Brandeis's drive and its appeal to Jewish traditions, and some younger professionals, notably social workers.[9]

Providing safe insurance to people of small means was particularly important to the last group, which was represented in the Committee of One Hundred by Max Mitchell, Meyer Bloomfield, and the same Robert Silverman who had fought against corruption in the public schools. Mitchell, the man who had persuaded Brandeis to defend Silverman in 1905, combined social work and administrative skills to become the superintendent of the Federation of Jewish Charities. Meyer Bloomfield, a close friend of Lincoln Filene, had only just graduated from Boston University School of Law in 1905 and now directed the Boston Civic House in the North End. Bloomfield led many campaigns supporting trade unionism, denouncing poverty, and recommending public intervention in matters of transportation. Supporting Brandeis's savings-bank insurance plan was in accord with the progressive spirit behind the Boston Civic House. Though not yet a central figure in Boston Jewish life, Bloomfield was already a member of the executive board of the Young Men's Hebrew Association and a constant contributor to the *Mt. Sinai Monthly*. Robert Silverman, besides practicing law and working for Zionism, devoted himself to Jewish social work in close cooperation with Mitchell and his assistant Martha Michaels (who later became Silverman's wife).[10]

Brandeis also realized that he would need a good public relations effort to overcome opposition to his plan. His appearance before the special Joint Recess Committee (appointed by the state's legislature) on November 8, 1906, was the first hurdle. He then enlisted the Publicity Bureau of Boston to prepare the propaganda of the Savings Bank Insurance League. Brandeis also called on Jacob Silverman of the New Century Club and Max Mitchell, who was influential in the Jewish *Boston Advocate*; he discussed with them the savings-bank insurance matter and consulted them throughout that winter. On February 22, 1907, the *Boston Advocate* published an editorial warmly endorsing Brandeis's insurance plan and calling him a great reformer:

Ever since the memorable Armstrong insurance investigation in New York, Mr. Louis D. Brandeis of Boston has been persistent in pointing out to the American people that no more wasteful institution imposes upon the poor, particularly the foreign poor, than so-called industrial or burial insurance, as it is at the present time carried on . . . Our purpose in presenting the matter in this issue is not so much to express our opinion of the plan as to call the attention of our readers to one of the most significant reforms proposed in our time. The matter is so important, so far-reaching, that we bespeak the earnest study of the subject on the part of our subscribers. We advise our readers to take up the matter, to devote a little time to this big subject. A busy man like Mr. Brandeis is devoting almost his life to it at the present time. Our columns will be open to any expression of opinion that the matter may call forth.[11]

In May 1907, before a vote was taken in the Massachusetts legislature, Brandeis met Mitchell in his firm's office together with Bloomfield and the rabbi of Temple Israel, Charles Fleischer, and maintained continual contact with them as well as with Mrs. Hecht until the vote in the House. Finally on June 5, 1907, the bill passed the House, and the *Advocate* congratulated its author and wished him well in the Senate vote (which he was to win):

> The great progress thus far made in the Legislature halls by the very important insurance bill drawn up by Mr. Louis D. Brandeis is marked enough to call for congratulations to the author.
>
> Our editorials on the subject of savings banks form of insurance have called forth warmest commendations clearly showing that our readers were following the proposed reform with acute interest.
>
> And why not? The insurance companies who make the tenement houses their hunting ground for industrial insurance business have for a long time caught the eye of workers among the poor. If the Senate of our State does its duty as well as the House has done, Mr. Brandeis will have achieved a great work for the working people of Massachusetts.[12]

Brandeis no doubt showed his appreciation for the editorial support of the Jewish press when he increased his donation (after a conversation with Pickert) for 1907-8 to the Federation of Jewish Charities to about double the sum he had given in the past. Though he gave less than his rich German-Jewish clients, his contribution was higher than that of most of the practicing Jewish lawyers in Boston. The amount of his contribution (he maintained this level in future years) also undoubtedly expressed Brandeis's new firm association with the Jewish community.[13]

This alliance, however, was not made principally with the German-Jewish elite or with the official Jewish community, but rather with the element represented by Max Mitchell, Robert Silverman, and Meyer Bloomfield. It was with Max Mitchell, and not with Pickert, that Brandeis developed a serious understanding on the savings-bank insurance issue, and it was Mitchell's *Boston Advocate* that represented Brandeis to the

Jewish community. Just as he had avoided the Elysium and spoken to the Jews for the first time at the New Century Club, so in 1907 Brandeis had chosen as his mouthpiece the *Advocate* (whose predecessor, the *Mount Sinai Monthly*, had been founded to arouse interest in and raise money for the first Jewish hospital in Boston), one of whose most conspicuous interests was movements of social progress.[14]

The success of savings-bank insurance, unlike Brandeis's earlier undertakings, depended upon continuous public support and action. The accomplishment of his objective consisted not merely in passing a single law, but in building up a whole alternative system — a project that would prove to be extremely difficult. The first savings-bank insurance department was opened in June 1908 in the small town of Whitman; in November another opened in the People's Bank of Brockton. No more were begun for the next two years and only two more after that, both in Pittsfield, between 1911 and 1921. Then and during the next decades (until the late 1930s) Brandeis's system did not reach Boston at all. By 1910 the savings-bank insurance system had 3,318 policies totaling $1,367,363; by contrast, the John Hancock Life Insurance Company of Boston alone had 1,941,106 industrial policies with a face value of $323,010,618.[15]

A major problem that had confronted Brandeis's system from the outset was one of supplying the necessary guaranty funds (provision of these had been confined to three shoe manufacturers). Another and even more difficult challenge was convincing the public that the system would work.[16] For this Brandeis needed a public receptive to his arguments and open to economic innovations; apparently he hoped to find it in the Jewish community through the intermediary of the *Boston Advocate*.

Jacob De Haas, the ex-secretary of the Federation of American Zionists who had visited Lewis Dembitz (sometime around 1902), came to Boston in 1906 as superintendent of the Young Men's Hebrew Association, a position he held for four years. A Zionist and a progressive, he was soon attracted to the *Boston Advocate*. Because it was for some time (during its early history) also the official organ of the YMHA, De Haas had some influence in the newspaper's affairs and connections with the people involved in it. One of these was Leo J. Lyons, until 1908 one of its editors as well as its business manager, who was like De Haas an early Zionist and a progressive. In August 1908 De Haas, Lyons, Mitchell, and two others purchased the *Advocate*. Lyons and De Haas made themselves editors, but gradually De Haas took over.[17]

In January 1909 De Haas wrote Brandeis asking what the *Advocate* could contribute to the support of the savings-bank insurance cause. They met at Brandeis's office on January 22; by February 5 an *Advocate* article appeared entitled "Saving at Small Expense" and subtitled "The Workings of Louis D. Brandeis Insurance Scheme." It outlined the details of the scheme and ended by strongly commending "the plan for which Louis D. Brandeis stands" as a means of avoiding socialistic legislation and improving savings methods at the same time. At the end of that month, the *Advocate* published a lecture by Dr. Lee K. Frankel, given at a Boston club under the auspices of, among others, the Federated Jewish Charities, on the subject of conditions of industrial workers. The address alluded to the insurance issue, and the lecturer expressed his "heartiest good wishes" for Massachusetts savings-bank insurance plans. Other similar publicity for Brandeis's cause followed throughout the spring. Now openly seeking public support, Brandeis at times gave speeches to Jewish groups. When, on March 13, 1909, he spoke at the Council of Jewish Women (whose invitations he had previously declined) on the subject of savings banks, he further cultivated his new relationship with the Jewish community.[18]

At the same time as Brandeis intensified his relationship with the progressive-minded *Boston Advocate*, he also utilized his old connections within the city's Jewish mercantile community to advance his plan.

Brandeis needed local agencies to sell policies for the two savings-bank insurance departments outside the Boston area. As always, his clients were useful. In September 1908, in addition to William Filene's Sons Company, the Henry Siegel Company and Conrad and Company were among those agents appointed to operate within their firms on behalf of the Whitman Savings Bank. A memo written by Brandeis's secretary Alice Grady, who became the financial secretary of the Savings Bank Insurance League, from the same period records that "Mr. Cory of Filene's telephoned me today and said that he had talked with Mr. Ferris of the Gilchrist Company [a department store owned by the Vorenbergs], who stated that he either had or would immediately apply for an agency from Whitman." Brandeis wrote that Abraham Ratshesky, a prosperous wholesale clothing merchant, authorized him "to apply on behalf of these two concerns for agencies for the Whitman Bank."[19]

A Jewish law student who was well connected in the city's mercantile circles, Abraham Pinanski, was also to help Brandeis in implementing the insurance plan. Brandeis met him through the businessman Louis E. Kirstein, who became an important person in Brandeis's life around this time. Kirstein's original business had been in Rochester, New York, but he had gradually developed business connections with the Filene company and from 1906 on lived in Boston. Brandeis advised Kirstein on the development of these relations until the time of Kirstein's joining William Filene's Sons Company as a vice president in 1911. Kirstein was very civic-minded; his father, who had left Germany after the failure of the 1848 revolution, was a follower of Carl Schurz. Like the Filenes, however, Kirstein developed his liberalism along the lines of the Progressives.[20]

During his first years in Boston, however, Kirstein was too busy to take much of a role in public affairs. Still he provided Brandeis with contacts in the Jewish community, including the competent and reliable Abraham Pinanski. Like his father (a merchant and a close friend of Kirstein), Abraham was active in the Jewish community. In particular he was interested in workingmen's insurance and served before 1909 as the secretary of the Boston Merchants Association Committee on Wage Earners' Insurance. In 1909 he was enrolled in the Harvard Law School, and he soon became a kind of agent for Brandeis at the university. (It was probably through him that Brandeis met his classmate Jacob Kaplan, whom he took into his law firm in 1910; Kaplan was a member of the Jewish students' organization and the Menorah Society, along with Pinanski.) Brandeis encouraged Pinanski to continue his public-service work "as far as you can without interfering with your law school program" and to mobilize Jewish organizations on behalf of the common cause:

> We have before us much educational work. We want to have the subject written up and talked on every possible occasion. Won't you do some writing and also join our corps of speakers, and among other things aid us in getting opportunities for presenting the subject before different audiences? It occurred to me that you might be in a way of getting the movement started among the various Jewish societies and clubs.[21]

Although Brandeis intensified his connections with the Jewish community from 1906 to 1909, he rather rarely addressed it directly. He probably felt a kinship with the progressive Jewish element, but he continued to identify primarily with the Yankees. The opposition of the savings-bank people and the animosity of some circles of the liberal financial community had surprised him — but had not loosened his attachment to the heritage of these people. Perhaps this was so because he *had* received considerable support from non-Jewish Boston, his plan had become a state law, and some beginnings of implementation, though meager, had been made. When Brandeis embarked on the next great political struggle, he still spoke in the name of New England tradition; but this time the struggle was to end in total defeat.

The history of Massachusetts legislation regulating corporations and especially railroads is a subject that has been well explored. The state pioneered many laws that were the goal of Progressive battles all over the country. When from 1903 to 1906 Charles Mellen, the president of the New York, New Haven, and Hartford Railroad Company, tried to acquire Massachusetts's interurban street railways, he encountered an old statute passed in 1874 that prohibited any railroad corporation from directly or indirectly holding the stock of another corporation unless authorized to do so by the legislature. The legislature defeated the New Haven's attempt to acquire this authorization in June 1906, for which they were roundly praised by Governor Curtis Guild, Jr.: "Let Massachusetts announce that transportation within her borders is in the future to be controlled by the people of Massachusetts and not by men beyond the reach of her law and the inspiration of her ideals." The New Haven's management was not discouraged, however, and continued its monopolizating efforts by buying up shares in the Boston and Maine Railroad, its chief rival.[22]

Brandeis soon became involved in the conflict. Samuel Crocker Lawrence (whose American ancestry went back to 1635) appeared with his son in Brandeis's office asking him to defend their large stockholding interest in the Boston and Maine against the "foreigners." In June 1907 Brandeis wrote to Edward Filene urging him to return at once from a trip to Yokohama because a question lay before them as to "whether the whole transportation system of Massachusetts shall be turned over to a single monopoly, and that one controlled by aliens — practically the Standard Oil and J.P. Morgan interests — parties who have great interests in other states and little in Massachusetts, and are foreign to our tradition."[23]

Later, in his lengthiest public criticism of the proposed merger between the New Haven system and the Boston and Maine, Brandeis struck his familiar theme: the importance of preserving the unique traditions of Massachusetts in the matter of business practices. Addressing the New England Dry Goods Association in February 1908, he pointed to the danger of "an alien monopoly" and stressed that "this monopoly by the New Haven in transportation within New England and from New England south and west would be controlled by persons alien to Massachusetts, not only in their financial interests, but in their traditions and aspirations." By contrast with what Brandeis depicted as the corrupt giant from New York, Massachusetts's Boston and Maine Railroad was highly commended: "the Boston & Maine system is a great system . . . it possesses a solid foundation . . . It is for Massachusetts to build up this distinctly Massachusetts railroad so that it shall be worthy of Massachusetts."[24]

Aside from the possibility of control by "foreign" interests, there were two further dangers, as Brandeis saw it, in the proposed merger: bigness and the weakening of free competition and democracy by finance capital.[25] But, as in the savings-bank life-insurance struggle, he saw these dangers in terms of their threat to New England tradition, and this precluded him for some time from publicly criticizing the role of the Boston Brahmins in the merger.

Though the New Haven system that Brandeis opposed was controlled by New York interests—J. P. Morgan had selected Charles Mellen to head the New Haven Railroad in 1903—Massachusetts financial interests had joined it in its efforts to monopolize New England transportation and stood to profit handsomely from the arrangement. Lee, Higginson and Company, the most powerful banking house in Boston, had sold the stock of Boston and Maine to the New Haven Railroad: "This has been engineered by Lee, Higginson & Company under an arrangement which is reported to be that the brokers get $1.50 per share for putting the transaction through," Brandeis wrote to Edward Filene. Not surprisingly, Lee, Higginson used all its tremendous power and far-reaching connections in attempting to put the merger through. In March 1908, when the Boston Chamber of Commerce decided against the merger, Gardiner M. Lane of the banking house called the president of the Chamber of Commerce and tried to pressure him into changing his mind.[26]

Brandeis contacted the secretary of the newly founded Massachusetts Anti-Merger League and suggested the counter tactic of disseminating one thousand copies of his own pamphlet on the subject; two months later he alerted the league's secretary that Lee, Higginson and Company had succeeded in placing one of its employees in the job of accountant for a legislative commission appointed to investigate the issue of railroad combinations. These efforts proved to be real threats to the proposed merger, and Henry Lee Higginson himself was prompt to act: Brandeis no longer seemed just another liberal campaigning against remote or common enemies, but a radical menacing business interests. To undermine Brandeis's influence and to secure the merger, Higginson allied himself with Senator Henry Cabot Lodge, the most conspicuous advocate of protectionism and imperialism in Massachusetts. Having heard that Brandeis had met with President Theodore Roosevelt to discuss the merger matter, Higginson wrote to Lodge on April 24, 1908, a letter which opened a continuing correspondence between them:

> My dear Cabot: So far as I know, Brandeis has been to see the President about the merger business, and I do not believe he has been speaking the truth. He has certainly said things here which were untrue . . . He has attacked and lied . . . Brandeis professes that he is working for the public good . . . Somebody, from July of last year, has been spending a good deal of money with his committees and agents throughout the state, and [he] hardly furnished that money himself. There is a deep-laid and skillful game going on which is very costly and very venomous, which is frightening our officials and our Legislature, which has a considerable amount of labor element behind it, and which means a good deal. Just what it means, it is difficult to say . . . He has endeavored to throw out the New Haven securities from the savings banks and to push the New Haven railroad out of the state . . . But the point to which I would call your attention is that Brandeis is not to be trusted.

Lodge's response was designed to hearten the banker, and thus the anti-Brandeis alliance among the Brahmins was established. Higginson's next letter said:

> What I would like to prevent if possible is Brandeis going up and down the State and saying things which are untrue, pushing his figures which are rotten and throwing discredit on men like those of this Commission . . . I have no question that he is trying to stir up the Democrats, make capital out of this merger and be elected. I should consider him a most dangerous man in office, as he is a dangerous man out of office . . . If anything can be done to put a damper on it, I wish it may be done but perhaps there is nothing.

If anything occurs to you, let me know and if you can in any way discredit Brandeis's statements, I shall be glad.[27]

The anti-Brandeis coalition soon included the Commonwealth's governor, Eben S. Draper, an ex-manufacturer of textile machines, an ultraprotectionist, and an archimperialist. Draper, who was acting governor of the state in 1908, and governor from 1909 to 1911, received a confidential five-page letter in June 1908 from Higginson extolling the advantages of "the union of the two corporations." Higginson wrote: "The Boston & Maine Railroad is carelessly managed, and much of it arises from lack of capital . . . We should not have thought of advising this union to be made if we had not studied the case carefully." To this he added: "I am perfectly clear that Brandeis and company have dragged this matter into politics and have demoralized the public very much." On the eve of the vote in the legislature on the Draper Bill, which provided for the approval of the merger, Higginson once more contacted Lodge: "I am very much afraid that the foolish men guided by Brandeis and White, of our Legislature, together with Rothwell, the President of the Chamber of Commerce, will defeat Governor Draper's excellent bill about the railroads . . . These men . . . are themselves in the habit of lying . . . I certainly should not believe Brandeis or Lawrence on oath."[28]

The merger's advocates found a powerful ally in the governor; on June 15, 1909, his "excellent bill" passed by 180 to 49 votes and three days later was signed into law. The bill provided for the establishment of a holding company empowered to acquire any or all the securities of the Boston and Maine; it allowed the New Haven to acquire the securities of the holding company. The holding-company device, long suspect in Massachusetts, thereby received an official stamp of approval.[29]

Alluding to Massachusetts's failure to defend itself in the New Haven case, Brandeis commented some years later: "A change has come in Massachusetts . . . The people have changed and the people who controlled industry have changed; we have no longer the same conditions." He was referring also to the New Haven Railroad's victories in the legislature on June

15, 1909 and June 13, 1913, the latter date marked by the passage of the Washburn Bill. This bill had originally been intended to mitigate the effects of the Draper Bill victory but was rendered totally ineffective in the form finally ratified by the assembly.[30]

Brandeis had bitter feelings toward those who had defeated him. In 1909 he wrote to his brother: "We got unmercifully licked but it took all the power of the Republican machine & of the Bankers' money to do it." That the leader of this group, Henry Lee Higginson, was thought by some to be Boston's leading citizen prompted Brandeis to remark in 1913, in summing up the "seven year war" against Mellen of the New Haven, that "the real disgrace to our community is the past attitude of our Pillars of Society—Higginson et al." In addition to being angry, Brandeis also knew moments of despair. "I am rapidly becoming a socialist," he wrote to his brother one month after the debacle: "What the bankers leave undone, their lawyer minions supply. After such experiences, an A.R.C. [American Red Cross] may claim me wholly his own." It was cause for depression that Brandeis's foes in the railroad fight had been his erstwhile allies. In the subway and gas controversies, the Lee, Higginson interests had stood to gain a great deal: Joseph Lee had consequently contributed substantial sums to the Public Franchise League. Laurence Minot, a member of the same business circle, had been chairman of the executive committee of the Good Government Association from its foundation in 1903 until 1910. The cooperation of these men had represented Brandeis's alliance with liberal State Street. That alliance, already weakened during the savings-bank life-insurance debate, was now shattered, as Brandeis was perfectly aware. In his letter to Edward Filene at the beginning of the antimerger fight, he had written: "The critical nature of the situation is due to the fact that those who ordinarily have worked with us in public matters have been either instrumental in bringing the merger about, or actually believe it desirable, or believe it to be inevitable." Brandeis had gone on to describe the New Haven's planned takeover and added: "This has been engineered by Lee, Higginson &

Company . . . All of State Street is of course in favor of the merger, and the larger trustee holders, including Laurence Minot, are exchanging their 7 per cent. Boston & Maine for 8 per cent. New Haven stock."[31]

These former allies of Brandeis had joined his traditional antagonists, the New England textile magnates, in the enemy camp. Others had not: the New England Shoe and Leather Association adopted strong resolutions against the merger in 1908 and again at the beginning of 1909. Both the president of the Massachusetts Anti-Merger League and its treasurer were shoe-manufacturer clients of Brandeis, Dunbar and Nutter. The mercantile community had been divided. Although in 1907-8 the Boston Merchants Association and the Chamber of Commerce opposed the railroad merger, by 1909 the new Chamber of Commerce (formed by a merger of the two groups) was split. Brandeis had correctly gauged the situation in June 1907 when he warned Edward Filene that "men like J. R. Carter, Jerome Jones, and others, whose impression was against the merger, are considerably hampered." These leaders of Boston's mercantile community, veterans of Brandeis's public fights, did not join the ranks of the Anti-Merger League. Even the Filenes, although lending their names to the organization, were not unwavering in their support.[32]

Support for the merger among Massachusetts businessmen reflected their apprehension about the declining New England economy. A growing number of businessmen had begun to believe that decreased control over corporations would improve the situation in general and particularly that a bigger, united railroad system would be more efficient and thus give Massachusetts a competitive advantage in national markets that used railroads. But not every Massachusetts industry had agreed with this solution to the state's economic problems. To the shoe manufacturers, who had vigorously opposed the merger, it seemed that for "continued growth and prosperity . . . the system of reasonable competition in transportation which has heretofore been maintained by the wise laws of the state . . . should be preserved and continued." This line of thought also found expression in the mercantile community.

Those confident of the success of their businesses and those leaning toward the philosophy of free competition and free trade tended to reject the merger and oppose the loosening of Massachusetts corporation laws. But these groups gradually lost ground and were decisively defeated in June 1909.[33]

New Alignments

Brandeis's struggles for savings-bank life insurance and against the state's capitalists in the railroad merger issue eventually forced him into labor's camp. John Tobin, president of the Boot and Shoe Workers Union, whom Brandeis had known from earlier dealings with the shoe industry, was an important ally in the expansion of the savings-bank insurance system and was active in the Anti-Merger League. John Golden, president of the United Textile Workers, helped mobilize public support for these causes and weaken the opposition of the textile manufacturers. An association between Brandeis and the secretary of the Boston Central Labor Union, Henry Abrahams, was initiated at the end of 1906 while both were involved in the insurance fight and grew gradually stronger during the railroad merger struggle. Edward Cohen of Lynn, president of the state branch of the American Federation of Labor, was also a valuable ally, having developed close ties with Brandeis in 1907 while working with him for savings-bank insurance; but this alliance was short lived—Cohen died at the end of that same year.[34]

Because in the insurance and antimerger efforts Brandeis was pitted against the large-capital interests represented mainly by Yankee Protestants in the textile, banking, and railroad industries, he was willy-nilly on the side of Boston's ethnic groups. The successful businessmen in these groups had not had access to the world of large capital and had begun their careers in industries where relatively little money was needed to make a start. Thomas Fitzpatrick, the leading Irish businessman in Boston and president of the Savings Bank Insurance League, had started as a dry-goods merchant, and even while he served as trustee of a savings institution had not been part of the inner circle of the Boston banking community. His modest beginnings made him a likely supporter for Brandeis's savings-bank insurance plan; he had important connections among the Irish through his involvement in many of their organizations, and he used these to further his adopted cause. Brandeis decided to follow in the Jewish community the example of Fitzgerald's method of operating among his fellow Irishmen, by activating Max Mitchell and the *Advocate* on behalf of the insurance plan. The strategy proved successful, soon became a habit, and was recommended to others. In February 1909, when David Tilley, a Catholic stockbroker, described to Brandeis how Lee Frankel, the Jewish vice president of Metropolitan Life had introduced reforms in company policy under the influence of Brandeis's ideas, the latter remarked: "I must not fail to ask you what progress you are making among your Catholic friends in regard to promoting the savings bank movement."[35]

Like Fitzpatrick, Bernard Joseph Rothwell, who was born in Dublin, achieved financial success through trade; he became influential in the Boston Chamber of Commerce and served as its president from 1908 to 1910. Though less active in the local community than Fitzpatrick, Rothwell was also a well-connected and self-conscious Irishman. With Fitzpatrick he served as a trustee of the Irish Union Institution for Savings and perhaps to an even greater extent than his coreligionist worked to disseminate his views, especially on the merger issue, among Boston's Irish. Brandeis was grateful; since he had begun his railroad merger fight, his backing even among the city's merchants had dwindled considerably. In the Chamber of Commerce, Rothwell, who did not like the Higginsons, faithfully and energetically worked with Brandeis to win over those members who disagreed with the antimerger course. Brandeis was aware of Rothwell's prominent position in the Irish community and found him particularly useful when Archbishop O'Connell refused to lend his authority to the antimerger movement.[36]

O'Connell's position reflected a new reactionary trend in Catholic Boston. When he became archbishop of Boston in

1907 (he was cardinal from 1911 to 1944), earlier efforts to liberalize the church came to an end; intolerance toward Yankees and Jews was encouraged. John Fitzgerald, Mayor of Boston in 1906-7 and 1910-13, went along with O'Connell's policy. With the more liberal Mayor Collins and Archbishop Williams both dead, the social atmosphere of Boston changed drastically.[37]

The Catholic Boston of O'Connell became a veritable font of bigotry. Michael Earls, a church leader who worked with the new archbishop, openly encouraged anti-Semitism, but since its effects and the attitude of O'Connell and Fitzgerald were not really felt until after 1910, it is doubtful that Brandeis himself was a target of Earls's attacks much earlier than that. He did, however, apparently endure before 1910 anti-Semitism that originated in the Protestant community. In 1916, writing to his brother regarding opposition to his nomination to the Supreme Court, Brandeis implied that anti-Semitic attacks upon him had begun in 1907, coincident with the beginning of his crusade to prevent the New Haven merger: "It is not as unpleasant to us as would seem to the outside. This attack continued throughout nine years has quite accustomed us to it and we are glad to have it out. At all events, the country including Boston will know what I have been 'up against.' I suppose eighteen centuries of Jewish persecution must have enured me to such hardships and developed the like of a duck's back." Brandeis's account seems to corroborate that of Jacob De Haas, who remarked that "the publicity agent for the railroad interests that he [Brandeis] often opposed described him as an 'oriental.' " The assaults upon Brandeis were sporadic and probably did not occur in writing. Still the new atmosphere in Catholic Boston coupled with even the mildest anti-Semitism from vested interests could only encourage Brandeis's growing alliance with the Jewish community.[38]

Although not many Jewish merchants supported Brandeis in the merger struggle, those that did held positions of prominence. The Filenes no longer stood alone as members of the German-Jewish elite dedicated to progressive causes. The second generation of German Jews were less materialistic and more at home in American politics than their parents and thus were not afraid to take antiestablishment stands. Felix Vorenberg, who had assisted Brandeis in the savings-bank movement, joined the ranks of the Anti-Merger League. The firm of Conrad and Company also first cooperated with Brandeis in the savings-bank insurance campaign, and later its chairman of the board, Sidney Conrad, joined Lincoln Filene as a vice president of the Massachusetts Anti-Merger League. Of the East European Jews, Meyer Bloomfield and Max Mitchell were important members of the community who gave Brandeis assistance. Bloomfield, the head of the Boston Civic House and a lawyer, screened a list of people for Brandeis, informing him of their attitude regarding the merger and suggesting if and how it was possible to influence them. Mitchell, the superintendent of the Federated Jewish Charities, who met with Brandeis rather often during the spring of 1909 on other public matters, undertook to send a letter (dictated by Brandeis) to a long list of Massachusetts Assembly members.[39]

While Bloomfield and Mitchell, heavily involved in social work and welfare, obviously represented for Brandeis the new Jewish Progressivism, Henry Abrahams, the Jewish secretary of the Massachusetts Anti-Merger League may have played a similar role, though it is doubtful, since in any case he was not closely associated with other Boston Jews. Edward Cohen of Lynn, the president of the state's American Federation of Labor, was helpful to Brandeis, but the briefness of their collaboration and lack of evidence make it hard to conclude that Brandeis thought of him as typical of his community. Thus it seems that Boston's Jewish professionals went furthest toward offering Brandeis affiliation with a group of Progressive Jews.[40]

The *Boston Advocate* did not take part in the New Haven merger controversy. It only rarely lent its pages to general political issues (savings-bank insurance was one such exception) and saw no particularly Jewish concern in this one; perhaps its editors also considered the matter too controversial and divisive to take a stand on. But the New Century Club invited

Brandeis to give an address on the merger issue, and he willingly did so. On this occasion he also had a chance to speak casually about politics with members of the club. He wrote to his brother afterwards: "I met at a Jewish club where I talked merger last evening [with] a man who had met a family of Philadelphia Dembitzes (not William)." Especially in the atmosphere of growing hostility to his public endeavors, it must have been encouraging to Brandeis that he was able to "talk merger" with his fellow Jews.[41]

In the early spring of 1909, Brandeis and Edward Filene launched the "Boston 1915" movement, a project aimed at the civic and social betterment of the city. As in the savings-bank insurance effort, while working for a general cause — an ideal city conducted in accordance with the vision of its Yankee founders — Brandeis came to depend more and more upon the Jews for help. Indeed the project can be said to have been sponsored by the Jewish community. And also as in the earlier campaign, Henry Abrahams and Meyer Bloomfield were notably helpful. Together with the Filenes, Mitchell, and Bloomfield, Brandeis (according to the latter's diary) "talked about Jewish organizations" and planned and evaluated their contribution to the civic project.[42]

The "Boston 1915" movement did not achieve very much, in part because of the indifference of Protestant Boston. Some Yankees must have been deterred from involvement in an organization with such an obvious Jewish leadership. The name of Louis D. Brandeis — now the enemy of a growing number of businessmen and of State Street — discouraged others. James J. Storrow, the standardbearer of the Protestant community in the 1909 city election and a partner in Lee, Higginson and Company, gave his support to the movement at first but dropped out in 1910.[43]

The *Advocate* was the only Boston paper to give the movement extensive coverage. Indeed this action represented a departure from its usual policy of dealing almost exclusively with Jewish subjects (when the *Advocate* did treat a general subject, it meant that a Jewish interest was somehow involved or that an election was about to occur). It had in fact supported Brandeis's savings-bank life-insurance plan, but mostly —as now with the "Boston 1915" movement—because it was Brandeis who was behind it.[44]

Brandeis had come to feel increasingly that the traditional leaders of Massachusetts were betraying their state. At the end of May 1909, two weeks before the defeat of the antimerger forces in the legislature, Lincoln Filene approached him on behalf of the Boston Merchants Association regarding the organization of a Massachusetts fire-insurance company. Brandeis was most willing to support such a project, referring to a letter that he had written to Edward Filene on this subject two months earlier and adding a scornful criticism of "Storrow's associates": "It is a strange fact, that although Lee, Higginson & Company are placing more security issues than any other concern in the City, and I think probably more than all the other banking concerns together, they have not, so far as I can recall, financed a single Massachusetts enterprise for many years." James Storrow, although a member of Lee, Higginson and Company, had at first supported Brandeis's savings-bank insurance plan, but by the middle of 1909 was back in Higginson's camp, leading the Businessmen's Merger League, and in 1909 he placed himself as a candidate for mayor against the incumbent Fitzgerald. This development put Brandeis in a real quandary.[45]

Storrow was backed by both the Good Government Association and the Citizens' Municipal League. His record merited that support: he had faithfully served on the Boston School Committee and other public organizations. Fitzgerald was, of course, anathema to the GGA people. He had also not supported Brandeis's savings-bank insurance plan and had come out strongly in favor of the Draper merger bill. Between these two men, Brandeis felt he had little choice and decided to side with Storrow. It is an index of the progress of Brandeis's disillusionment with Yankee society that in the 1905 election he

had actively supported the GGA candidate opposing Fitzgerald, Louis Frothingham, but now halfheartedly did so. He
responded coolly to a letter from the old liberal Charles Hamlin by saying that the city needed "a man of large ability" and
that Storrow was only a "man of marked ability."[46]

As in the election of 1905, most of Jewish Boston now opposed John Fitzgerald, and most supported the GGA candidate. The *Jewish Advocate* (its name had been changed from
Boston Advocate in May of 1909) began to mobilize Jewish
public opinion on behalf of its favorites for the mayoralty and
city council, all candidates endorsed by the GGA. David Ellis,
a favorite of the *Advocate* since 1905, had the support of the
Public School Association and of its activist Leo Lyons (who
was also an editor of the *Advocate*). In addition the *Advocate*
strongly supported Plan Two, a project sponsored by the GGA
as a means of achieving more honest and efficient electoral
procedures in the city. Max Mitchell was active in the Hebrew
Independent Club in support of Plan Two and lent his name in
endorsement of Storrow. By the end of 1909, the *Jewish Advocate* and the Jewish professional and progressive circles had
won Brandeis over.[47]

In three consecutive issues of the *Advocate*, on October 15,
22, and 29, a political advertisement was published endorsing
Arthur D. Hill for District Attorney. Hill had been a clean,
bold and efficient district attorney, and especially successful in
prosecuting the city's grafters. But there was yet another reason for the *Advocate*'s supporting him, and the signers of the
petition, headed by Brandeis (whose name appeared first, out
of the otherwise strict alphabetical order), spelled it out: "One
of his assistants in whom we have every confidence is Philip
Rubenstein, who is a well-known co-religionist who enjoyed a
reputation for probity of character and interest in communal
affairs for years before he was appointed to office by Mr. Hill."
Brandeis may have participated in this Jewish petition more
out of interest in the election of Hill than of Rubenstein; nonetheless he had allowed his name to be used in what was clearly
a partisan Jewish cause. Moreover the number of times Bran-

deis was mentioned elsewhere in the pages of these same issues indicates his growing importance and involvement in the Jewish community during this period.[48]

Beyond the Yankee Domain

Disappointed in the turn New England's politics and business were taking, Brandeis had become interested in social experiments being conducted elsewhere. In 1908 he read H. G. Wells's *New Worlds for Old*, and, according to Elizabeth Glendower Evans, it "immensely interested Mr. and Mrs. Brandeis and me, and led them to urge me . . . to make a dash to England and tell them about the New World, with Old Age Pensions and meals for maintaining school children of which Mr. Wells spoke." Mrs. Evans explained that "Brandeis had insisted . . . [she] should make [the trip] to find out what English Socialism was like" and at his behest she toured Britain for three months — and apparently suffered a case of culture shock on her return: "When I returned to the United States, Oh, but I found it bleak and cold! 'Is this the land of my fathers,' I said, 'which I have thought of as fit to redeem the world? The ideals of a former generation as I knew them in Boston seem simply bent on making money.' I came home feeling myself a lost soul in a perishing land."[49]

It was probably through Brandeis that Mrs. Evans came to address the Jewish community on the achievements of English socialism. The *Advocate* reported to its readers that "Mrs. Glendower Evans delivered a very interesting lecture [to the Jewish People's Institute] on 'Industrial Conditions in Europe.' "[50]

In June of 1909 Brandeis, too, started to travel. In November he was "entering Kansas, en route" and writing to his brother: "I feel that I have overcome much of my lamentable ignorance of the United States, and have now seen its most wonderful parts. West of Lincoln, my previous ultima Thule, the remarkable America really begins." He urged Alfred to "take your family west soon and widen your American Horizon," and in a subsequent letter recommended: "Don't fail to keep in mind seeing the West with your family. It is the real thing."[51]

Mrs. Evans had in the meantime forged a great friendship with the Progressive leaders of the agrarian Midwest, Robert and Belle La Follette. After attending a convention in Chicago of the Women's Trade Union League, she, together with fellow delegate Mary O'Sullivan, visited the La Follettes at their farm in Wisconsin. "When I got back to Boston," she recounts, "Mr. Brandeis had much to ask about my experiences in Wisconsin. It happened that winter [1909-10] he passed many weeks in Washington [in connection with the Ballinger case] . . . from my discourse of the La Follettes he struck up an intimacy with both the Senator and his family, then in Washington. Mrs. La Follette often told how one evening there came a ring at the door-bell and Mr. Brandeis called up: 'Have you got a cold potato to give a wayfarer?' " A friendship had quickly developed, characterized from its inception by warmth and a meeting of the minds. To Mrs. Evans's question (upon Brandeis's returning from Washington) whether La Follette knew much about railroads, Brandeis answered: "He knows all there is to know. He is the great expert upon that subject in this country." With Brandeis's urging, La Follette reopened the New Haven merger issue on April 12, 1910, in the Senate of the United States. The abandoned heritage of New England, Brandeis hoped, would be redeemed by "Fighting Bob."[52]

By April 1910, when La Follette and Brandeis were trying to restore good Yankee values to Massachusetts business practices through the agency of the United States Senate, Brandeis's ties with Boston society had become very limited indeed. Furthermore Samuel D. Warren, his closest Yankee friend and first law partner, had died on February 19, 1910. The *Boston American* reported that Warren died at age fifty-eight, a healthy and energetic man:

A great deal of mystery shrouds the sudden and unexpected death of Samuel D. Warren at midnight Saturday night, at his

121

beautiful home on the Charles River in Dedham . . . Louis D. Brandeis . . . who was in Washington in connection with the Pinchot-Ballinger controversy, hurried home and was in charge of things at the Warren House Today . . . Mr. Brandeis stood as a guard between newspaper reporters and any members of the family. The lawyer made this statement: "Mr. Warren died from apoplexy. I think that exhaustion, following the suit that has been started against him, was largely responsible for his death. He came here to rest for a few days."

Brandeis stood guard to conceal from the newspapermen the real cause of Warren's death—the millionaire lawyer turned manufacturer had shot himself.[53]

The suit referred to in the *Boston American* was in fact the result of a struggle over money that had developed within the Warren family. After 1901 there had been a rift between the heirs of the elder Samuel Warren, and their conflict had become steadily more bitter, noisy, and ugly. At the end of 1909, Edward Warren brought suit against his brother Samuel. The later retained the Brandeis law firm (which previously had been counsel for all the concerned parties), but instead of defending Samuel himself, Brandeis sent Edward F. McClennen to the trial. "He told me," wrote Norman Hapgood a few years later, "how much he disliked to leave this Warren case to his partners on account of his own personal feeling for Warren, although he felt that his partners were as able to conduct it as he was." Other responsibilities were obviously now of more importance to Brandeis. He was busy at this time with the famous Ballinger-Pinchot case, trying to keep America's resources out of the hands of monopolists. He was forging his alliance with La Follette to restore the economic independence of Massachusetts. These seemed more significant matters than a protracted contest over an inheritance.[54]

Certainly the death of Samuel Warren was of great social as well as personal significance for Brandeis. From the first years of their association, Warren had provided Brandeis what acceptance he did have in Yankee society, as well as launching his legal career. The years spent living in Dedham, during which Brandeis made his somewhat thwarted attempt to join the clubs and generally live the life of the Brahmins, were made possible by his relationship to Warren. Samuel Warren mixed with the most elite of Boston society, and Brandeis's connection with him afforded the latter a degree of social prestige he could not otherwise have attained during the early years. When Warren died, Brandeis was already on rather bad terms with the Brahmins owing to the Progressive causes he had pursued at State Street's expense. Warren's death drastically reduced what remaining bond Brandeis had with that group.

Nevertheless it seems that Warren's privileged social position would inevitably have led to tension between him and Brandeis when the latter began his various fights against the vested financial interests in Boston. This was in fact the case and helps explain why Brandeis declined to handle personally the Warren lawsuit. Before 1905 Warren had willingly supported Brandeis's causes—the good government movement, the Boston Elevated struggle, and unionization for workers. But after that date, he ceased to follow Brandeis's lead. When Brandeis began the savings-bank insurance drive and later when he headed the antimerger forces in the railroad conflict, Warren did not take his part: he had too many ties with State Street. Warren evidently did not accept Brandeis's invitation in November 1905 to attend a meeting on the "subject of insurance of working men" despite his earlier interest in the conditions of labor. He is not mentioned in the literature or surviving papers concerning the savings-bank insurance movement. Nor is Warren mentioned in the voluminous papers connected with the fight against the New Haven merger. Warren's evasiveness in these matters undoubtedly caused his friendship with Brandeis to degenerate.[55]

At the time of Warren's death, Brandeis had just been badly beaten in the railroad merger controversy by the "pillars" of Boston society (while Warren stood by). Thus it seems likely that Brandeis had become disillusioned with his friend just as he had with the Yankees in general, who were no longer in his eyes the upholders of their own ethical tradition. In addition he might have seen the sordid Warren family lawsuit and the suicide as symptoms of what he now suspected old Boston to be: a deteriorating society.

Beginning in 1906 a circle of Jewish social workers had supported Brandeis in his savings-bank life-insurance and anti-New Haven struggles; some of them also cooperated with him in promoting the causes of industrial education and arbitration. Associated with this group and very much involved in these efforts was Meyer Bloomfield, who had the active support of Lincoln Filene. The three men often discussed the possible role of the United States Industrial Commission, the National Civic Federation, and the Commission on Industrial Education in furthering their interests. In the spring of 1910, Brandeis's law firm advised Filene in his plan to establish a Vocation Bureau aimed at providing vocational guidance for youth; Bloomfield was to be the director. Filene guaranteed the director's budget and, when the bureau was formed, served on the executive board. Brandeis was a member of the bureau's advisory board.[56]

In July 1910 Filene and Bloomfield contacted Brandeis regarding a garment workers' strike then under way in New York. As a clothing merchant, Filene was of course concerned about a steady supply of goods from the garment district, but there was also another reason for his interest. The New York garment workers' strike was a Jewish affair: both employers and employees were by and large Jews. Thus in addition to their general interest in labor matters, Filene and Bloomfield may well have felt it was their responsibility as Jews to help resolve the conflict. Brandeis agreed to lend his services, and on July 23 he left for New York. The strike represented to Brandeis an opportunity to test some of his ideas about labor-management relations; the fact that Jews were on both sides of the fence made this an especially interesting case. He earlier had taken part in the Filene company's experiments in cooperation between employees and management (perhaps for this reason he was all the more willing now to answer Lincoln Filene's call). In December 1906 Brandeis, along with Lincoln and Edward Filene, had become a trustee of the new Cooperative League, whose purpose was "promoting the investigation and study of and providing instruction as to economic and industrial questions and aiding in improving the relations between employers and employees." Brandeis had been very close to the development of this organization. A month before approaching him in reference to the garment workers' strike, Lincoln Filene (who was the league's treasurer) had met with Brandeis to set new goals for the Cooperative League: These were to be "promoting the investigation and study of all matters relating to civic democracy and industrial democracy, including methods of civic and industrial organization and improvement . . . advancing and aiding the progress of and improving civic and industrial conditions."[57]

In New York Brandeis succeeded, with considerable effort, in bringing both sides to accept the solution of a preferential shop. A protocol of agreement was signed that established self-government in the industry: a board to standardize working conditions, a grievance board to settle disputes, and an arbitration board as the highest authority, were organized all representing milestones in the history of labor-management relations.[58]

Jewish workers in the New York garment industry typically identified with their ethnic origins. Furthermore, many of them were followers of the Bund (abbreviation of the Yiddish name of the influential Jewish socialist party founded in Russia in 1897), which in America meant that they believed that wherever Jews lived, they should struggle, as Jews, for the cause of democracy and social justice. During the strike Brandeis was made aware of this particular brand of Jewish idealism. According to a monograph on the subject of his involvement in the negotiations between garment workers and their bosses,

Brandeis at times heard a man shout in Yiddish: *'Ihr darft sich shemen! Passt dost far a Idn?'* (Shame! Is this worthy of a Jew?) On one occasion he heard a shopworker confront his employer with a quotation in Hebrew from the prophet Isaiah (3:14-15): "It is you who have devoured the vineyard/ The spoil of the poor is in your houses./ What do you mean by crushing My People/ By grinding the face of the poor?/ Saith the Lord God of hosts."[59]

Brandeis was deeply moved by his New York experience. Several years later he described how, while striving for "the American ideals of democracy and social justice" in connection with this strike, he came "into close and almost continuous relations with Jews en masse, with employees and employers and with many who were but recent immigrants." He added: "I was impressed, deeply impressed, that these Jews with whom I dealt showed in a striking degree the qualities which, to my mind, make for the best American citizenship, that within them there was a true democratic feeling and a deep appreciation of the elements of social justice . . . Observation and study revealed to me that this was not an accident, that it was due to the fact that twentieth century ideals of America had been the age-old ideals of the Jews."[60]

Brandeis was as much impressed by the workers' intelligence and understanding as by their passion for justice. Several years after the strike, Brandeis, who had remained in constant contact with the garment workers' unions, referred to the Jewish workers as "thinkers" and as possessing "many good qualities, intellectual and moral."[61]

Brandeis's association of Judaism with a social ethos was furthered by the fact that the Jewish employers had also demonstrated a unique attitude:

> What struck me most was that each side had a great capacity for placing themselves in the other fellows' shoes. There was the usual bitterness and rancor but despite this, each side was willing to admit the reality of the other fellows' predicament. They really understood each other, and admitted the understanding. They argued, but they were willing to listen to argument. That set these people apart in my experience in labor disputes.[62]

Those who had introduced Brandeis to the strike and worked with him toward its resolution were also, of course, Jews, and one of them was even a leader in the field of ethical Judaism that Brandeis had been brought up on. "The success obtained in New York was due in a very large measure to the admirable team work of A. Lincoln Filene, Meyer Bloomfield, and Dr. Henry W. Moskowitz," wrote Brandeis: "They are entitled to far more credit than I am." Moskowitz, the secretary of the Board of Arbitration, was also the director of the Down Town Ethical Society. Like Felix Adler's original New York Ethical Culture Society, the Down Town Ethical Society was composed mainly of Jews, and its leadership was completely Jewish. (Max Meyer, the secretary of the Cloak, Suit and Skirt Manufacturers' Protective Association, with whom Brandeis closely cooperated on the New York strike, was a trustee of the Down Town Ethical Society.) Moskowitz himself was active in a variety of Jewish causes. He was an important and tireless social worker and active in industrial relations, the settlement house movement, and civic reform. When at the end of the summer of 1910 Brandeis was asked to write an article about the strike for the Progressive weekly *The Outlook*, he deferred to Henry Moskowitz. Moskowitz and Brandeis continued to cooperate on garment industry matters and on other labor issues and remained friends.[63]

As a result of Brandeis's activities in New York, Boston's Jews became increasingly inclined to see him as their leader. Articles in the *Advocate* took note of him and covered the progress of his activities among the Jewish workers of New York. For Brandeis's part, the detailed and sympathetic account of his work in the garment workers' strike, coupled with the emergence of his Jewish ethnic pride as a result of his contact with the Jewish workers, served to strengthen his connection with the *Advocate*. In mid-September of 1910, there was an important meeting between Brandeis and editor De Haas — once more on the subject of savings-bank insurance. De Haas provides this account:

At that time, the early fall of 1910, Brandeis was still carrying on his propaganda for Savings Bank Insurance in Boston, and it was with the desire to obtain some publicity for the workings of the new law that the insurance publicity representative called on the author in his capacity as editor of the *Jewish Advocate*. Cooperation was offered but the theme seemed both dry and remote. It was suggested that if certain new features could be introduced into

the working plan, the system might be made attractive to his readers. A few days later, these remarks led to a request that the editor
meet the father of the new insurance law. The problem of creating
dowry and college tuition endowment was discussed with characteristic directness. Jewish habits of thrift were examined imperson-
ally and objectively.

In the wake of the meeting, the *Jewish Advocate* published on
September 30 a comprehensive article entitled "Insurance and
the Savings Banks" which described to its readers the history of
the movement, its problems, and especially its successes and
future prospects.[64]

Prelude to the 1912 Election

By 1910 Brandeis could have fair confidence in his support
among Jews. He regarded the preferential union shop as an
epochal achievement, and the savings-bank life-insurance
movement, despite its great difficulties, seemed to be making
progress. Brandeis now became bolder in his overtures to the
Jewish community. Brandeis's diary entry of October 4, 1910,
records: "Max Mitchell in about Jewish organizations for political purposes."[65] Mitchell, superintendent of the Federated
Jewish Charities and co-owner of the *Advocate*, was becoming
more and more important as an ally.

In the autumn of 1909, Brandeis began to expand his interests to include national politics. In large measure by way of his
connection with Norman Hapgood, the editor of *Collier's
Magazine*, Brandeis aligned himself with western Progressives.
He had already formed an association with La Follette's group;
now he also drew close to Gifford and Amos Pinchot and other
Republicans whose political hero was Theodore Roosevelt.
Brandeis himself admired Roosevelt, despite his reservations
about the latter's imperialistic foreign policy. But Roosevelt
maneuvered skillfully between the midwestern insurgents and
President Taft, a course that not only confused La Follette
and his friends but also hampered their organization on the
national level. The question for them was how to make use of
the widespread and growing dissatisfaction in many parts of

the country with Taft's policies so as to defeat his nomination in 1912. Without knowing whether or not to back Roosevelt, they could not devise a national strategy for channeling that dissatisfaction or for capturing the leadership of the party.[66]

At the Republican New York State Convention in Saratoga on September 28, Roosevelt gave a keynote address in which he commended Taft for his achievements in the first eighteen months of his administration. The state party platform also praised the president's treatment of the trust issue and even endorsed the protectionist Payne-Aldrich tariff. The Midwesterners now had their answer regarding Roosevelt's official position and began to organize independently. The founding meeting of the resulting National Progressive Republican League was held at La Follette's home on January 21, 1911.[67]

Brandeis was, not surprisingly, also irritated by the Saratoga platform, but publicly he chose not to take sides so as to leave open the possibility of cooperation between Roosevelt and the La Follette group. Privately he was in the La Follette camp, believing that "of course, Roosevelt with his good trusts and bad trusts has always stood for monopoly." Seasoned in the political struggles of city and state, Brandeis was now ready to plan his course backing the midwest insurgents on the national stage. He was already known nationally, but mainly as an attorney—as the Bostonian "people's lawyer." To enhance his political image, he began a series of interviews with Ernest Poole (an early admirer of the midwest Progressives) for publication in the *American Magazine*. The resulting article, which finally appeared in February 1911, dealt with Brandeis's personal life, thoughts, and feelings on many issues of interest to American readers, as well as the important public services he had rendered. His Jewishness was openly and sympathetically discussed: "He is a Jew. For a century back his family were made up of men of means, education, social ideals."[68]

Brandeis also enlisted the aid of the *Advocate* for the La Follette movement during the elections of 1912. The *Advocate* was far more conservative than the *American Magazine*, but its stand on social justice questions made it antithetical to "stand-pattism." Even Teddy Roosevelt, the hero of the Jewish professionals, was occasionally censured in its pages. On the eve of Roosevelt's return to America, the *Advocate* criticized him for his endorsement of power politics at the expense of the rights of small nations, suggesting that, according to Roosevelt's philosophy, the right of the Jewish people to exist would be called into question. Although these judgments did not amount to comprehensive editorial policy, they did create a certain climate of opinion.[69]

To this were added, at times, attacks on the country's financial elite. The September 30, 1910, issue had printed on its front page: "J.P. Morgan does not like Jews on Wall St." An article on "The Money Power" contended that the major non-Jewish financiers were anti-Semites and did not allow Jews to participate in the management of the money market; in the same article, Jewish financiers were hailed as liberals and independents. The newspaper often attacked Senator Henry Cabot Lodge for his position on immigration. These sporadic attacks on the "money power" and Lodge, and the general social concerns of the *Advocate*, did not give its readers any guidelines in national politics, but did place it generally in the Progressive camp.[70]

The *Advocate* also continued to cover Brandeis's political course after the New York garment workers' strike. It followed his assistance to the trade organizations of the Atlantic seaboard in opposing high railroad rates, which included his showing the railroads how they could introduce efficient management to avoid raising rates. The *Advocate* was led to remark: "And now it is the railroads that Louis D. Brandeis is to teach their business to." On the front page of the November 11 *Advocate*, in the section "News on Jews in Congress," there appeared an item that said: "Mr. Louis D. Brandeis has been mentioned as a possible successor to Senator Lodge."[71]

An interview with Brandeis by an *Advocate* representative was published in the December 9 issue. Like the *American Magazine* interview, this one served to support the Progressives' independent alignment in the 1912 campaign and to further their goal of making Brandeis a spokesman for their cause. It seems that the strategy Mitchell and Brandeis had agreed upon in their October 4 conference "about Jewish organizations for political purposes" had two objectives: to discredit Roosevelt in the eyes of the Jewish public and to acquaint them with Brandeis as a Progressive Jewish leader.[72]

The November 11 issue of the *Advocate* contained a story claiming that, according to the head of the anthropology department at Clark University in Worcester, Roosevelt was anti-Semitic. This accusation caused the *Advocate* to attract national attention at least briefly. Editors across the country sent clippings from the Boston newspaper to Roosevelt, asking him to refute or explain. Roosevelt, through his secretary, labeled the story "an absurd falsehood." On December 16 the *Advocate* published a letter from the Clark anthropologist, accusing Roosevelt of being unstable, a liar, and, again, an anti-Semite. Appearing between these two issues was one containing Brandeis's interview which, though it took place in Boston (with L. H. Semonoff, a student who evidently was assigned by Mitchell and De Haas), was obviously meant to have an impact on Jews nationwide (as one version was first published in the New York *American Hebrew*). Its rationale was made clear at the outset: "While leading a splendid battle for lower railroad rates . . . Louis D. Brandeis granted the writer an interview in which he defined his position as a Jew." The interview continued: "Ever since the beginning of the Pinchot-Glavis affair, when Brandeis as the attorney for Glavis shook the prestige of the Taft administration, the question has been asked, 'Who is Brandeis?' . . . It has been said that he had been brought up in a Christian Unitarian family and had received his early training under Gentile auspices. It was doubted whether he was an adherent of Judaism." These were, of course, rumors that could only have arisen outside Boston, but setting the record straight was precisely the reason for the interview. "There should be no doubt as to where I stand. Of course I am a Jew," Brandeis was quoted as saying. He then recounted the history of his Jewish ancestry, the scholarship of his uncle, Lewis Dembitz, in "Jewish lore" and his mastery of "certain phases of Jewish scholarship" and concluded by telling of his family connection to Felix Adler.[73]

It was to the theme of Judaism's great moral and social mission, associated for him with the person of Felix Adler, that Brandeis devoted his longest answer during the interview. "Do you believe in a Jewish mission; that is, do you agree with those who say that the Jews are a chosen people whose mission it is to preserve and spread their religion?" asked the interviewer. Brandeis replied affirmatively and added:

> I believe further that the Jews can be just as much of a priest people to-day as they ever were in the prophetic days. Their mission is one that will endure forever. The Jewish prophet may struggle for truth and righteousness to-day just as the ancient prophets did. Nobody takes greater pride than I do in the success of the individual Jews. I mean success in the higher sense, not success that spells dollars. And the opportunity for Jewish success was never greater here than it is to-day. The Jews in America will be what they themselves decide. America has done its share for the Jew, just as it has done its part for others. It is now for the Jew to say where he will stand in American life. America needs his help.

It was a new Brandeis who now spoke in the name of a unique Jewish heritage, of the ancient Jewish prophets, and of present Jewish spiritual contributions.[74]

On a slightly different subject, Brandeis also willingly expressed his sympathy for Zionism, although not as a solution to the persecution of Jews in Eastern Europe or prejudice elsewhere. It did not need to fill the latter function, he felt, pointing out that in America, his Jewish descent did not "embarrass [him] in the slightest" as far as his career was concerned. He did not applaud Zionism as a movement to create a home for Jews or to restore Jewish sovereignty; he was willing to support it simply to draw attention to his own Jewishness and perhaps as an example of the social and moral mission of the Jews. "I have a great deal of sympathy with the Zionists . . . The movement is an exceedingly deserving one. These so-called dreamers are entitled to the respect and appreciation of the entire Jewish people."[75]

On the same day that the Brandeis interview was published in the *American Hebrew*, the *Jewish Advocate* devoted a special editorial to Brandeis, commending him for the service rendered to the eastern shippers in their fight against the railroads:

> The action of Mr. Louis D. Brandeis . . . is the kind of patriotism that means more than a battle won by the firing of cannon. Mr. Brandeis has accumulated what Sir Moses Montefiore once described as "a crust of bread and cheese, and a glass of port for a friend." He can afford to champion the people's causes, but there are other lawyers who can afford the luxury of the higher citizenship. But they do not indulge themselves.
>
> Mr. Brandeis has the courage to do this. Let us hope that others will follow his example. It would make our country look different if they did so.

The *American Hebrew*'s editors also found Brandeis's representation of the shippers "a splendid battle for lower railroad rates in this country," while the *Advocate* declared that his whole life set an example worthy of emulation.[76]

A whole array of trade and commerce organizations had backed Brandeis in the successful fight against the railroads' demands. The great talent that Brandeis exhibited in this struggle, the publicity that accrued to the idea of "scientific management," and the final victory had all added to his national prestige. (Locally, though, far from broadening his base of support, the defeat of the railroads only increased the animosity of their owners for him.) It seems, however, that it was not specifically the struggle against the railroads that had prompted Brandeis to increase his standing in the Jewish community. He had something even greater in mind.[77]

The interview with Brandeis appeared in the *Advocate* with the title "Thinks the Jews Should Still Be a Moral Ensign to the Nations" and the subtitle: "Louis Dembitz Brandeis Sympathizes with Zionism and Believes in the Theory of a Jewish Mission." But the theme of Zionism was downplayed in the text ("I believe that the opportunities for members of my race are greater here than in any other country"). Brandeis instead emphasized the mission of his people to be carried out in the United States. The earlier *American Hebrew* version of the interview had likewise revealed Brandeis's focus on the current American situation ("And the opportunity for Jewish success was never greater here than it is today"). The *Advocate* version further stressed the "mission" theme by including in the article Brandeis's address before the New Century Club in 1905.[78]

That Brandeis allowed the five-year-old address to be used suggests that he regarded both it and the interview as reflecting the same line of thought, namely, that the Jews should defend the threatened ideals of American society. A conspicuous thread of belief in a Jewish mission connected the two public statements. The *Advocate* interviewer evidently shared the view, at least as far as Brandeis was concerned: "I asked my last question, and rose to leave. Extending his hand, he said, 'I wish you success.' I responded, 'And I can fairly say, Mr. Brandeis, the American people wish you success and long life, because they need you today,' " referring to Brandeis's having fought "so strongly and effectively against corporate greed, and [for] higher living and for greater humanity of man to man."[79]

Readers of the article could also discern Brandeis's sense of mission in another detail, in terms supplied by the representative of the *Advocate*: "And Brandeis found his prototype [among the prophets] in Daniel. And how much like the great Daniel, prophet of old, who struggled against historic wrong and injustice, is this mighty modern Jewish prophet." Daniel's situation, indeed, of that of all the ancient prophets, best characterized Brandeis's position in 1910. The Daniel stories took place not in the Jewish homeland but in Babylon. The Jews there were respected and their God honored. Daniel and his friends underwent many trials but finally triumphed. Moreover no one was wiser than Daniel; only he was able to read the menacing writing on the wall at Belshazzar's feast, indicating the imminent death of the king. The image of Daniel whose famous trials in the lions' den were a universal symbol, may have been more immediately appealing to Brandeis than that of other prophetic figures like Isaiah who, although exhibiting far greater social concern, lived in Palestine and prophesied the ingathering of the exiles. Like Daniel's, Brandeis's battlefield was outside of Palestine; Brandeis, too, was a man with a mission to pursue in the framework of a non-Jewish society. The qualities of wisdom and boldness characterized the modern Daniel as they had the ancient prophet from Babylon. Both were proud of their Jewishness in the Diaspora, and both trusted that their loyalty to their people and heritage would sustain them.[80]

But whether or not he was aware of it, Brandeis's concept of the Jewish mission had changed since 1905. As a result he (or possibly, the editor of the *Advocate*) did change the 1905 address somewhat, so that of Brandeis's original statement that American Jews should demonstrate "loyalty to American institutions and ideals" had the last word deleted from the 1910 article. The change suggests that perhaps in Brandeis's view American society in general was not sufficiently idealistic, and that only certain well-defined American ideals should evoke the Jews' support. In the 1905 speech, the Jewish mission was said to be distinct from Jewish nationalism. In the 1910 recapitulation of the address, this point (comprising almost one-fifth of the address) was almost entirely omitted. The deleted sections included references to the "brotherhood of man" and the following passage on the Jewish law: " 'Ye shall have one manner of law as well for the stranger as for one of your own country,' declared its code. For as the demands of Jewish law 'knew no restrictions of race, so its privileges were open to all.' " In 1910 the following was substituted: "I believe the Jews can be just as much of a priest people today as they ever were in the prophetic days." Also deleted from the earlier version was: " 'And long after the Jewish State had fallen' their [the Jews'] religion became 'that of civilized humanity.' " In 1910 Brandeis expressed sympathy and respect for the "movement looking towards a revival of the Jewish state in Palentine." In short, acknowledgments of Jewish uniqueness and Jewish nationalism were the new threads interwoven into Brandeis's philosophy of the Jewish mission.[81]

But the future Jewish state, as he seems to have perceived it then, would be merely another aspect of the worldwide Jewish mission whose main stage would remain in the United States. He still saw Jewish and American ideals fundamentally akin, and "he believed . . . in the theory of Jewish Mission, that it was given the race to assert the inexorable moral law."[82]

5

The New Zion

Zionism as a Mission

BRANDEIS took great pride in the Massachusetts legislative record in protecting the rights of workers. Introducing his sister-in-law, Pauline Goldmark, who was secretary of the Consumer League in New York, to a Bostonian in 1907, he remarked that she had had to "come to Boston to make inquiries into the operation of our 58-hour law." But five years later he concluded that there was much more to be done. During the Lawrence textile workers' strike, he censured the strikers but also severely criticized the Massachusetts mill owners who had arrogantly defied a new hour-labor law. He accused them of abrogating the civil rights of their workers, tampering with the law to suppress a strike, and creating "conditions of workers in the [textile] industry where, as in the steel industry, tariff and combinations have protected the product, and left the workers without protection." He suggested that the preferential union shop, which had proved itself workable in the garment industry in New York, was the "way out of our present serious difficulty."[1]

During his successful drive to spread the preferential-shop system to various branches of the garment trade after its introduction in New York in the early autumn of 1910, Brandeis found himself very often dealing with Jews. He maintained close and continuous contact with the Jewish social workers who were at the center of the movement—Meyer Bloomfield of

Boston and Henry Moskowitz of New York. In mid-September, when Brandeis was called upon to mediate a strike by the New York Ladies' Tailors and Dressmakers, he immediately contacted Bloomfield, who, together with Moskowitz, was later to help introduce the preferential shop into this branch of the garment industry. Later that autumn, when a strike broke out in the Cleveland garment industry, Brandeis told Moskowitz: "Bloomfield says that Meyer London has asked you to go to Cleveland to look over the situation." Brandeis discussed his ideas on the matter in detail with Moskowitz. He often met with the social worker in New York at meetings of the Society for Ethical Culture. When Moskowitz published an article entitled "The Power for Constructive Reform in the Trade Union Movement" in the January 1912 issue of *Life and Labor*, Brandeis recommended it as the most important argument yet made on behalf of the preferential union shop.[2]

Brandeis's connection with the preferential-union-shop movement was only one aspect of his contact with the social movements that were having an increasingly conspicuous place in the American Jewish community. His initial alliance with the Boston Jewish community had taken place during the life-insurance drive; Brandeis now allied himself with Jewish reformers in other cities as well to address the issue of labor-capital relations on a national level (and in the process was developing his view, publicized in the 1910 *Advocate* interview, of the Jews as a "moral ensign to the nations"). It was in connection with this enterprise that he first met the people who would later become his closest associates in the American Zionist movement.

Beginning in November 1907, Brandeis and Josephine Goldmark worked together on the famous labor case, *Muller v. Oregon*, in which that state's ten-hour-day law for women was upheld. The outcome of the case was a victory for the National Consumers' League, which had brought the case to Brandeis, and for several members of Brandeis's family as well. Pauline Goldmark, who was an active league member, wrote *Women and Children in the Canning Industry*. Another relative of

Brandeis, Frank W. Taussig, served as one of the league's nine honorary vice-presidents. But there were other prominent Jews in the league's leadership aside from members of the Brandeis clan, including Edwin R. Seligman, a professor at Columbia University, and Mrs. Frederick Nathan of New York City.[3]

Brandeis's efforts on behalf of the Oregon hour law brought him in touch with Stephen Samuel Wise, the Zionist rabbi and social reformer who occupied the pulpit in Portland for several years and provided Brandeis, through the mediation of Josephine Goldmark, with advice based on his own experiences in getting the ten-hour-day law passed in Oregon in 1903. Wise had closely followed Brandeis's career, especially his battles to further the cause of social legislation. In November 1911 Wise and Maurice Wertheim of New York selected Brandeis to deliver an address on "Courts and Social Justice," believing that he was "the one man in the country most qualified to speak on this subject." Brandeis declined, but his answer was cordial and complimentary of Wertheim's "good work." Of the trial of the union men James and Joseph McNamara, accused of dynamiting the *Los Angeles Times* building, Brandeis stated: "The recent dynamite outrages are to be attributed to the feeling of despair among laboring men inspired by the great controlling trusts." Wise agreed and asked permission to quote him. Both Brandeis and Wise, along with several other Jewish reformers including Moskowitz and Seligman, were among the signers of a letter written to President Taft deploring the social conditions underlying this case.[4]

The following year Wise wrote Brandeis:

> I write to ask you whether you have anything in print on this question which might be of service to me in the preparation of my address [on "Social Progress through Political Action"]. If you have not, I should indeed welcome a line from you in which you would give me your own thought . . . concerning the question. I think it of great importance that the Democratic side be put as vigorously and convincingly as possible and it is for that reason that I should be glad to consider your own thought on the question.

To this Brandeis replied: "I am delighted to know that the Democratic side [they were by now both supporters of Woodrow Wilson] is to be presented by one so competent to do so as yourself. I doubt whether there is much which I can contribute to what you already know." He attached some of the requested material and added: "I wish I might be present to hear you." Wise responded in a similarly warm vein: "It will be good to be able to cite your word in the course of my remarks."[5]

Brandeis's role in *Muller* v. *Oregon* also led to the renewal of his connections with liberal Jewish circles in Louisville. Abraham Flexner—of the "Louisville Library" group which had been headed by Lewis N. Dembitz—asked Brandeis in February 1908 to send him a copy of the Oregon brief, saying he had found it "absolutely convincing"; Brandeis did so, adding a warm invitation to visit him in Boston. In December 1912 Abraham Flexner invited Brandeis to present before an important academic meeting "some utterance bearing on the problems in regard to which you have become leader." Flexner continued to follow Brandeis's career through his years on the Supreme Court and assisted in financing Samuel Konefsky's liberal-Progressive study, *The Legacy of Holmes and Brandeis.*[6]

Brandeis's relations with Abraham Flexner's brother Bernard also grew closer; a lawyer himself, Bernard Flexner followed Brandeis's legal battles in every detail. In 1909 an Illinois statute comparable to the one involved in the Muller action was contested before the state supreme court, and Brandeis went to Illinois to argue the case. Afterwards Bernard Flexner wrote to Brandeis that he was "exceedingly anxious to get a copy of your brief in the Illinois Ten Hour law case, pending in the Court of Appeals" and rejoiced at Brandeis's victory. When Brandeis won the Interstate Commerce Commission freight-rate case in February 1911, Flexner congratulated him: "The whole country is again indebted to you for your generous service in these cases."[7]

From the outset of his career, Bernard Flexner had devoted much of his time to social welfare and labor problems. He was prominent in the development of the juvenile-court system, first in Kentucky and later nationally, and frequently wrote on the subject, as well as on workmen's compensation and employer's liability. Many of his numerous articles were published in *Charities* (later the *Survey*), in the pages of which many articles by or about Brandeis were also to be found. In February 1912 Bernard Flexner arranged a "Child's Welfare Exhibit and Conference" in Louisville and invited Brandeis to give the main address on the subject of the conditions of female labor. Brandeis thanked him heartily and emphasized his "great satisfaction to speak on such an occasion" although adding that he would not be able to attend. Brandeis respected Flexner and considered him to be a true Progressive deeply committed to social justice.[8]

In the course of his defense of the Illinois ten-hour-day law, Brandeis broadened his circle of acquaintances among eminent Jewish professionals with Progressive leanings. Ernst Freund, professor of law at the University of Chicago, was instrumental in having Brandeis invited to assist the state's attorney in October 1909. Their cooperation in the Illinois case continued through the winter of 1909-10 and again from December 1911 to June 1912. Freund, a well-known legal scholar, was especially sensitive to the injustices that accompanied social growth and change in the country. The similarity between Freund's and Brandeis's legal philosophy united them when they served as coofficers of the American Association for Labor Legislation. Freund was president of the Illinois chapter and a member of the national executive committee; Brandeis served on the general council. In 1910, when Brandeis became a vice president of the Association for Labor Legislation, he came into still closer contact with Freund's work.[9]

Though Freund was not especially active in the Chicago Jewish community, through him Brandeis expanded his connections there. Following Freund's suggestion, Brandeis sent his Illinois case brief to Levy Mayer—a lawyer and prominent member of this community—with the comment: "I was delighted to hear through Professor Ernst Freund that you were desirous of having the law sustained, and I wish we might have the benefit of your assistance in oral argument." Mayer was hardly in a position to do so, having successfully argued against the legislation in 1895, though he had since, along with many others in his Jewish community, changed his position on this as well as other social issues. Mayer wrote to Brandeis that he admired his brief and was ready to help in other ways; Brandeis in any case respected Mayer for having the courage openly to reject his own earlier opinion.[10]

In the midst of the Illinois case, Brandeis received a request for a brief from the City Club of Chicago. It may have originated with Lessing Rosenthal, a Jewish lawyer active in Chicago civic affairs and powerful in the City Club, or perhaps with Julian W. Mack, judge of the Circuit Court of Cook County from 1903 to 1911 and United States Circuit Court judge from 1913 to 1943. Mack was close to the Rosenthal family, especially to Lessing, and was a director of the City Club. Brandeis knew both of them, but his earlier and more important connection was with Mack because of the latter's interest in Progressive labor legislation. They had first met in 1886-87, when Mack was the *Harvard Law Review*'s business manager. A closer association began to develop in the winter of 1893-94, when Mack did some legal work in Boston for Levy Mayer. Mack saw Brandeis and obtained from him the synopsis of his M.I.T. lectures given in 1892-93, which, since rewritten in light of the Homestead strike, stressed the need for realistic and responsive labor legislation. They represent the beginning of a new legal style that had made Brandeis the victor in the Oregon and Illinois labor legislation cases. Years later, when Mack asked for Brandeis's help in preparing a course on business law, he was still expressing appreciation for those lectures. Mack's interest in social problems was to keep the relationship alive despite the geographical distance between them.[11]

The Illinois case brought Brandeis into contact with yet another Jewish legal scholar—Felix Frankfurter—with whom he formed an acquaintance that gradually developed into friendship and political alliance. As a student at Harvard Law School, Frankfurter had heard Brandeis's address before the Harvard Ethical Society, "The Opportunity in the Law" and had very much admired it. He came to value Brandeis not so much because of his fight against the trusts as for his efforts to make the legal system more responsive to human and social needs; in his memoirs he calls himself a follower of Brandeis in the field of labor legislation. When Frankfurter received Brandeis's Illinois brief in March of 1910, he responded:

> I am very glad indeed, to have your brief, for its extensive treatment of a social-economic question, in which I am very much interested. From a purely lawyer's standpoint, I am glad to have it, because I have already realized from your prior brief in the Muller case that the method you have pursued is the most effective and successful in presenting to the Court a purely social-economic question in its constitutional aspect. I am sure that the Supreme Court of Illinois will have to yield to your inexorable logic and facts; as readily as did the Supreme Court of the United States.[12]

Like Wise, Freund, and Flexner, Frankfurter had more to offer Brandeis than mere admiration: he was also an ally in Progressive causes. Brandeis's first letter to Frankfurter, acknowledging congratulations on the Illinois case and attaching a brief in the Ballinger case, ended: "You, too, have had a great victory," in reference to Frankfurter's successful prosecution of the sugar corporations accused of tampering with scales at the port of New York. In February 1911 Frankfurter wrote to Brandeis about the railroad freight-rate case: "Of course I was delighted with your notable success again, though I'm somewhat disappointed to infer from the abstract of the Commission's opinion, that the efficiency line of argument did not receive attention." Brandeis's response was more optimistic about the success of the efficiency line of argument, and Frankfurter's next letter included some relevant clippings. Later that year Frankfurter sent Brandeis more material on scientific management, and in the spring of 1912 the two finally met. Frankfurter asked Brandeis for suggestions for a "productive leadership" for the new Children's Bureau (Brandeis offered four names, including those of Felix Adler and Julian Mack). In the summer they exchanged views (in letters) on the trust issue. Frankfurter's voting for Roosevelt in the

1912 presidential election did not at all disturb the bond with Brandeis; by the beginning of 1913 they were cordially sharing opinions on desirable ways to mobilize the public behind programs of social reform.[13]

Brandeis's collaboration with Josephine Goldmark (along with Florence Kelley, the leader of the National Consumers' League), which had begun with the *Muller* v. *Oregon* case in 1907, remained active. In December 1908 she asked for Brandeis's help in defending Ohio's nine-hour-day law for women, which he gave. It was also in part as a result of his sister-in-law's activities that Brandeis became involved in the Illinois case. In January 1911 Brandeis was approached by a California attorney regarding the drafting of "a bill for an eight-hour work day for women in California along the lines of the Oregon and Illinois statutes"; Josephine Goldmark was involved in this battle as well. Furthermore as secretary of the Consumers' League she was able to keep Brandeis informed of general news and developments pertaining to labor legislation.[14]

It was in 1910 that Joseph Fels, a Philadelphia Jewish soap manufacturer who was devoted to finding a solution to the problem of unemployment, entered Brandeis's life. Although Fels considered Brandeis's approach to social issues to be merely "philanthropically palliative work," the connections between Brandeis and the Fels circle steadily developed so that by 1914 Samuel Fels (Joseph's younger brother) felt that he could ask Brandeis to lecture on the topic of the "money trust" before the American Academy of Political and Social Science.[15]

Most of the Jewish social reformers that Brandeis knew he had met through the *Survey*, the major journal of social work in the United States and a magazine that Brandeis found to be an appropriate vehicle for his opinions. In June 1909 the *Survey* published Brandeis's comprehensive articles dealing with the "Boston 1915" movement and with a Massachusetts old-age pension system. The journal soon became the main disseminator of Brandeis's views on labor conditions and social reform; Bernard Flexner and Julian Mack were also long-standing and prolific contributors, and Mack served on its publication committee; Meyer Bloomfield and Henry Moskowitz often worked with the magazine as well. At the end of 1911, when Brandeis and Stephen Wise along with the Kellogg brothers (who were, respectively, managing editor and business manager of the *Survey*) signed a petition to President Taft about the McNamara dynamiting case, the *Survey* had already printed a great deal on the subject and had held a symposium on "The Larger Bearings of the McNamara Case." The creation of the Federal Commission on Industrial Relations — which development Brandeis and Felix Frankfurter closely watched — was a direct outgrowth of the symposium.[16]

Serving with Julian Mack on the publication committee of the *Survey* was the noted Jewish leader from New York, Lee Kaufer Frankel. Frankel, who was involved in a number of philanthropic and social agencies, had favored Brandeis's savings-bank insurance plan, as Brandeis learned in February 1909 when a Boston businessman sent him a letter about Frankel. Later in the same month, Frankel lectured in Boston on the conditions of industrial workers and publicly expressed his "heartiest good wishes" for Brandeis's insurance plan. (Brandeis was not convinced that Frankel was qualified to further legislation in the insurance field but still regarded him as an ally "of Old Savings Bank Insurance days").[17]

The image of Jews as pursuers of social justice was perhaps further impressed upon Brandeis by his involvement in the American Association for Labor Legislation, organized in 1906. In the *Survey*'s first years, the journal was the house organ for the association; later the association's writings took up only a few of its pages. When Brandeis joined the association in 1907, he could see that Jews were conspicuous among its membership. His dues were sent to Isaac N. Seligman (of J. W. Seligman and Company, bankers) who was its treasurer; among the small number of vice presidents was Samuel Gompers, the president of the American Federation of Labor. In 1910 Brandeis himself became a vice president of the association. In that same year its headquarters were transferred from Madison, Wisconsin, to New York City, and this move may have brought more Jews into its ranks. Among the vice presidents added in that year, along with Brandeis and Gompers, was Paul M. Warburg (of Kuhn, Loeb and Company). On the association council were three Brandeis relatives: Felix Adler, Josephine Goldmark, and Frank Taussig. Among its members were Lee Frankel, Edward Filene, and Bernard Flexner, and — perhaps less well known to Brandeis at that time — I. M. Rubinow, a social worker from New York City. The association already had a branch in Massachusetts, where Henry Abrahams, Meyer Bloomfield, the Filene brothers, Sidney Conrad, and Louis Kirstein were members.[18]

The Jews whom Brandeis met in the course of his efforts to protect working men and women varied in their degree of Jewish affiliation. Some, such as Samuel Gompers and the Goldmark sisters (the latter being followers of Felix Adler), were Jews in name only. Others, like Brandeis himself, considered themselves Jews but were not active in Jewish affairs; these included Ernst Freund, Julius Mayer, and the Flexner brothers. Some, like Felix Frankfurter and especially Stephen Wise, Julian Mack, and Henry Moskowitz, had more active ethnic ties. But there is no doubt that Brandeis considered them all Jews. In his *Advocate* interview of December 1910, in listing his Jewish credentials, he mentioned in one breath the Zionist leader Lewis Dembitz and the founder of the Society for Ethical Culture, Felix Adler. All Brandeis's Jewish contacts in the labor movement strengthened his convictions about the high moral caliber of the Jews, and those who were active in Jewish life undoubtedly confirmed his notion of a unique Jewish "peoplehood," of a Jewish mission.[19]

Some of these Jews joined the Zionist movement in 1914 with the outbreak of war; others, already Zionists, became active again. In the first group were Julian Mack and Felix Frankfurter, Mrs. Joseph Fels, and Louis Kirstein; in the second, Stephen Wise and Jacob De Haas. In a few years Brandeis had become "the chief" for a circle within the Zionist organization consisting of De Haas, Mack, Frankfurter, Wise, and Bernard Flexner.[20] Although the bond between Brandeis and this group had originated outside the Jewish orbit, these people had played a part in the Judaization and Zionization of Bran-

deis, insofar as they embodied for him the Jewish social ethos
and invoked his ethnic pride. And since it was through the
American social-reform movement that Brandeis had developed his Jewish consciousness, that consciousness was governed
by the notion that the Jews' contribution to the welfare of the
society at large principally justified their survival as a nation.

The theory of cultural pluralism found a considerable
amount of support in Boston. The sharp ethnic divisions, the
libertarian Emersonian tradition, and the rich intellectual life
of the city all contributed to the development of a philosophy
according to which the United States was, in the words of one
proponent of cultural pluralism, "a federal state not merely as
a union of geographical and administrative unities, but also a
cooperation of cultural diversities, as a federation or commonwealth of national cultures." One source of this belief was the
settlement house movement. Settlement workers had long
since discovered that respecting the cultures of immigrant
groups made their work easier than trying to impress upon
them a too rapid Americanization. Appreciation of their original culture gave a sense of dignity to the older people, helped
prevent delinquency among the young, and prevented the dis-
integration of families; it also encouraged the immigrants to
be active and productive American citizens. Thus, as in Jane
Addams's Hull House, the course that encouraged the per-
petuation of ethnic cultures was followed in Boston from the
early days of settlement work. Robert Woods, the renowned
social worker of the South End House, urged his staff "to appreciate the distinctive genius of each type [of racial or national loyalties] and to sympathize with its traditions." In his
comprehensive article, "Assimilation: Two-Edged Sword,"
published in 1902, he called on the various nationalities to be
"affected by the American spirit, but also to have the American spirit affected by what is real in them. The loyal American, honoring and seeking to preserve much in the genius of
each nationality, will thus stimulate each racial type to seek for
what is worthy in all the others."[21]
In time Woods became even more emphatic in his rejection

of outright assimilation. In a paper read before the Harvard
Ethical Society in October 1905, he concluded: "Social work
has to do with the building-up of a natural federation among
all our different racial groups, which will in reasonable degree
preserve all that is valuable in the heredity and traditions of
each type, but will link all types together into a universal yet
coherent and distinctively American nationality." Gradually
Woods began to insist on the importance of the local neighborhood to maintaining cultural diversity and pride. The way to
preserve the American neighborhood system was by "holding
together the fabric of all that is best in the immigrant home."
The idea of a nation made up of neighborhoods was interwoven in Woods's philosophy with the concept of America as a
federation of "different racial groups."[22]

Woods's ideas, especially those concerning cultural pluralism, were buttressed in Boston by the work of Albert J. Kennedy. Kennedy, who from 1907 headed investigations for and
was associate director of the South End House, recommended
"national groupings" as the only way to "true Americanization." Kennedy emphasized the idea that those communities
based on ethnic bonds represented values to be fostered in
American society. "We must be thankful that simple people so
adequately build up a social structure of their own through
which are preserved those community values which America
itself neglects." Preserving what was worthwhile in the immigrants' heritage gradually became more than mere educational strategy on the part of social workers; it developed in
some respects into an independent goal.[23]

The prominent position of these early adherents of cultural
pluralism guaranteed its wide dissemination in Boston. Joseph
Eastman, the secretary of the Public Franchise League — in
which Brandeis was a leading figure — was a follower, though a
moderate one, of this movement; he came directly to the PFL
from Woods's South End House in 1905 with Brandeis's bless-
ing. Woods himself, in addition to exerting a tremendous influence on Boston's social workers, had become an important
figure in the affairs of the city. Woods and Brandeis had cooperated in the struggle against Boston Elevated and also in the

savings-bank insurance drive. After the railroad merger fight, the Woods-Brandeis team was less active, but the two men still worked together occasionally on civic and labor matters. Woods supported the "Boston 1915" movement and was connected with the Vocation Bureau, the Association for Labor Legislation, and the *Survey*.[24]

As Brandeis had become preoccupied with the savings-bank insurance and antimerger efforts, his involvement with the settlement house movement had weakened. But important links remained. Some of the wives of Brandeis's close clients were active on the executive committee of Denison House; D. Blakely Hoar of Brandeis's law firm was on its extension committee, and Samuel D. Warren's sister Cornelia was chairman of the executive committee and consulted Brandeis on occasion. Some of the Irish labor leaders with whom Brandeis had cooperated were also connected with the Denison and South End Houses and with Woods himself. The workers of Denison House eventually arrived at the same conclusions as Woods and Kennedy. In *A Listener in Babel* (1903), Vida Scudder, the founder of this settlement house, supported cultural pluralism as the best way to acculturate immigrants and revive neglected American values. Denison House came gradually to deal for the most part with a large and concentrated Italian constituency, in which it found according to Scudder "the sincere recognition of qualities which America desperately needed, qualities indefinable perhaps, such as can be possessed only by an ancient race . . . They [the Italian immigrants] had an instantaneous response to values which America too often disregarded." Denison House did much to further the cause of cultural pluralism in Boston.[25]

More than the social workers, however, it was Harvard's leading liberal thinkers who led Brandeis to embrace cultural pluralism. During his student years, Brandeis had absorbed the ideas of Nathaniel S. Shaler on man and society. Shaler elaborated on the connection between different geographical environments and the development of the diversity of races, ethnic groups, and nations, and came to the conclusion that diversity was both unavoidable and a spur to human progress. He predicted (in 1891) that peoples of Celtic stock (mainly the Irish) would in another fifty years greatly outnumber the original New Englanders and concluded: "We may look forward to another element in the diversification of New England conditions." Brandeis's notebook often makes mention of Shaler, including comments such as "Cosmopolitanism, centralization, is objectionable, is to be avoided. It diminishes the probabilities of greatness. It contravenes Nature which stamps on all its creatures a local impression . . . Every person, as every animal or plant, should upon examination disclose his habitation." The whole course of Brandeis's life proved to be a reaction against "cosmopolitanism, centralization." Indeed Brandeis always felt himself to be a citizen of the state of Massachusetts more than of America. And in the years after Brandeis shifted his allegiance from the Yankees to the Jews, his views still reflected this aspect of the nineteenth-century liberalism of Nathaniel Shaler.[26]

Brandeis also came into contact with the ideas of William James, through the Evanses, who were close to the philosopher. James was a cultural pluralist of a sort, and his antiimperialism was in line with his concept of the world as a composite of different nationalities. An opponent of "bigness and greatness in all their forms," James saw American society as ideally diversified, divided into many subsocieties. Although he did not specifically talk about race and ethnicity in the United States, his attitude toward national and racial differences and his belief in a pluralistic society lent themselves to the arguments of the cultural pluralists.[27]

Horace M. Kallen was in the midst of this philosophical-political debate and was in fact the first to expound a comprehensive theory of cultural pluralism. His ideology, even more than Brandeis's, was very much shaped while he was a student at Harvard College. The son of a German Orthodox rabbi, he had become an almost entirely assimilated Jew before entering college. At Harvard the general regard for Hebrew culture and the liberal-pluralistic political atmosphere influenced Kallen toward Zionism and the concept of America as a federation of peoples. He was greatly affected during his first year at college by the views of George Santayana, who perceived pluralism by pointing to the distinctiveness of the New England culture. During Kallen's second year, "a Yankee, named Barrett Wendell, re-Judaized" him. Wendell taught Kallen English literature and through his admiration for the Bible inspired Kallen to take an interest in Judaism and his ethnic origins. The philosophical pluralism of William James, who directed his Ph.D. dissertation, completed the process of Kallen's development along these lines. In 1905 he began to formulate his version of cultural pluralism.[28]

The Menorah Society of Harvard, organized by him and Henry Hurwitz, was the rostrum for Kallen's ideas. The society had grown out of a series of informal meetings where Jewish students read Hebrew and Yiddish literature and encouraged literary efforts on Jewish subjects. Although there was already a new Zionist Club at Harvard, some of its members wanted a more open framework for the study of Jewish culture and discussion of Jewish problems; the Menorah Society was the result.[29]

From its inception the new society was idealistic. Its constitution stated: "The object of this Society shall be to study and to promote the culture and ideals of the Jewish people." Its first meeting characteristically included a lecture on "Jewish Idealism." The founders skillfully blended social concerns with ethnic pride: "And this is the second purpose of a Menorah Society—the moral purpose. For a knowledge of the history and culture which are their own heritage must stir young men with red Jewish blood in their veins to endeavor to be worthy of that heritage . . . Noblesse oblige!" "The third purpose of a Menorah Society [is] its patriotic purpose." And because "to the Jews . . . American democracy offers the opportunity to develop in freedom their virtue and their ideals, to cherish and to cultivate their heritage and traditions," they in return had, in addition to the regular duties of citizenship, "a special spiritual obligation . . . to contribute to the civilization of America that faith, that culture, that individuality, which are the products of a civilized history of three thousand years."

The civilization of America is a composition of the cultures and ideals of the various peoples that constitute the American nation. To the common treasury of American culture and ideals each constituent element of the nation must bring the full measure of its resources . . . For the glory of American civilization can arise, not out of a suppression of individuality, a tyrannical levelling of all distinctions within the nation, but rather out of the freest functioning of democracy and the harmonization of the various cultures and traditions that may have the strength to flourish in the sun of America. Herein lies the true spiritual significance of *e pluribus unum.*[30]

With such arguments the Menorah Society connected the Jewish sense of mission with a theory of cultural pluralism. The society's name — chosen "after a lively discussion of several names proposed" — was symbolic: "For 'Menorah' means, in Hebrew, a bearer of light, a candelabrum . . . the Menorah can still . . . fire the blood of Jewish youth as the symbol of their race, of its glories, of its invincible spirit through defeat, of unquenched hope, of renaissance, and of freshly radiant service to mankind." This rationale for the Jews' survival can best be termed "missionist."[31]

The society's avowed sense of mission functioned as a standing invitation to non-Zionists to participate; this fact explains the apparent contradiction in Kallen's memoirs, when he stresses the important role that people "warm to Zionism" had in the establishment of Menorah but adds: "Now that [the objects of the society] impressed anti-Zionists, who at that time were constituting the American Jewish Committee, as something desirable," they were attracted to participate. At an important annual dinner of the society (in May 1910), both Horace Kallen the devoted Zionist and Jacob Schiff the ardent non-Zionist leader spoke. Schiff in fact was one of the two honorary vice presidents of Harvard Menorah. Cultural pluralism, interwoven as it was with belief in a Jewish mission in the minds of the Menorah leaders, seems to have formed the common meeting ground for adherents and opponents of Zionism.[32]

Horace Kallen remained close to the Menorah movement. He himelf was a missionist Zionist. According to him, the Jews' right to nationhood stemmed from their pledge to use it to fulfill a noble social mission. In his first article on Zionism, published in *The Maccabaean* in August 1906, he presented the case for "The Ethics of Zionism" and concluded:

> Not religion, then, nor philanthropy, nor physical vigor, nor sentiment can together or each alone constitute a warrant for rehabilitating the Jewish nation. That warrant must lie deeper than all of these, which must themselves, since they are secondary, receive from it their sanction . . . If it is the Jew's right to survive, and Zionism asserts it is, it is his right by the vigor of his achievement and the effectiveness of his ideals, by his gifts to the world and his power for good in the world.

This idea by no means exhausted Kallen's Zionist philosophy, but it was a strong enough part of it to lead him to establish a society like the Menorah where cultural pluralism and Zionist missionism could coexist.[33]

Brandeis and Horace Kallen first met in 1905 while Brandeis was defending Kallen's sister, Mildred, and Robert Silverman, the two who had challenged corruption in the Boston school system. Kallen was working in the Civic Service House directed by Meyer Bloomfield, and Robert Silverman, then just finishing his law studies, belonged to a youth club in that settlement house. Kallen thus had a double interest in the case through which he met Brandeis. The two did not meet again for some years (Kallen left Boston in 1911), but when Kallen heard in 1914 that Brandeis was interested in his ideas, he sent him his treatise on the "Ethics of Zionism."[34] Brandeis's interest in the Menorah Society, however, originated largely apart from his relations with Kallen or, for that matter, any other Jew. More important to him was the fact that the society was connected with his alma mater and looked favorably upon by President Eliot.

Eliot, like Brandeis, was something more than a liberal. He sided with Progressive legislation introduced by Theodore Roosevelt to protect workingmen and consumers. A long-time advocate of conservation, he was the president of the National Conservation Association when Brandeis fought for the pro-conservation forces in the Ballinger case. Despite differences

over the role of trade unions, Eliot and Brandeis found themselves serving together as officers in the National Civic Federation, the most prestigious organization mediating between
management and labor. Both represented "the part of the
public": Brandeis was a vice president of the New England
branch of the federation, while Eliot served on its national
executive committee. Eliot also served on the advisory council
of the Massachusetts Association for Labor Legislation, in
which Brandeis was active. When Eliot "announced his wish to
have the choice made of his successor" as Harvard's president,
Norman Hapgood, a friend of both, suggested Brandeis. Hapgood reports that "Dr. Eliot was delighted. The question of
social prejudice was far from giving him concern. Rather it
added to his enthusiasm . . . 'I am a Unitarian, [he said]. It
would please me to be followed by a Jew. You know those seven
men [the Overseers] and what chance he will have, but I shall
be pleased to put his name before them.' " In 1916 Eliot also
enthusiastically supported Brandeis's nomination to the
Supreme Court—that time with more success.[35]

Eliot began by assuming, like most educators at the beginning of the century, that the newly arrived ethnic groups
would eventually become totally assimilated, an outcome he
favored. But in time he, too, came to support the preservation
of ethnic variety. In 1905, when he addressed a group celebrat-
ing in Boston's Faneuil Hall the two hundred and fiftieth anniversary of the landing of the Jews in America, he called for the
encouragement of cultural pluralism in the United States and
expressed admiration for the Jews and their heritage: "For the
whole civilized world this race [the Jews] has been the source of
all the highest conceptions of God, man, and nature." Toward
the end of his address he said: "Let all the other national stocks
which have met on the fresh territory of the Republic welcome
the Jewish stock to a free competition in racial intelligence,
morality, and honor," and he finished with the following
words: "Let all the other races in America recognize the fact
that the prodigious vitality of the Jews is due at bottom to a
sublime religious idealism."[36]

The next year, Eliot gave his approval to the founding of

Harvard's Menorah Society. In 1907 he participated in the December 20 conference during which society members acquainted students from other colleges and universities in the area with Menorah's purposes. Eliot spoke on this occasion, commending the Jews for their great capacity for hard work, their pure and devoted family life, and their high religious ideals, and called upon the Jewish students to help their people to flourish in America: "What a wonderful survival it has been through all these Christian centuries; and when freedom came, what sudden blooming up of the race long suppressed! The development of the power of the Jewish race in this country entirely within my remembrance has been most striking. How can it be furthered and promoted? What can you do for the strengthening of your race in this free land?" He said that he hoped to see Jews competing successfully in a pluralistic society: "By so doing you will win the respect of the other races with which you are going to live."[37]

Eliot's ethnical pluralism was carried to such an extreme that it soon got him into trouble. During a tour of the South in the early spring of 1909, he declared himself in favor of the region's antimiscegenation laws and expressed his conviction "that the Irish should not intermarry with the Americans of English descent; that the Germans should not marry the Italians; that the Jews should not marry the French. Each race should maintain its own individuality." The outcry from newspapers across Massachusetts compelled Eliot to send them a clarifying telegram. Even the *Jewish Advocate* was shocked: "President Eliot speaking in the South has, it is claimed, declared for nonadmixture, a view that rather contradicts some things he has said within recent years." At the same time the weekly suggested that his attitude was spreading and becoming acceptable: "But on the whole, this is the doctrine that is coming to be held more and more in America, as against the once almost universal theory of absorption." The *Advocate* suggested that tolerance and cooperation between races and ethnic groups rather than coerced unification were the solutions to America's diversity. A biographer of Eliot suggests that Eliot may not have been entirely clear on the question: "He may . . . have been groping toward a concept of 'primary' and 'secondary' culture, seeing the first as learned at home and continuing to vary by ethnic group, and the second as an increasingly shared pattern of public life." But Eliot's fundamental idea of preserving some degree of ethnicity was clear enough. He continued to defend and publicize it in 1910-11, when he boldly opposed immigration restriction.[38]

Cultural pluralism was also an enthusiasm of Norman Hapgood, the Progressive publicist who from the spring of 1908 had been Brandeis's intimate political ally. The Hapgood family was of old Puritan stock—Norman's father had been the first to move from Massachusetts and Norman himself grew up in Illinois. But being New Englanders at heart, he and his brother aspired to attend Harvard, because it was the only "proper" college and was a family tradition. Norman, who earned his A.B. and law degrees from Harvard, admired William James's pluralistic views and esteemed Charles Eliot's liberalism and developed lasting friendships with both men. In 1897 he joined the *New York Commercial Advertiser*, where he expanded the departments of education, literature, and especially drama: according to one scholar, "he was the first to crash the boundaries between cultures and to find artistic inspiration in the flourishing Chinese, German, Italian, and Yiddish theaters." Himself a Unitarian and a friend of Abraham Cahan, who was then on the staff of the *Advertiser* and later edited the *Jewish Daily Forward*, as well as of other East European Jews, Hapgood was especially sensitive to the Jewish culture. But he took an interest in all ethnic groups, and the blooming of a diversity of cultures in America was part of his image of the United States. His younger brother Hutchins joined the *Advertiser*'s staff some time after him and was also inspired by the differences among New York's various ethnic groups. "Hutchins followed in Norman's steps, but with far greater intensity. The result was *The Spirit of the Ghetto*, the *Commercial Advertiser*'s most lasting contribution to literature, and the product of Hutchins Hapgood's special friendship with Abraham Cahan." *The Spirit of the Ghetto* (1902) expressed the two brothers' respect for communal values:

"What distinguishes *The Spirit of the Ghetto* . . . is its sharp focus on a true community. Hapgood wrote, 'What we need at the present time more than anything else is a spiritual unity . . . similar to the spirit underlying the national and religious unity of the Jewish culture.' " More political and methodical than his younger brother, Norman became a theoretician of cultural pluralism, a development whose sources lay in his *Commercial Advertiser* days. Toward the end of his life he became editor of the *Christian Register*, a Boston Unitarian publication.[39]

Brandeis's cultural pluralism, coupled with his belief in a Jewish moral mission, made it natural for him eventually to become associated with the Menorah Society, although he tended to stress more than the society did the social-political claims of Jewish identity. Still, he had been reluctant to join at first. In April 1910 the secretary of the society, Herbert B. Ehrmann, invited Brandeis to be its guest at the annual banquet; this invitation probably represented Brandeis's first contact with the society, for Ehrmann found it appropriate to explain its aims ("the study and promotion of Hebraic culture and ideals"). Ehrmann came from Louisville and knew Brandeis's uncle, Lewis Dembitz. But in spite of this personal connection and his indicated approval for the work of the organization, Brandeis found he had to refuse. In the following year the Menorah Society renewed its efforts to enlist Brandeis. Ehrmann, who was by then president, approached him early in March and invited him to speak at the annual meeting in May. Again Brandeis did not accept, although he discussed the organization with Ehrmann in his office. Ehrmann then asked Julian Mack instead, and the chain of events that brought Brandeis to demonstrate his kinship with the society is related by Ehrmann:

The day before the banquet, however, we received a telegram from Judge Mack regretting that he could not come because of the illness of his wife. We were in a panic. Many tickets had been sold on Judge Mack's reputation to awesome law school students.

Reservations had been made at the hotel for a guaranteed number of dinners. A major tragedy of youth impended.

In this quandary I consulted my friend, Max Lowenthal, then one of the demigods attending the Harvard Law School. Max did not hesitate.

"Get Felix Frankfurter!" he said immediately.[40]

But Ehrmann decided to try Brandeis again. "I do not know whether [Frankfurter] would have come on one day's notice," concluded Ehrmann, "because Brandeis surprised all of us by accepting the invitation."[41]

It is likely that Brandeis made this gesture in part to help Mack out, since the two had supported each other in various causes. In the following month Brandeis and Mack appeared before the convention held in Boston of the National Conference of Charities and Correction, the most important social work organization in the United States. Mack was elected its president (succeeding Jane Addams), and Brandeis delivered a lecture on "Workingmen's Insurance — The Road to Social Efficiency."[42]

In his address to the Menorah Society, which he had little time to prepare, Brandeis began:

> I came here, less to speak to you than to testify to my appreciation and admiration of your Society and the work it is doing. My own education has been such that I could contribute little to that subject. But I have looked with the greatest of satisfaction to the development of this movement, as I have upon the development of Zionism — far as it was from me — as indicating that the spirit of idealism, that one product of Judaism which has surely survived, is as strong as ever, and in this America has much to hope for.

He supported the idea that "there is in the Jew's character, point of view, and tradition, just those qualities which will enable America to solve the crying problems of social justice . . . The Jew is essentially a democrat, and as a democrat a man whose tradition and training should particularly fit him to carry out this work of social regeneration." He called upon his audience to "prove to America, by your example, that the Jew is of all things an idealist, a lover of justice, and that it is this

. . . problem in which you are going to endeavor to play a part."[43]

The speech was followed by the reading of a poem, a moving testimony to missionist Jewish nationalism, composed and read by Harry Wolfson, who was later to become one of Harvard's most distinguished scholars. Ehrmann reported that "years later Brandeis stated that Wolfson's fervor and eloquence were the start of a series of experiences which kindled within him an interest in Jewish affairs leading eventually to his historic espousal of Zionism." Wolfson, then a third-year student, was an enthusiastic Menorah Society member who had been reading his poems in Hebrew to the society from his first year at Harvard College. The social idealism apparent in his writings reflected the fact that he was also a member of the Harvard Socialist Club. The poem that Wolfson read on this occasion was entitled "The Spirit of Hebraism," and it dismissed those who said that the Jew was bereft of spirit and "that no inspiration is left." The Jewish spirit "will live . . . to the last generation of man" and, as in the glorious past, bear an eloquent message for the world: "It will speak from the lips of new Prophets, / And their truth from the heights will be hurled, / From a model city of Justice / Where its flag will blazon unfurled."[44]

Impressed by "The Spirit of Hebraism"—with its yearning for a Jewish "model city of Justice"—Brandeis arranged an informal meeting at his home with members of the society. Wolfson came, along with Ehrmann, Henry Hurwitz (a previous president), and several others. Brandeis asked the students about their backgrounds, ideas, and the workings of the society, and in effect offered to help the Jewish student movement.[45]

The day after the Menorah address, Brandeis began to work on his speech to the National Conference of Charities and Correction to take place the following month. During the week-long meeting, Brandeis deepened his relations with Julian Mack: a biographer of Mack notes that "Julian presided over a section on juvenile problems in which Brandeis also participated. Likewise, they had had some association when Julian was active in the National Conference on Social Work, meetings which Brandeis attended from time to time, frequently as a featured speaker who would be introduced by Julian." Brandeis probably was present when Mack was elected president of the organization and delivered an address in which he identified social justice as fundamental to the Jewish heritage. In his speech Mack said: "I take it [the presidency], too, as a tribute to a religion which is so in accord with the spirit that prevails in this Conference that in the ancient Hebrew tongue there was no word for charity except the word which also signified justice. Justice and charity were ever one among the Jews."[46]

Brandeis's participation in the conference appears also to have been connected with his interest in workingmen's insurance. Furthermore he was at the same time attending a Jewish social workers' conference, where he gave advice on the establishment of a retirement and pension fund for Jewish social workers. The president of the Society of Jewish Social Workers of New York then asked him to address that group. That June his connections with the Jewish social work community became intensified when his friend Max Mitchell was elected secretary of the National Conference of Charities and Corrections and treasurer of the Association of Jewish Social Workers. The *Advocate* reported the news and expressed admiration for the social workers and the hope that they would have in the future a greater role in community policy making.[47]

Meanwhile the news of Brandeis's appearance before the Menorah Society had spread across the country, and in February 1912 the president of the Menorah club at the University of Minnesota invited Brandeis to speak "should you be in the west at some time before the close of the present college year." Brandeis replied: "There is no likelihood of my being in Minnesota this Spring . . . But I shall bear your request in mind, and it will give me great pleasure to aid in securing a speaker for you." The following December the president of the Minnesota group organized a Western Intercollegiate Menorah Association as part of an attempt to establish the movement on the national level; he wrote Brandeis a long letter about this effort, to which Brandeis responded in words obviously meant for publication: "Every good American must sympathize heartily with its aims and its purposes . . . [the Menorah's] lofty aspirations will tend to protect the educated Jew from the more sordid ambitions which are apt to engross those engaged in the competitive struggle. It will bring a proper appreciation of the higher aims demanded by self-respect and a noble past. It will make us appreciate better the noblesse oblige." (For the Menorah Society noblesse oblige meant, as we have seen, fulfilling the Jewish mission.) "Thus the Menorah must become an important factor in the development of the Jews in America, and prove of great service to the Country," concluded Brandeis.[48]

At about the same time, Brandeis sent a letter to the founding convention of the national Intercollegiate Menorah Society (the role of Harvard people in this organization was significant; both the new president and the secretary were from that university). When it was read, Brandeis's interest in the Menorah was brought to the attention of L. H. Semonoff, who had interviewed Brandeis in December 1910 for the *Advocate* article. If Semonoff read Brandeis's letter carefully, he found a salient theme uniting it with the 1910 statement: this was the idea that Jews should redeem their heritage and organize themselves in order better to contribute to Progressivism in American society. "It [the Menorah movement] will tend to make the Jew appreciate better the *noblesse oblige,* and as the Menorah thus becomes an important factor in the development of the Jew in America, it must prove of great service to the country."[49]

Brandeis finally joined the Harvard Menorah Society on May 24, 1913, and became a member of a committee set up to aid the intercollegiate Menorah. Another member was Julian Mack (Irving Lehman, a distinguished New York jurist and advocate of the same kind of flexible and liberalizing jurisprudence as Brandeis, was chairman).[50]

When the first issue of the *Menorah Journal* was published in January 1915, it included an article by Brandeis which was a revised version of a recent Menorah address. The biographical note, probably written by editor-in-chief Henry Hurwitz, summed up Brandeis's relationship with Menorah: "His extraordinary record of unselfish, genuine achievement in behalf of public interest — for shorter hours of labor, savings bank insurance, protection against monopoly, against increase in railroad rates, etc. — gives peculiar aptness to the appeal for community service made in this article." And the writer added: "From the beginning Mr. Brandeis has taken a keen interest in the Menorah movement as a promotive force for the ideals he has at heart." Brandeis's belief in a Jewish mission was sustained by the theory of cultural pluralism already common among Menorah members. During 1911-13 he thus further developed a philosophy according to which the Jews — by living up to their tradition — could contribute to a pluralistic America. When in August 1914 Horace Kallen, the society's founder, outlined for Brandeis his now mature concept of cultural pluralism, Brandeis was immediately receptive; he had already been made ready.[51]

Although in his December 1910 *Advocate* interview Brandeis had expressed sympathy "with those Jews who are working for the revival of a Jewish state in Palestine," he neither knew much about the Zionist movement and its ideology nor was much interested in it. Zionism probably appeared to him to be merely the creation of one of the more vociferous of those Jewish organizations committed to the preservation of the Jewish people. It could only begin to command Brandeis's fuller attention when he saw it in relation to his own social philosophy, as he began to do shortly after the interview took place.

At the beginning of February 1911, Brandeis received a letter from Bernard Richards, who was editor of the *Maccabaean*, the magazine of the Federation of American Zionists. Richards explained that he had read with interest the interview published in the *American Hebrew* and noted Brandeis's reference to the Zionist movement and to his uncle, Lewis Dembitz. He enclosed a copy of the first number of the *Maccabaean*, which contained an article by Dembitz, along with the most recent issue. Richards, "noting [Brandeis's] expressions of sympathy with our movement," invited him "to deliver a short address on any phase of the Zionist movement" for the approaching celebration of the tenth anniversary of the founding of the magazine. Brandeis refused, adding expressions of general sympathy for the cause, and this would have been the end of it had not Richards also made the following remarks: "I may say that as one who has lived in Boston for many years, I have watched with great interest and admiration, the work which you have done for the public good . . . While living in Boston, I was working as reporter on The Boston Post, and afterwards contributed extensively to The Evening Transcript. Mr. Frank B. Tracy and Mr. Rollin Lynde Hartt, of that paper, who are doubtless known to you, are among the many good friends which I have in Boston." To all this Brandeis responded: "My sympathy with the Zionist movement rests primarily upon the noble idealism which underlies it, and the conviction that a great people, stirred by enthusiasm for such an ideal, must bear important part in the betterment of the world." These phrases, which expressed Brandeis's concept of the Jewish mission, corresponded with Richards's own variety of Zionism.[52]

It seems that the Zionist Council of Boston had no role in Brandeis's conversion to Zionism. Founded in 1898, it had grown steadily during its first five years but had declined suddenly apparently following the involvement of its leaders in some unsavory local politics.[53] Those on the staff of the *Jewish Advocate* who subscribed to the Zionist ideology, such as Jacob De Haas and Leo Lyons, were not directly connected with the council; neither was Max Mitchell. Still others, such as A. Lincoln Filene and Meyer Bloomfield, actively opposed it. Robert Silverman was active in the local Zionist movement, but Brandeis knew him primarily as a Progressive-minded social worker. All had helped make Brandeis an active Jew, but none had stimulated his Zionism.

When Brandeis received an invitation (dated June 23, 1911) from Isadore Kronstein, vice president of the Zionist Council of Boston, to be the principal speaker at a meeting to commemorate Theodore Herzl, the founder of modern Zionism, he responded curtly that it was impossible for him to come but added his "appreciation of the fine idealism represented by the movement of which he [Herzl] is the founder."[54]

At the same time Brandeis was being considered to lead the national Federation of American Zionists. On June 22, 1911, Israel Friedlander, the intellectual leader whose cultural Zionism affirmed the principles of "Diaspora plus Palestine, religion plus nationalism," wrote to Judah Magnes: "If no president can be secured it seems to me that it would be best to keep the present arrangement of an honorary president (candidates: Dr. [Solomon] Schecter, Samuel Strauss, Louis Brandeis, Dr. S. Cohen)."[55] But there is no evidence that as far as Brandeis was concerned anything came of this plan.

The Zionist movement was undergoing a significant transformation. Magnes, also a cultural Zionist who was then a member of the American Jewish Committee's Executive Committee, and Friedlander were trying to establish a comprehensive community organization, the New York Kehillah, in collaboration with the AJC. Downtown opposition to the Kehillah as a rubber-stamp for the local Jewish plutocracy was shared by a group of FAZ leaders, who were more concerned with social reform than the committee had shown itself to be. They were headed by Louis Lipsky, editor of the *Maccabaean*, and Abraham Goldberg, previously associated with labor Zionism and since 1908 a member of the governing board of the FAZ. With Senior Abel, Goldberg had founded the FAZ weekly, *Dos Yiddishe Folk*, in 1910. Control of the Federation of American Zionists passed into the hands of Lipsky and Goldberg's group at the Tannersville Convention of 1911. No honorary president was chosen; instead Louis Lipsky was elected chairman of the executive committee and became the leader of the federation. The administrative committee, which managed the routine work of the FAZ, included Goldberg and Senior Abel in addition to Lipsky; the honorary secretary was Bernard Rosenblatt, a young lawyer of pronounced Progressive views, who in his student days had organized the Columbia University Zionist Society. Bernard Richards, although not an officer of the FAZ, helped his fellow journalists Lipsky and Goldberg in making decisions and shared their antipathy toward the "uptown, aristocratic *yahudim*."[56]

This new leadership kept in close touch with local activists, as it was the first in the history of the Zionist Federation to emerge from the rank and file of the movement. This fact, coupled with the East European origins of virtually all its members, gave the FAZ of 1912 a new complexion that was in strong contrast with that of the American Jewish Committee, whose leaders were of German origins, were appointed or nominated by their fellow notables, and included a powerful group of big capitalists. The AJC was financed mainly by these wealthy contributors.[57]

Even an outsider such as Brandeis could see the difference between the two organizations. And since Brandeis's politics had antagonized some of the AJC leaders, he was not likely to gravitate toward that group. Jacob Schiff, a dominant figure in the committee and head of the investment banking house of Kuhn, Loeb and Company, had been criticized by Brandeis in 1905 for his mismanagement of the Equitable Life Assurance Society. Brandeis's censuring of railroad tycoon Averell Harriman further antagonized Schiff, who was allied with the Harriman interests. Daniel Guggenheim, another influential figure in the AJC, was the owner of large mining interests, and Brandeis had bitterly fought against him in the Ballinger case, calling attention to his exploitation of Alaska's resources. Investment bankers were also numbered among AJC leaders, and Brandeis had long been critical of investment (as distinguished from commercial) bankers. But neither the American Jewish Committee nor the Federation of American Zionists represented a homogeneous group, and neither was particularly militant. Both had members with diverse social and political views. Besides the big capitalists, the AJC included professionals such as Julian Mack, who supported the social and labor legislation of Theodore Roosevelt, Oscar Straus, Roosevelt's Secretary of Commerce and Labor, and Louis Marshall, one of the founders of the AJC, its second president (1912-29), and a Taft supporter. Jacob Schiff not only had voted for Woodrow Wilson, but had contributed to his preconvention fund as early as December 1911. Still in Brandeis's view the AJC represented big business, big banking, railroads, and policies that he opposed. By contrast the picture that Brandeis had of the Zionist federation was formed by his contact with Bernard Richards and Bernard Rosenblatt, both of whom conspicuously represented the FAZ's Progressive and democratic element. He was eventually to choose the Zionists, considering them to be more in harmony with the goals that had brought him earlier to Jewish affiliation.[58]

In April 1912 Richards invited Brandeis to participate in the coming Zionist annual convention to be held in Cleveland the following June. Now with increased authority he spoke to Brandeis in the language of what later became known as "social Zionism": "We should be glad to have you speak on the struggle for the re-establishment of the Jewish nationality and its relation to the general democratic ideal, or some similar theme which would emphasize the Jewish belief in the rule of the people." Brandeis responded: "I sympathize with the high idealism expressed in this movement and with the fine democratic spirit which pervades it." He declined with apologies and sent a check as a "contribution to the cause." Richards pursued the contact: "I was sorry to learn that you could not be with us on the occasion of the Fourteenth Annual Convention of the Federation of American Zionists, but I will not abandon hope of having you speak for us at some other time in the future." Several days later Louis Lipsky, the chairman of the executive committee of the FAZ, thanked Brandeis "in the name of the cause to which we are devoted" for the contribution forwarded to him "through Mr. Richards, a member of our committee." "We need not assure you that we are appreciative of your interest in and sympathy with the Zionist ideal . . . May we not hope that in time, as Jewish problems press themselves into the circle of your intellectual and spiritual activities, we may be able to gain for Zionism your interest, your sympathy, and also yourself."[59]

Brandeis received this letter on May 14. That evening he met for the first time with Bernard Rosenblatt, whom he knew to be the honorary secretary of the American Federation of Zionists from Lipsky's organization letterhead. The meeting had been scheduled before Lipsky's letter arrived, and its subject was labor, not Zionism; but it affected Brandeis more strongly than a direct appeal to join the ranks. Brandeis had long been known for his interest in what he called the irregularity of employment, and during the recession of 1910-11 (which by 1913-14 had developed into a depression), his concern had grown. On this question, as generally in labor matters, he worked especially with Jews. In June 1911 he asked Lincoln Filene and Meyer Bloomfield for their opinion of his formulation of the issue, declaring that "irregularity of employment is . . . the greatest of industrial wastes, and one of the main causes of social demoralization." He proposed to them, in seven full pages of writing, a solution whereby wages would be put on a sliding scale.[60]

Bernard Rosenblatt suggested in his "Unemployment and the Competitive System" (which he sent to Brandeis in April 1912) that unemployment resulting from increasing productivity could be solved by establishing "work colonies" for the unemployed where they could produce necessary goods for themselves. Ideas about cooperative government of these colonies and guaranteed annual income were interwoven with the main thesis. Brandeis was intrigued; on May 3 he wrote to Rosenblatt: "Your paper is able, and closely reasoned. The suggestion was very interesting, and you have faced courageously certain objections which suggested themselves." He thought the paper should be widely read and commented: "I am hoping to take up later the general subject of employment, or irregularity of employment, which you properly state is one of our fundamental questions; and I may be able later to make more definite suggestions in regard to your valuable paper." Rosenblatt's *Recollections* record the continuation of that paper and of the contact between him and Brandeis:

> In the early summer of 1912, before the election of President Woodrow Wilson, I had the good fortune to meet Louis D. Brandeis, at the Harvard University Club in New York City, at his invitation, to discuss a book I was then writing (later published, in 1914, under the title "The Social Commonwealth") and dedicated to "LOUIS D. BRANDEIS, a Leader of the people in the Battle for Social Justice". The book was the result of Sociological studies in the Post Graduate Department of Columbia University, and

dealt largely with the recurring problem of mass unemployment and its possible solution through the fostering of an organization of agricultural "Labor Colonies," and a collateral program of the nationalization of land values (by Government purchases) to safeguard the interest of the public as consumers.

This meeting was followed by further correspondence between the two, recorded in Brandeis's diary under the heading "Labor. Irregularity of Employment."[61]

Rosenblatt, as Brandeis undoubtedly knew, was a Zionist leader. Rosenblatt recalls: "I inevitably touched upon the problem of Zionism. Later I was agreeably surprised to receive a message from [Brandeis], addressed to me as Honorary Secretary, at the Zionist Convention in Cleveland that summer with his first initial gift to the Zionist cause." At that time, however, Brandeis avoided discussing Zionism with Rosenblatt. But the latter's social Zionism helped Brandeis to see the connection between Zionism and American Progressivism.[62]

It was Brandeis's letter to Bernard Richards of the *Maccabaean* that publicly committed him to the Zionist movement in America. The *Jewish Advocate* of May 17, 1912, which announced the forthcoming Zionist Convention in Cleveland, also contained an article entitled "Brandeis Zionist."

> A communication has also been received by the Convention Committee from Mr. Louis D. Brandeis, a letter regretting his inability to attend the Convention, owing to the pressure of public business, but expressing his whole hearty [*sic*] sympathy with the Zionist cause, and enclosing a donation towards the funds of the Convention. The letter, which is of great public interest, will be read together with other communications at the opening session of the Convention.

Later, at the beginning of July, when the *Advocate* reported on its front page the opening of the convention, the article's subtitle ran: "Louis D. Brandeis and Nathan Straus Join the Ranks." The letter Brandeis had written to Richards on April 26 had been read to those assembled.[63]

Jews Are Not Welcome

As in other parts of the country, social anti-Semitism in Boston preceded its political and ideological expressions. During the first decade of the twentieth century, the social exclusion of Jews took increasingly aggressive forms. The growing number of Jews in Boston and their migration to the suburbs of Dorchester and Roxbury (especially after the fire that destroyed the Chelsea ghetto in 1908) provoked hostile reactions to the "invaders." The *Jewish Advocate* of August 1910 ran a sensational story on the refusal of real estate agents to rent apartments to Jews in Roxbury and Dorchester; the same practices were employed in Brookline, Brighton, and Allston. Jewish real estate men had paved the way for that migration and also demonstrated the Jews' rapid success in business; they thus became a particular target of anti-Semitism. The memoirs of a Protestant Roxbury resident described the influx led by "a builder named Feldman" and the transformation of the local school, which "began to fill with precocious Jewish children, all of whom seemed to be taking either piano or violin lessons."[64]

Their increasing numbers in the colleges and professions aroused animosity not only against the "Feldmans" but also against the Jews' achieving, ambitious children. "Every Jewish junk-dealer from Chelsea, every shopkeeper or delicatessen proprietor in Dorchester, every tailor or fur-worker in Mattapan above all else wanted his son to become a professional man. And because nearby Harvard was America's oldest and most illustrious university he wanted him to go there and to no lesser place." Nathaniel Shaler in 1904 described how anti-Semitism had spread since the end of the nineteenth century into the confines of Harvard itself: "Of this resurgence of dislike the Hebrew students in Harvard College had some, though not a serious, share. Thirty years ago, when the Jews first began to be an appreciable element among the students of this University, there was no evidence whatever of dislike to them," but now it "is sufficient to be noticeable and to awaken keen regret in all those who love the catholic and humane motive which so long has inspired the school."[65]

It was against this background of anti-Semitism that Joseph Bergman, Brandeis's acquaintance from Mt. Sinai Hospital and the Good Government Association, was tried for assault in 1910-11. Bergman, who had first come to Boston as a sailor, had accumulated almost half a million dollars within a dozen years or so in the real estate business. Part of the fortune was made by moving Jews to Dorchester and Roxbury. As the first president of the Mount Sinai Hospital Dispensary, he was among the rising Jewish professionals in the city. His elder son was an able young attorney; his younger son would later be a noted physician. But this success story was disturbed in 1904 when Joseph Bergman was brought to court on charges that he had assaulted the adopted daughter of Richard and Mary Welch when they were his neighbors in Roxbury. The Welches asked for twenty-five thousand dollars in damages. In 1910, after enduring many legal entanglements and much anguish, Bergman engaged Brandeis, Dunbar and Nutter to take up his defense.[66]

Brandeis and his partners, hoping to demonstrate the innocence of the man, took on the case, although it was outside the firm's usual line of business. Bergman had a strong alibi. At the time that the alleged assault took place, he claimed to have been at a meeting to discuss the founding of a Jewish hospital in Boston. His story was supported by physicians and public figures who were there or knew about the meeting. Dr. Philip S. Sumner (Sosnoski), the founder of the *Mount Sinai Monthly* (the *Advocate*'s predecessor), headed a long and distinguished list of witnesses. With this impressive defense, Edward McClennen of Brandeis, Dunbar and Nutter hoped to convince the Massachusetts Superior Court of the innocence of Joseph Bergman. The bench was not impressed, however, and the defendant was found guilty. Bergman intended to appeal the case, but his health failed, and in May 1912 he died at the age of 53.[67]

Almost no one was immune to the social barriers erected

against Jews, though some hoped to be. The eccentric Edward A. Filene constantly tried to avoid being classified as a Jew. "He asked me once how he could overcome the class, race and religious differences which split up Boston so that the city could not act as a unit on anything," recalls Lincoln Steffens in his autobiography. "I suggested humorously [that] a City Club where all these varieties of Bostonese would meet and learn to know one another [would be the solution]. We talked about it; he was serious." In 1906, Filene founded the Boston City Club with himself as chairman of the executive committee and an Irish fellow merchant as president. Some Brahmins also joined and the club seemed to flourish. It soon became primarily a political club, where lectures and debates regularly took place. Outside, however, no doors were opened to Jews by Boston society. Brandeis and other important members of the Jewish community were among the early members of the City Club, but elsewhere their social environment remained unchanged.[68]

The New Century Club continued to be a refuge for Jewish professionals. Although the Elysium, the favorite club of the German Jews, lasted until 1930, the new country clubs somewhat overshadowed its appeal. The Kernwood Country Club, a Jewish social haven, was established in 1914 under the presidency of Louis Kirstein. Brandeis knew many of its members, but the club apparently was politically too conservative and socially too dull for him, and he and Alice never joined it.[69]

Thus the Boston of 1910 restricted the Jews to their own social circles. Even Lincoln Filene (though not Edward) finally gave up trying to avoid a clear-cut Jewish affiliation and joined the Kernwood Club. Some of the feeling of this period is reflected in Santayana's *The Last Puritan*, in which the Boscovitz family try to conceal their Jewish origins but are finally sorted out and rejected. The non-Jewish Mrs. Boscovitz "thought that in America, no one had any prejudices about race or religion, and there were no social distinctions; and she sighs when she tells me so and adds, *Quelle erreur!* . . . There was a pause, long enough for [Brahmin] Oliver to feel distinctly that he would never like the Boscovitzes."[70]

Brandeis intended to retain his membership in the Dedham

Polo Club even after the death of Samuel D. Warren, but other events soon led him to resign. A week after Warren took his life, the club was partially destroyed by fire. Some of its members had wanted to merge it with the Norfolk Country Club of Westwood, and the fire provided a pretext to do so. Joshua Crane of Westwood (who was prominent also in the Dedham Polo Club) wrote to Brandeis about the plan in March 1910; anticipating that Brandeis might oppose the merger, he covered five pages with his explanations and arguments. The letter was forwarded to Brandeis in Washington, where he was in the midst of his efforts to expose Attorney General George Wickersham's cover-up in the Ballinger case. Busy as he was, he promptly replied to Crane: "I am strenuously opposed to giving up the present club. If necessary I should be quite willing to pay increased dues to the Dedham Club, or if the funds are insufficient for rebuilding, take an additional bond." Four days after Crane's letter arrived, Brandeis's friend in Dedham, Herbert Maynard, wrote to him: "The majority of the prime-movers [toward amalgamation] are men whose interests in the Country Club are greater than in the Polo Club. There is a strong feeling on both sides and before long the question will no doubt be presented to each club to vote on." Maynard wanted to rebuild the Dedham clubhouse, and only "then give consideration to the question of amalgamation or liquidation . . . I believe, that a fairer conclusion can be arrived at by the Club at large if it is not asked to vote on the question while the house is in a partially destroyed condition." Brandeis replied to Maynard as he had to Crane. But at a meeting of the Dedham Polo Club the motion was passed "to transfer to the Norfolk Country Club the Polo interest, that club to assume all responsibility and management." Several weeks later the Norfolk Country Club of Westwood changed its name to the Dedham Country and Polo Club, and Brandeis resigned.[71]

Alterations to the Norfolk Country Club began in the autumn of 1910. Located on Westfield Street, on the border of Westwood and Dedham, the new club drew its leadership from Westwood. Most of the former members of the Dedham Polo

Club were satisfied with the merger, and even many of those who opposed it submitted to the situation. The new club flourished: it included the prominent members of the old Dedham club and offered polo besides. By contrast the club that remained on High Street in Dedham gradually declined. Its name curtailed to Dedham Club, it lingered on for several years, but local residents gradually forgot it. Brandeis's Dedham life had faded in any case after Warren's death, although he had continued to pay his club dues.[72]

It was not only sentimental attachment to the club founded by his friend Warren that had caused Brandeis to be strenuously opposed to the merger: he was also aware that the merger would change the club's atmosphere. Though he was something of an outsider at the Dedham Polo Club, he had some standing as a long-time member, and the club reflected, in some measure, the social arrangements of nineteenth-century Boston. But the people of Westwood (the town came into being in 1897) brought to the new club the values of a less liberal Boston society. The generation of Brahmins who had bought their estates in this area restricted their social life much more than had their earlier counterparts in Dedham. What had simply been pride among Dedham Yankees often became arrogance in Westwood; the new suburbanites were aggressively exclusive. A son of one of the leaders of the Westwood group recalls that anti-Semitism in general and dislike for Brandeis in particular were both common.[73]

The Saga of the Palestinian Jews

Beginning in late May of 1911, Brandeis became involved in a bitter struggle and public confrontation with the Massachusetts-based United Shoe Machinery Company. He had first become associated with the manufacturers of shoe machinery in the mid 1890s as a result of legal services rendered to important shoe-manufacturing clients. Two of these, Charles H. Jones and Jenry B. Endicott, brought Brandeis into contact with USM, and his relations with the company gradually increased. He acted as their counsel and eventually became one of its nineteen directors.[74]

In May 1906 two of Brandeis's clients, W. H. McElwain and C. H. Jones, complained about the "tying clauses" in their leases with United Shoe Machinery, which forbade the lessees to use machinery manufactured by USM's competitors. After investigating the matter, Brandeis resigned as a director of USM. In 1910, when an alternative shoe machinery system invented by Thomas Plant was eliminated by the credit power of USM, Brandeis "concluded that the time had come when I could no longer properly remain passive in the shoe-machinery controversy, and that I ought, if called upon, to so lend aid in any effort that might be made to restore competitive condition [*sic*] in the industry."[75]

In testimony before a Senate committee in December 1911, Brandeis violently attacked USM's business and financial position: "As a matter of fact this shoe machinery corporation is a financial power as much as it is an industrial power. The managers of the shoe machinery corporation are practically the controlling influence in the First National Bank of Boston. They are a very large influence in our leading trust company." In a letter to the Wisconsin Progressive La Follette, Brandeis made the same point and especially emphasized the role played by Sidney Winslow, the organizer and president of USM, in the affairs of the First National Bank. He also noted that USM had connections with financial Boston through James J. Storrow of the law firm Fish, Richardson and Storrow. Storrow, a member of the banking firm of Lee, Higginson and Company, was an important USM director. In short, USM's governance was thoroughly intertwined with the industrial and financial powers of Boston. As an outsider to these interest groups, Brandeis was especially willing to take his clients' part against USM when a conflict arose. As in the New Haven case, he was ready to embark upon an all-out struggle against an uncontrolled industrial-financial power.[76]

Brandeis was granted an opportunity to end the unfair practices on May 27, 1911, when "officers of the Shoe Manufacturers' Alliance asked me to act as their legal adviser . . . The Shoe Manufacturers' Alliance is an association of shoe manufacturers who, it is said, manufacture in the aggregate over one-third of all the shoes made in the United States." Of the sixty members of the alliance, only two were from New England; the rest were from St. Louis, Cincinnati, and Milwaukee. Although a few local organizations and large companies in New England were protesting USM practices, they refused to join the alliance. Included among them was the firm of W. H. McElwain and Company which, along with the Commonwealth Shoe and Leather Company, introduced Brandeis to the case. The New England Shoe and Leather Association did not take a stand on the issue. "In Massachusetts the allegiance of the shoe manufacturers to the United Shoe Machinery Co. is due in many cases to the financial power," according to Brandeis, and USM was a powerful company indeed. Its treasurer was one of the vice presidents of the New England Shoe and Leather Association; its lawyers succeeded in nullifying the federal government's efforts to declare the tying clauses illegal, and they remained in effect until 1922. By 1912 it was apparent to Brandeis that despite the opportunity his old relationship with Massachusetts shoe manufacturers had not been invigorated at all; no more than the original two firms had joined the Shoe Manufacturers' Alliance, though there were approximately two hundred member firms in the New England Shoe and Leather Association. The alliance's headquarters continued to be in St. Louis, as were most of its officers; the rest were in Cincinnati.[77]

This case proved even more disappointing to Brandeis than the New Haven struggle. In the railroad case he had at least been able to gain allies by claiming to represent old and cherished Yankee values; in the fight against USM, there was no such emotional issue around which to organize any kind of "league." Politicians and businessmen both failed him. Governor Eugene Foss, a professed Progressive, gave only token assistance. In a message to the legislature, Foss asked for a statute applicable to the USM monopoly, but the legislative committee on rules claimed that an antimonopoly statute already in existence took care of the situation. The governor then ordered an immediate investigation into the methods of the Massachusetts shoe-machinery industry. The attorney general asked for evidence. Foss replied that it was not his job to supply evidence and sent a second message to the legislature accompanied by a letter from the president of a Massachusetts shoe manufacturing company. Desultory public hearings finally began. Brandeis and Charles Jones spoke, but the futility of the situation was clear; an order providing for a recess committee to begin a probe was killed in the House.[78]

Since the time when Massachusetts submitted in the New Haven case, Brandeis had shifted his hopes for antimonopoly legislation to Washington and the Wisconsin Progressives there. From the summer of 1911 he worked closely with La Follette's group, in the wake of the Supreme Court's disappointing ruling on Standard Oil's violation of the Sherman Antitrust Act. As an amendment to that law he suggested a section designed to make tying clauses illegal. His collaborator in this case was Irving Lenroot, who represented Wisconsin in the House of Representatives from 1909 to 1918, and until 1914 served as La Follette's lieutenant.[79]

In the New Haven Railroad case, it had seemed that the forces of evil came from without to threaten the old Yankee virtues. But the USM leaders were all Yankees; Brandeis now saw the innovative spirit of Massachusetts being threatened from within. It was the suppression of the Plant system — of a new and more efficient method of manufacturing — that propelled Brandeis into action. When he associated himself with the midwestern shoe manufacturers, he saw to it that one purpose of the alliance was defined as removing "conditions which now discourage the invention and development of shoe machinery." When he testified on the trust question before the Senate committee later in 1911 he attributed to the USM monopoly the stifling of the inventive spirit. This theme was taken up in Judson Welliver's article in *Hampton's Magazine*, which Brandeis recommended as the best on the USM case. "Since the days of Benjamin Franklin we have prided ourselves upon our inventive genius. For decades we have led the world in the production of mechanical marvels," the article declared, and asked: "What is Happening to the 'Ingenious Yankees?' "

It continued: "We are the 'ingenious Yankees' who for years have taken the breath of the Old World. A new people, face to face with new conditions, we have invented short cuts. To overcome natural obstacles we have made the ideal practical. Steamboats, railways, telegraphs, electric lights, aeroplanes, wooden nutmegs, and predigested food, all have followed in the train of our national ingenuity."[80]

As Brandeis began his attack on the United Shoe Machinery Company he simultaneously joined, as noted earlier, La Follette's effort to amend the now threatened Sherman Antitrust Act. His antagonism toward trusts and big business steadily sharpened. His antitrust views were not based on close analysis but rather on his general sense of social justice, which originated in part in the nature of his legal practice. Brandeis's law firm did not do business among the state's bigger industries or banks: he thus sought fair treatment for those smaller businessmen who were represented by his clientele. He rejected the assumption "that with increase of size comes increase of efficiency," claiming instead that bigness beyond a certain size led to inefficiency and that "the circumstances attending business to-day are such that the temptation is toward the creation of too large units of efficiency . . . Success or failure of an enterprise depends usually upon one man; upon the quality of one man's judgment, and, above all things, his capacity to see what is needed and his capacity to direct others."[81]

The political and moral aspects of Brandeis's objection to bigness became apparent in remarks such as "You can not have true American citizenship, you can not preserve political liberty, you can not secure American standards of living unless some degree of industrial liberty accompanie[s] it." In his January 1912 testimony before the House's Stanley Committee, which was investigating steel industry practices, Brandeis continued in the same vein, stressing the need to save the "manhood" of the American people and of American workers. Discussing the antipathy felt toward Congress by Carnegie Steel's directors, Brandeis declared: "[It] adds to the many dangers to democracy which are inherent in these huge aggregations." At óne point he spoke for over two hours to a crowded audience at the Ethical Culture Society in New York City about "Big Business and Industrial Liberty."[82]

During this period Brandeis shuttled back and forth between Washington and the Midwest. In Chicago he helped to organize the anti-Taft insurgency of midwestern Republican Progressives; in Washington he assisted Congressmen Lenroot of Wisconsin and Augustus Stanley of Kentucky in their anti-trust campaign.[83] He still hoped that "manhood," freedom, and ingenuity could be restored to American life. And then he learned that in Palestine — where Jewish pioneers worked and strived — these values had been achieved.

On the evening of January 6, 1912, Brandeis attended a dinner about which he reported enthusiastically to his brother:

> I met your friend Glaeser Saturday at Dinner — talk on "wild wheat" given by Julius Rosenwald for Aaron Aaronsohn of the Jewish Agricultural Experiment Station in Palestine. Aaronsohn is a Roumainian [*sic*] Jew who at the age of 5 emigrated to Palestine with his father who is now a farmer there.
>
> The talk was the most thrillingly interesting I have ever heard, showing the possibilities of scientific agriculture and utilization of arid or supposedly exhausted land.
>
> I am told the U.S. Agricultural Department has issued a Bulletin by Aaronsohn on wild wheat. Send for it.[84]

When Aaronsohn — a noted agronomist and Zionist statesman — visited the United States in 1909, he came with a letter of introduction to Julian Mack. Judge Mack took Aaronsohn to call on the Rosenwald family, who were fascinated by him. Rosenwald spent the day absorbed in Aaronsohn's stories of Palestine and its agricultural potential. Rosenwald and Judge Mack took Aaronsohn to dinner with a group of botanists from the University of Chicago, and the botanists were so interested in Aaronsohn's researches that they asked him to deliver a lecture the next day before their botanical society. Before he left Aaronsohn had obtained the incorporation (in 1910) of the Jewish Agricultural Experiment Station, with Julius Rosenwald as president, had developed a lasting friendship with Mack,

who remained close to the project, and had established connections with a wide circle of non-Zionist Jews, Felix Frankfurter among them.[85]

Aaronsohn had an important place in Brandeis's conversion
to Zionism—Mrs. Julius Rosenwald claimed to have heard
Brandeis say that Aaronsohn had to be credited with it. In his
reminiscences Norman Hapgood writes that "the seed of Zionism was first sown in [Brandeis's] mind" by the story of Aaronsohn and his wild wheat. Hapgood was close to Brandeis at the
time, and it is possible that Brandeis said something to support
this idea. But Hapgood could also readily have sensed the impact that Aaronsohn's story might have had on Brandeis. The
Zionist effort in Palestine would have appealed to him as the
embodiment of his ideal society: "Two of his basic principles
soon presented themselves to him as connected with the dream
of making Palestine again the home of a culture ages long . . .
Zionism became an outstanding idea in his mind . . . because it
is an idea that is creatively democratic . . . Democracy, as he
dreams it . . . [is] not controlled from great centers, but a force
to add vitality, vigor, and profusion to human experience, by
the method of free experiment and unchecked expression
whether it be qualities of the individual or of the group." Hapgood concludes by noting that Brandeis was never a party
man: "he is always a Jeffersonian. It happens that the little
country of Palestine made a contribution to the race of man
that is among our most precious assets." Thus, it seems that
ingenuity, experimentation, and smallness were the elements
in Aaronsohn's Palestine that appealed to Brandeis.[86]

In October 1912 Aaronsohn returned to the United States,
and in early 1913 he went on a lecture tour along the East
Coast. He and Brandeis finally met through Mack and Frank-
furter at Brandeis's home on the evening of May 4; Charles W.
Eliot was also present. Lief's biography of Brandeis states:
"The guests were thrilled and Brandeis beamed."[87]

Some of Aaronsohn's remarks that evening were recounted
several days later to the Jewish audience who heard Brandeis's
first full-fledged Zionist statement. His address, given to the
Young Men's Hebrew Association of Chelsea, Massachusetts on

May 18, 1913, began as if it were a continuation of the letter to his brother written the previous January:

> A fortnight ago it was my privilege to spend the evening with one of the most interesting, brilliant and remarkable men that I have ever met. He is the son of a poor Rumanian Jew who migrated from his native land thirty-two years ago to take up his residence in the land of his fathers in Palestine. This man who is now at the head of the Jewish Agricultural Experiment Station in Palestine is Prof. Aaronsohn. He made what is considered one of the most remarkable and useful discoveries in recent years and possibly of all times. He has discovered what is known as the "Wild Wheat" which botanists all over the world have been trying to discover for years.

Brandeis went on to praise Aaronsohn for his persistence and ingeniousness and to describe his contribution as one of worldwide importance. Then he told his listeners of something even more notable:

> [Aaronsohn] went on and he told a story even more remarkable than the first. We were telling of a series of unpleasant acts with which the Jewish name was connected last year in New York City. Then this Mr. Aaronsohn told us: 'That in Palestine, the little communities which have grown up in the last thirty two years and now number 150,000 Jewish souls, not a single crime was known to have been committed by one of our people during all that time.' . . . There has developed there, and there can develop still more in that old land to a higher degree, that spirit of which Mr. Aaronsohn speaks . . . this manhood.[88]

The morality and industry of the pioneer Zionists in Palestine completed for Brandeis the picture of his own people as the new "Puritans." He could now shift his allegiance, for he had decided that the values of the Massachusetts founders were being carried on in far-off Palestine. Like the New England Puritans, the settlers in the Land of Israel were courageous, hard working, and uncorrupted; they lived in "little communities" and displayed a Yankee-like ingenuity in overcoming obstacles. "The very lack of wealth in Palestine — the impossibility of there ever being wrung from that soil much luxury—has been an attraction to Mr. Brandeis," observed Norman Hapgood. "[Brandeis's] contempt for material excess for anybody . . . his dislike of passive entertainment" also helped him to identify New England's tradition with the epic of the new Palestine.[89]

In subsequent public statements, Brandeis continued to equate the New England Puritans with the new Zionists. In a speech delivered in September 1914, entitled "The Rebirth of the Jewish Nation," he stated: "These new Pilgrim Fathers sought, therefore, to restore in the land of their fathers the Jewish national life." In an address two months later, he likened "the re-birth of the Jewish nation in Palestine . . . to the birth of the new England" and spoke about "our Pilgrim Jewish fathers [who] started to the Holy Land to make the attempt." In mid-1915, by then a committed and nationally known Zionist leader, he repeated: "Zionism is the Pilgrim inspiration and impulse over again; the descendants of the Pilgrim Fathers should not find it hard to understand and sympathize with it."[90]

Lessons in Zionism

Along with his fascination for the Zionists in Palestine, Brandeis's alliance with the local Jewish community continued to grow, thanks in large part to Max Mitchell, his oldest and most reliable Jewish ally in Boston. Mitchell was politically important for Brandeis because, as an East European working among German Jews, he was in touch with the entire community. In 1911 Brandeis helped him to found a new bank, a daring step in a banking community dominated by Yankee business. It was in fact the second Jewish bank to be established in Boston: in 1887 the brothers Abraham and Israel Ratshesky had founded the United States Trust Company there, but Brandeis had taken no interest because the Ratshesky brothers were members of the community's old elite and politically conservative. Mitchell succeeded in arousing Brandeis's interest in part because he approached him in the wake of Brandeis's bitter confrontation with State Street. Brandeis felt that he could use a Jewish ally in banking circles, and like many Jewish businessmen (especially East Europeans) he regarded Mitchell as deserving of help. The new bank, named the Cosmopolitan Trust Company, opened on April 3, 1912; Brandeis closed his account with the New England Trust Company and opened one there the same day. By moving from the Protestant to the Jewish bank, Brandeis meant to show his solidarity with his ethnic group. He also took care to commit the Cosmopolitan Trust to the cause of savings-bank insurance. Following his discussions with Mitchell and others from the Cosmopolitan during April and May, the *Jewish Advocate* informed its readers on May 31, 1912, that "The Cosmopolitan Trust Company of Boston has recently become a public agency for Savings Bank Life Insurance."[91]

By 1912 Brandeis had cut most of his ties with the German community. Now a full-fledged Progressive, he found its members too conservative, and having a large and stable clientele for his practice, he no longer needed their social connections. He had also drawn closer to the East European Jews in Boston, and following his conversion to Zionism he did not depend upon the philo-German milieu for his sense of ethnic identity. His enthusiasm for the Jewish ethos and his "thrill" at the accomplishments of Zionist pioneers in Palestine gradually displaced his earlier passion for German culture and weakened his previously keen interest in its social and economic achievements.[92]

Around 1906 Brandeis had resigned his directorship in the Germanic Museum Association; his contact with that organization further declined and finally ended in May 1912 when he was invited to attend the laying of the cornerstone of its new building at Harvard. He refused and had no further communication with the association.[93]

In February 1912, in the midst of his presidential nomination campaign, Robert La Follette suffered a physical collapse, and in July the Democrats nominated Woodrow Wilson. "It seems to me that those Progressives who do not consider themselves bound by party affiliations ought to give Wilson thorough support," Brandeis wrote to La Follette the next day. The *Jewish Advocate* also called on independent voters to support Wilson; an editorial on July 12 suggested that having a scholar in politics would bring enlightenment to government, making it more responsive to the public's interests. And in October the *Advocate* wrote: "Governor Wilson . . . is an idealist, in words, actions, and in his personality . . . Jews should do their individual utmost to place the guidance of the United States in the hands of a man who has made culture the shining purpose of his life."[94]

With Wilson's candidacy, well-off and established Jews began to move away from their traditional support of the Republican party. The *Advocate* reported after Wilson's victory that "Mr. Wilson received an unusual amount of avowed financial and political support from Jewish citizens." Henry Morgenthau, for example, was a heavy contributor to Wilson's preconvention campaign, and he subsequently became chairman of the Democratic campaign finance committee; other supporters were the noted lawyers Samuel Untermyer and Abram I. Elkus.[95]

Brandeis wrote to his brother while campaigning for Wilson in the West: "Had invitations from Rabbis in St. Paul, Minneapolis, and Omaha to occupy their pulpits this Friday. So you see I am making headway in Judaism. Also have a very urgent Jewish appeal from Newark, N.J."[96]

The Jewish community became a political home for Brandeis. For the first time in his life he also found himself asking the Jewish community for help in a nonpublic matter. He wrote in November 1912 to the superintendent of the Federated Jewish Charities, requesting assistance for a needy Jew who had approached him: "I have been a contributor to the Federation since its organization, but I think this is the first time that I have called upon the society for a similar service." He was subsequently notified that the person was being assisted.[97]

Brandeis met *Advocate* editor Jacob De Haas in August 1912 to discuss ethnic politics. They had met twice before — in January 1909 and in the early fall of 1910 — in reference to savings-bank life insurance. The *Advocate* had been responsive. As editor, De Haas ensured that the paper was sympathetic to social reform and Zionism. He argued (in 1907) that American Zionism was comparable to American-Irish support for an Irish Free State and in no way detracted from a citizen's loyalty to the United States. When Charles Eliot spoke out for cultural pluralism, he found in De Haas a supporter well versed in the subject.[98]

De Haas was something of a hero worshiper. He was a staunch admirer of Theodor Herzl; he had acted for some time as Herzl's secretary in England ([he] "always seemed to be the automatic choice for secretary . . . he was generally in a position to carry out policies") and came to America still under his spell. From his first meeting with Brandeis in January 1909 (Herzl had died several years before), De Haas hoped Brandeis would become active in the American Zionist movement. When Brandeis's letter was read at the Zionist convention in Cleveland, the *Advocate* commented: "Mr. Brandeis represents the intellectual force which has been favorable to the movement since its inception, at least in Europe . . . the adhesion of Mr. Brandeis to Zionism must make a profound impression on the Jews of New England, who have come to look upon this brilliant legal luminary as a great Jew." It went on to say that the Jews of New England "cannot fail to observe that a Brandeis in the most Jewish of Jewish movements, implies a new asset, not only for this cause, but for the whole of Jewry." Before De Haas met with Brandeis in mid-August 1912 to plan a strategy for the Wilson campaign, he saw to it that an issue of the *Advocate* included a front-page article on Brandeis, commending his public work and emphasizing his ethnic commitment. Brandeis was seen in this article as living up to the Jewish and Zionist heritage of his famous uncle, Lewis Dembitz.[99]

In a letter of August 13 to Governor Eugene Foss of Massachusetts, Brandeis wrote: "Mr. Jacob De Haas called upon me today with a letter from . . . the Dem[ocratic] Nat[ional] Com[mittee] in reference to work among the nationalized citizens in the interest of the Dem. candidates. I think it would be helpful if you would send for Mr. De Haas (258 Washington

St., Boston) & talk over the plans with him." It was De Haas's assignment to deliver the Jewish vote to Wilson that caused him to visit Brandeis at his summer house on Cape Cod. Mason's account of the meeting (based on Brandeis's recollection) says they were fund-raising at William G. McAdoo's request. (McAdoo was of the inner circle of the Wilson organization; later he became Wilson's treasury secretary and son-in-law). Between that meeting and election day, the *Advocate* published lavish advertisements on Wilson's behalf.[100]

De Haas was of course an old hand at ethnic politics, and in August 1912 he could approach Brandeis with the backing of the Democratic National Committee. Wilson himself (like any other contender for the presidency) was not above playing ethnic politics; he, according to a biographer, was "making [in December 1911] a bold bid for Jewish support." Abram I. Elkus, Wilson's friend from Democratic national headquarters and a member of Rabbi Wise's Free Synagogue, had brought De Haas and Brandeis together. A fellow lawyer from New York and well known in Jewish circles, Elkus had an impressive record as a Progressive.[101]

Since Brandeis seemed well disposed to him, De Haas decided to try during their August 1912 meeting to complete Brandeis's induction into the Zionist ranks. When the conference was over, Brandeis accompanied him to the station. In his biography of Brandeis, De Haas recounts that he "ventured to identify the Boston attorney with the Louisville uncle for whom he [Brandeis] was named. Brandeis's admission came readily enough, and upon repetition of the sentence 'Louis N. Dembitz was a noble Jew,' there was instant demand for explanation of that term." According to Brandeis's recollection (through Mason), "De Haas made some mention of Lewis Dembitz as a 'noble Jew,' and on being further questioned launched into the subject nearest his heart—Zionism." Thus there was a question and a response, and De Haas tells it: "It was in explanation of our [American Zionists'] esteem of Louis [*sic*] Dembitz that we proceeded in the next hour to unfold the epic story of Theodor Herzl, the founder of the Zionist movement." Brandeis was intrigued by De Haas's connections in

Brahmin Boston, and "when De Haas told further that he had been London secretary to Theodor Herzl, his interest in De Haas' story was so profoundly aroused that he forgot vacation plans and invited his caller to stay for lunch and take a later train."[102]

De Haas next suggested that he would make a good assistant to Brandeis, being knowledgeable about Zionist politics: Brandeis himself did not know much about Zionism, despite his support for the movement. De Haas became his secretary and instructor in the history of Zionism. In 1916 Brandeis referred to him as the one "who was active originally in bringing me into the [Zionist] Cause." He presented De Haas with his portrait in 1924, writing on it: "For Jacob De Haas Teacher and Companion through years of struggle at a great Cause, 1912-1924 with every fond wish." In 1940 he recalled (according to Mason) that "it was not until De Haas' South Yarmouth visit in August 1912 that his interest in Zionism was fully awakened." It is also possible, although not documented, that De Haas reinforced Brandeis's leanings toward cultural pluralism and assisted him in coping with the problem of dual loyalty. Still, it was De Haas's experiences as a Zionist that interested Brandeis most about him: "That story [of Theodor Herzl], [was] told chapter by chapter in a series of interviews during the following winter [1912-13]," writes De Haas. According to Mason, on August 14, 1912, Brandeis related to his brother: "I had, by chance, one of the original Zionists at luncheon yesterday, who told a better story (Susan and Elizabeth will so testify) even than Capt. Baker [a South Yarmouth 'sea captain']."[103]

The results that winter of Brandeis's conversations with the "original Zionist" were not dramatic: he did not take advantage of several opportunities to express himself on Jewish subjects. He renewed his public role in Zionist matters when he spoke to the New Century Club on March 22, 1913: "In the privacy of the monthly dinner . . . Brandeis made his first serious utterance on Zionism," recounts De Haas. "He . . . unfolded his deep solicitude for the spiritual and moral welfare of the Jews. He explained his interest in Zionism and identified himself in unqualified terms with the cause." In this summary of the address, which is all that remains, Brandeis spoke primarily of "his deep solicitude for the spiritual and moral welfare of the Jews" as, apparently, giving rise to "his interest in Zionism." Whereas De Haas thought that a sovereign national state was the essential goal of modern Zionism, Brandeis emphasized that the movement was committed to social ideals, and he felt that Zionists should be judged chiefly by their loyalty to them.[104]

6

The Burden of
His Jewishness

Left Off the Cabinet

AFTER Woodrow Wilson's election to office in 1912, he considered Brandeis as a possible candidate for attorney general. "Wilson thought almost instinctively of Louis D. Brandeis of Boston, who had emerged as the most trenchant critic of industrial monopoly and had been Wilson's only really important advisor during the campaign of 1912," writes one historian. "No man mentioned for appointment to any position, not even Bryan, had such wide support from all elements in the progressive movement." But Brandeis was not appointed. Although Wilson and his close advisor Edward M. House felt the need to have a Jew in their administration, certain powerful Jews, especially those in American Jewish Committee circles, opposed Brandeis as being too radical in economic matters. They were also interested in promoting into positions of power Jews who were conspicuously affiliated with the Jewish community. According to Henry Moskowitz, the noted New York social worker and Brandeis's friend, "Jewish bankers and Jewish corporate interests" tried to eliminate Brandeis from any cabinet consideration on the grounds that he was "not a representative Jew." The opposition of Jacob Schiff, the investment banker and leader of the AJC, was especially effective, since he had contributed to Wilson's preconvention fund and supported his presidential campaign. In reply to a question from Brandeis's friend Max Mitchell, Schiff stated: "I have been asked from time to time recently whether Mr. Brandeis may be considered a representative Jew, and to this I was able to give a qualified reply only, but he is, without doubt, a representative American." Jewish opposition helped to convince Wilson and House to remove Brandeis from consideration.[1]

Brandeis was in any case not an office-seeker. After his name had been crossed off the list of possible appointees, he wrote to his brother: "Today's papers will have removed the mystery as to the cabinet. As you know I had great doubts as to its being desirable for me, so I concluded to literally let nature take its course and to do nothing either to get called or to stop the talk, although some of my friends were quite active." During the winter of 1912-13, Brandeis indeed "let nature take its course." He did nothing to bolster his image as a "representative Jew," neglecting those Jewish groups with which he had maintained contact since the end of 1905 and which now offered to emphasize publicly the fact that he did represent them. He declined an invitation to address the convention of the Intercollegiate Menorah Societies in Chicago on January 1, 1913. He also declined an invitation from Bernard Richards of the Federation of American Zionists to address a mass meeting in honor of Nahum Sokolow at Carnegie Hall in New York and thus denied himself the benefit of the publicity that would have preceded such an event. He wrote to Richards: "It is possible that I may be in New York while Mr. Nahum Sokolow is here; and if so, I shall be very glad to meet him and you then." He did not participate when De Haas, with the cooperation of Louis Lipsky and Bernard Rosenblatt of the Federation of American Zionists, initiated letters of support to Wilson from FAZ and several other Jewish organizations.[2]

Brandeis's supporters among Boston Jews also tried to publicize his affiliation with their community. (And privately, Max Mitchell made contacts with Schiff and Louis Marshall, president of the AJC, in early February 1913 in an attempt to mitigate their opposition to Brandeis.) During the crucial postelection months, Brandeis was invited to address prominent Jewish organizations in the city, and he refused them all. The established lawyer Edward Goulston wanted him to speak at the

Elysium Club, the most prestigious Jewish club in Boston, where he would have had a superb opportunity to present himself as a "representative Jew," but he did not do so. His diary also records that on January 27, 1913, "[Edward] Bromberg asked me to speak at the New Century Club on Saturday; declined." Brandeis stopped declining Jewish invitations only after Wilson's inauguration, when the cabinet list had been published: he addressed the New Century Club eighteen days after its announcement.[3]

The decisive role in defeating Brandeis's appointment was played not by Jacob Schiff but by members of the Boston financial community, especially Henry Lee Higginson, the banker who had opposed Brandeis in his drive for savings-bank insurance and had been his enemy since the New Haven fight. He exerted constant pressure on Wilson and people close to him from the autumn of 1912, pressure that was effective despite the fact that Brandeis was Wilson's chief adviser on economic issues. Wilson's connection with Higginson can be traced back to the years 1905-10, when the banker generously supported Princeton University, of which Wilson was then president. When Wilson became governor of New Jersey in November 1910, Higginson sent his congratulations. He continued to show interest in Wilson's political course: in October 1912 he contributed one thousand dollars to Wilson's campaign and, in the next month, his vote as well.[4]

Although Higginson was not an unequivocal Wilson supporter, both men were liberals of the free-trade, gold-standard, antiimperialist school. This trilogy of interests had also connected Brandeis with Higginson until about 1905; Wilson had turned Progressive at a slower pace than Brandeis. In 1906 Wilson was an avowed conservative, a nineteenth-century liberal. In 1908, however, he began to change his mind, and his final conversion to Progressivism can be dated to sometime in 1910, after his nomination as governor of New Jersey. Higginson, who himself was rather indifferent to social reform, continued to regard Wilson (though not without suspicion) as a potential ally. Several weeks after Wilson's nomination by the

Democratic party, Higginson wrote a signed editorial in the *Boston Herald* evaluating the three presidential candidates: he discounted Roosevelt for his severe criticism of Wall Street as well as for his egotism and eliminated Taft because of his association with the "tariff tag" and his undue loyalty to the Sherman Act. About Wilson he wrote: "We do not know him and his qualities." But he wrote this before Wilson met Brandeis on August 28: after that the tariff was relegated to second place among Wilson's concerns, and the trust issue became his primary interest. Higginson seemed not to notice, however; in his view Wilson remained a fellow liberal.[5]

After the election Higginson organized his Democratic friends in Boston to stop Brandeis from gaining a cabinet appointment. In Washington Wilson behaved equivocally in the face of their opposition. First he received a long letter in which Higginson systematically listed Brandeis's Progressive sins, including the savings-bank insurance effort, the antirailroad campaign, and his economic views in general. "I know no reputable lawyer here who has a good word for him," Higginson reported, concluding that "what I say to you in this letter is as from one comrade who wishes another well." Wilson's responses, though always carefully phrased, did not discourage Higginson from writing more. In the last of his letters (February 27, 1913), written just before the cabinet list was made final, Higginson no longer had even to mention Brandeis by name: "I have 'rung the changes' about one man who is named for your cabinet, and I can assure you that the men here with whom you would associate and whom you would trust, have but one opinion about that man: — no. If he goes into your cabinet, it will be a distinct injury to the cabinet. He may do all sorts of good services, but, like Mr. Untermyer, he is a great injury to the cause."[6]

Higginson's weight with Wilson came partly from his influence at Doubleday Page and Company, publishers of the magazine *World's Work*, which had shown early and strong support for Wilson. Higginson was on excellent terms with its editor, Walter Hines Page, who had been one of the "original" little group that supported Wilson's bid for the Democratic candidacy in March 1911 (he was later appointed ambassador to Britain by Wilson).[7]

Higginson also knew Cleveland H. Dodge, the largest contributor to Wilson's campaign. The connection between the Higginson and Dodge families went back to 1803, when the first New York member of the Dodges became a partner in the firm of Higginson and Dodge, the largest dry-goods wholesaler in New York. At the time of the 1912 election, Dodge and Higginson served together as directors of the Old Dominion Copper Company, a huge mining company with headquarters in Boston.[8]

In their 1912-13 correspondence Dodge encouraged Higginson's animosity to Brandeis: "I agree with all you say about your distinguished fellow citizen, Mr. Brandeis, whom I have known in connection with the Old Dominion suit. He is undoubtedly a very able man, but I agree with you that it would be unfortunate if Governor Wilson trusted to him [*sic*] too much . . . Fortunately, if he is elected, he will have some wise and sensible advisors, and I am very hopeful that he will be able to select the right men for his Cabinet." After Wilson was elected, blocking Brandeis seemed even more imperative. Dodge informed Higginson: "I did not get an opportunity to talk freely with him before he left but did have some little talk about Mr. Brandeis, and I do not think that he has made up his mind at all, and is still open to just such information as you give." He hoped that "the Governor would be guided aright to make a wise decision." The pressure of old figures from Brandeis's liberal past told against him now: those who had once been his collaborators saw him as a traitor and fought to prevent his appointment.[9]

The New Boston

Brandeis knew that State Street, especially in the form of Henry Lee Higginson, opposed him. Higginson was also a member of the Immigration Restriction League, a powerful organization with racist and anti-Semitic overtones. From 1907 on, Higginson was active in the restriction crusade. His business partner, Joseph Lee, facilitated this development. He was the league's vice president and treasurer, and he prodded Higginson into joining: "I want to interest you again in the Immigration Restriction League . . . we are doing [now] very effective work in getting the immigration laws enforced and in organizing the sentiment for effective restriction . . . this is the most important work for the future of this country that is being done." The following year Lee asked him "to drop a line to Lodge in behalf of immigration restriction, especially the illiteracy test." "We are getting *more* aliens than we can assimilate . . . we are getting the *less desirable races* from . . . southern and eastern Europe . . . we are getting the *lower strata* of various races." In February 1912 Lee induced Higginson to join the advisory council of the league and during several months prepared him for the impending struggle in Congress over immigration-restriction legislation. Higginson wrote to the secretary of the treasury urging him to act on the literacy test bill. President Taft's veto frustrated their efforts, but the restrictionists remained powerful and intensified their campaign. On March 12, 1913, Lee wrote to Higginson: "Last year you consented to serve on the Advisory Committee of the Immigration Restriction League. We are now making it a National Committee and want you to serve on that. If I don't receive any kick from you, I shall assume that we may do so—I mean print your name." The kick did not come, and the next day it was reported at a meeting of the executive committee of the league that Higginson had accepted the position.[10]

Joseph Lee's interest in the Immigration Restriction League was not a matter of chance; one historian notes that the core of the founding group "belonged to the Mugwump-Democrat-Free Trade element of the community." In time, after about 1910, the political make-up of the membership became more heterogeneous.[11]

As was noted in an earlier chapter, at first the idea of restricting immigration had grown out of concern for preserving the democratic process and the social welfare system, which threatened to be overwhelmed by large influxes of poor immigrants. Brandeis himself had only gradually come to oppose it. In 1904 he wrote to a leader of the Immigration Restriction League that his "masterly argument on Selection of Immigration" had "nearly convinced" him that further restrictive legislation was necessary. In 1909 Samuel D. Warren wrote to him: "I enclose an appeal from Joseph Lee. Do you know whether he is proceeding on sensible lines or not? There is much that I should be willing to do, and much that I should be unwilling to do, in the way of the restriction of immigration." Brandeis's response to this query was rather evasive. Ordinarily he trusted Lee's judgment, but in this case he said: "I do not know what lines [*sic*] he is proceeding . . . I have not been wholly convinced by the arguments of the Immigration Restriction League." When in 1911 Paul Kellogg of the *Survey* approached him on the question of immigration, he still wavered: "I have not thought out the immigration problem sufficiently to have reached a definite conclusion, but I am not particularly troubled with the suggestion that by restriction we should close our doors to the oppressed. There are a great many other doors open, and besides it may be the best way to end oppression by denying to enterprising individuals an easy escape."[12]

But between the beginning of 1911 and the spring of 1912, Brandeis formed a more definite opinion. On April 1, 1912, a publishing house sent him an advance copy of Mary Antin's *The Promised Land*: "We believe that this is a book which you will find of unusual interest as showing what America has meant to those who have felt the scourge of despotism." Brandeis later wrote to the publisher that he found "Mary Antin's 'The Promised Land' . . . simple, vivid, powerful. It is a lesson in Democracy which will prove a serious obstacle to immigration restriction. It teaches anew the blessings of freedom, and will enkindle the latent patriotism in many a native American." He now saw the United States as a home for the oppressed, and he tried to educate the natives about this new meaning of patriotism. A year later he became a member of the advisory board of the Hebrew Sheltering and Immigrant

Aid Society, an organization devoted to aiding Jewish immigrants in America.[13]

By the time Brandeis was imparting this belated lesson, the Immigration Restriction League had become a powerful and bigoted organization, and by 1912 the early nativist leanings of the Massachusetts reform movement had become even stronger. William B. Munro, a civic leader and professor of municipal government at Harvard, wrote in a book published in 1912 that there was "an undoubted relation between chromosomes and politics." "The various watchdog groups had to see to it that the right chromosomes remained dominant."[14]

During the municipal election of January 1910, the *Jewish Advocate* accused the Good Government Association of anti-Semitism, claiming that the association's refusal to endorse a Jewish candidate was a symptom of its bias. The targets of the *Advocate*'s criticism were Edmund Billings, secretary of the GGA, and Laurence Minot, chairman of the executive committee of the association from its inception. They had labeled a deserving Jewish public servant a "Sheeny candidate," reported the weekly, and added: "The Billings-Minot crowd must be taught that prejudice is resented, and undoubtedly every Jew will carry that idea with him into the polling booth." When the Jewish candidate lost the election, the *Advocate* interpreted the defeat as "clear evidence of the mischief that can be done to an honest man who fails to win the applause of the Good Government Association."[15]

In January 1916, when President Wilson nominated Brandeis for a seat on the Supreme Court, anti-Semitism again surfaced. The signers of the February 1916 declaration opposing the nomination included Laurence Minot and others whose roots went deep into Massachusetts Mugwumpery.[16]

In the Boston of 1912, anti-Semitism in Brahmin circles clearly affected Brandeis's political prospects. Henry Lee Higginson spoke not only for State Street but for a good part of Boston. Furthermore, A. Lawrence Lowell, the president of Harvard who had replaced Charles Eliot in May 1909, was very different from his predecessor who had supported cultural pluralism. An early member of the Immigration Restriction League and a national vice president since 1912, he notified Wilson immediately after the election that Brandeis did not "stand very high in the opinion of the best judges in Massachusetts." (In 1922 Lowell investigated the "race distribution" within Harvard College and suggested a quota for Jews.) The vehement opposition to Brandeis in Boston, expressed as early as November 16, 1912, led Wilson and Edward House temporarily to eliminate him from their list of potential cabinet members. They reconsidered him only after a wave of support reached the White House, not from Boston, but from Progressives in other parts of the country. "I feel very lonesome in our little provincial town and long to see our friends in the Capitol," Brandeis wrote in February 1913.[17]

Brandeis was not unaware of the anti-Semitic aspect of the opposition to him. In a letter to Norman Hapgood he wrote that "the Massachusetts opposition to my going into the Cabinet was not in its essence political." When in December 1912 Alex Kanter of the University of Minnesota asked him for his opinion on some aspects of the Menorah organization, Brandeis said in his answer that "its refining and ennobling influence will present the best argument and defense against anti-Semitism." The same phrase appears in Brandeis's public letter to the founding conference of the Intercollegiate Menorah Association.[18]

In the years prior to the First World War, nativism prospered as a result of increasing Progressive innovations and social unrest. In the face of the strikes and violent labor upheavals, even manufacturers were skeptical about continuing uncontrolled immigration. The Boston presidents of the National Association of Cotton Manufacturers considered socialism a crime and advised its members not to trust the "ignorant and clumsy foreigners," warning that they would become "self-respecting educated Americans" only through strict discipline in the cotton mills. In 1913 a new name appeared among the major contributors to the Immigration Restriction League: it was that of Henry B. Cabot, secretary and treasurer of the

Boston and Lowell Railroad and a director of the Lawrence Manufacturing Company.[19]

The heavy involvement of Jews in social welfare and in the struggle for labor rights had turned the old stereotype of Jew as prophet into a new one of Jew as radical and subversive. Oliver Alden, the "last Puritan" of Santayana's book, saw them as "outsiders who hung loosely on the fringes of college life: odd persons going out alone, or in little knots, looking intellectual, or looking dissipated. They were likely to be Jews or radicals or to take drugs." For the anti-Semitism of Boston's "last Puritans," Brandeis was a particularly good target: he was a radical reformer who took part in the Lawrence textile strike, and at the same time he was a millionaire. He had always been labeled "not to be trusted"; now he was considered dangerous.[20]

Through 1912 Brandeis continued his strenuous efforts, begun in 1911, to break the monopoly of United Shoe Machinery. His antagonists in this case were formidable and shrewd: USM was notorious for its practice of bribing newspapermen and for aggressive use of the press. Brandeis loved a good fight and toured America organizing the shoe manufacturers' opposition. Nor was Sidney W. Winslow, USM's president, one to sit idly by. Neither well educated, cultivated, nor part of Boston society, he was happy to use anti-Semitism as a weapon in the struggle. In July 1912, when Brandeis was in Washington assisting Augustus Stanley, a Kentucky congressman, in drafting antitrust legislation aimed at breaking USM's monopoly, an article entitled "Brandeis the Reformer" was published by the *Washington Post*. Inspired by Winslow, it was simple, shrewd, and biting. Its theme was that Brandeis, while pretending to care about free competition in the shoe industry, had himself built up a trust of midwestern shoe manufacturers. This two-faced "crook" lawyer, said the article, had something peculiar in his very name:

> How does Brandeis do it? Not many men can impress themselves upon the public as real reformers while assisting their particular friends to form trusts.

No, sir; Looey Brandeis is in a class by himself. All other reformers are fakers or pikers. No other lawyer can act the double
role of attorney for the people and attorney for the trusts, and
make both sides happy. Looey is the incarnation of scientific management. He gets them coming and going.

"Looey," then, was the Jewish lawyer who thrived while exacer-
bating conflicts in society.[21]

Brandeis continued to fight against United Shoe Machinery
through the rest of the year, both indirectly by assisting in anti-
trust legislation and directly by helping the Shoe Manufacturers' Alliance. In the meantime Winslow, the "Czar of Footwear," his warning signal having gone unheeded, prepared his
forces. The journalist who had contributed the article to the
Washington Post in July and a second newspaperman were
now approached by USM with the idea of starting a new
weekly. Both were already employed by the *Boston Herald*, a
daily that had shown itself to be especially compliant with the
policies of USM (as well as those of the New Haven Railroad).
Winslow and the journalists went into action immediately after
Woodrow Wilson's election: Brandeis's appointment as attorney general would be very detrimental to USM's interests. On
November 16, 1912, the first issue of *Truth* was published,
edited by George R. Conroy and Joseph Smith. The financial
backers of the weekly remained anonymous for the first few
months, but after February 1, 1913, each issue included a
quarter-page advertisement by Hornblower and Weeks, an
investment banking house closely allied with USM. Later full-
page advertisements for the USM itself appeared in *Truth* and
continued to appear until its last issue.[22]

The New Haven Railroad collaborated with United Shoe
Machinery in the *Truth* venture. In April 1912 Brandeis opposed a consolidation measure recommended by Governor
Foss which, though intended to modernize Boston's transportation system, also had the effect of buttressing New Haven's
monopoly. One newspaper stated that "the proposal of closer
union was met with a fierce attack from Brandeis, who suddenly revived the old 'obstructive' tactics that had been dor-

mant since the passage of the holding company act [of 1909]."
That summer he persuaded the Interstate Commerce Commission to open a new investigation of the New Haven and in the fall convinced a competitor of the New Haven, the Grand Trunk, to extend its lines into Massachusetts. Attacks on Brandeis and the Grand Trunk were the main themes of *Truth*; little wonder that several weeks after the weekly was established, full-page advertisements by the New Haven began to appear on its pages. Later on it was discovered that the railroad had made direct payments to *Truth*'s "editor and publisher," G. R. Conroy.[23]

Charles S. Mellen, the president of the New Haven, had a background similar to Winslow's. He had been born in a Massachusetts town outside of Boston, and his formal education had ended with high school. Mellen had reached his powerful position through hard work and tireless ambition. And his economic success, like Winslow's, did not earn him entry into Boston's society; neither he nor Winslow was included in the *Social Register*. Reckless like Winslow, and of an even more belligerent temperament, Mellen was equally unreluctant to use anti-Semitism as a political weapon.[24]

Changes in the Catholic community helped Mellen and Winslow in their enterprise. The conservative and intolerant reign of William Cardinal O'Connell (1911-44) that had just begun encouraged prejudice against the Jews. Michael Earls, Jesuit leader and associate of O'Connell, wrote stories and novels saturated with anti-Semitism. A recent work on the subject of Boston's priests tells that "Earls also openly encouraged popular anti-Semitism and blind scorn of 'socialists.' In *Marie of the House d'Antres* [1916] he mercilessly typed the Jews, even ridiculing their physical characteristics. They were 'men of medium height, generally inclining toward corpulency as they become prosperous.' They were inherently villainous, likely to be socialists and generally advocates of free-love."[25]

The Irish nationalism of Joseph Smith, one of the two editors of *Truth*, was Catholic and socially conservative (he wrote the article in the *Washington Post*). His fellow editor George

R. Conroy was a Protestant from Nova Scotia but was none-theless a strong nativist.[26]

In its first issue *Truth* sarcastically suggested that Brandeis be appointed "Consulting Attorney General" for Wilson's cabinet. And alongside its declaration of antireform and anti-labor principles, in which the specter of the Lawrence strike was raised, was printed "the Sabotageur." According to this article, a covert, sinister sabotageur had activated industrial unrest and social tension. He was an intellectual, active in public councils, and a combination of social worker and pro-fessional reformer. But, the story assured, *Truth* and its loyal readers would salvage society's peace: "The moral sabotageur of Boston has got to go: he is seldom a politician less seldom a manufacturer or merchant; and he is quite frequently a mem-ber of the parasitic professions or a barnacle on the side lines of the community. Look around; pick him out; mark him; Truth wants his scalp." Brandeis was either mentioned by name or clearly alluded to in each issue. Cartoons, poems, and satirical articles suggested that he was a hypocrite, pretending to pro-tect the public while actually bent on accumulating millions, and a dangerous radical, plotting to wreck New England's economy.[27]

Truth constantly reminded its readers that Brandeis was a Jew and thus implied that his unpleasant traits were character-istic of Jews. In the second issue, for example, he was depicted in a cartoon as a Jewish tailor and was accused in a neighbor-ing piece of plotting to destroy society as head of the Public Franchise League. The dangers to peace and prosperity come from the "fakirs and pharisees" or the "Pharisees of Jeru-salem," declared *Truth*. The names of Louis Brandeis and Samuel Untermyer, the successful Jewish attorney from New York who often worked for Progressive causes, were repeatedly linked; "Samuel Untermeyr, the Brandeis of New York, ought to have a contest with Louis Dembitz Brandeis, the Untermeyr of Boston, to see which can destroy the most credit, bankrupt the most enterprises, and pluck the most pigeons in a given time."[28]

The "modern veiled prophet of Khorassan" was the subject of an article entitled "Brandeisism." In another, "St. Louis of

Boston," readers learned about the machinations of one who
"was born somewhere between Frankfort-on-Main and Kentucky" to destroy, with the help of "western plutocratic shoe-
makers," the good old Yankee United Shoe Machinery. In the
Christmas issue, an editorial entitled "Let Us Have Peace"
called for an end to "the dishonest and mercenary campaign
. . . injurious to every energy and interest of the Commonwealth" and ended with: "Let us have peace! To your tents,
O Israel!" Putting the Israelites in their place would bring
peace, implied *Truth*, which on another page even offered the
suggestion: "If Massachusetts has a Christmas tree it would be
an excellent idea to hang a lot of our vociferous reformers and
railroad wreckers on it." In the same issue Brandeis was the
main figure in a two-page cartoon; he was awaiting some present from a Christmas wagon full of political appointments and
being driven by Woodrow Wilson.[29]

In January and February of 1913, *Truth* intensified its war
against Brandeis's appointment; in March it celebrated victory. In an article entitled "Truth and Brandeis," the magazine detailed its own contributions to the rejection of Brandeis's candidacy and concluded: "In a word, it was the first to
strip the garb of sanctity from Brandeis and Brandeisism, and
expose them in all their nakedness to the public gaze." In the
March 15 issue, a two-page cartoon depicted Brandeis bent
under the load of "his Record," leaving the White House for
the desert; the cartoon was entitled "Ishmael": the Israelite
had finally received his due, had been driven back to the tents
of his people, and peace and prosperity would be restored to
the land.[30]

Truth in fact had little to do with keeping Brandeis out of
the cabinet; its circulation was small, and two years after its
founding it was out of business. But it may have played a role
in Brandeis's conversion to Zionism. According to Mason, "For
the first time . . . [in 1912 or 1913] he felt the sting of anti-
Semitism. The obscure magazine, with the intriguing title
Truth, may have influenced his thinking and action."[31]

The waxing of anti-Semitism in Boston was also reflected in
Brandeis's address as chairman of the public reception for the

East European Zionist leader, Nahum Sokolow, on March 30, 1913. Brandeis sat on the dais to honor Sokolow, who came from a world where Zionism meant emancipation, a home, and political independence to millions. The *Jewish Advocate* reported: "[Sokolow] began his speech by saying that he had the right to assert that the Jews had the right to live as a people without a question of a mission. The right of life was theirs as much as any other people." In this spirit Sokolow spoke of "the millions of Jews who still must emigrate from Russia, Roumania, and Galicia" and called on American Jews to help them and to participate "in the effort to recreate Zion for the Jews." "The chairman . . . had been deeply moved," recorded the reporter. In the Boston of the Immigration Restriction League, of Cardinal O'Connell and Michael Earls, and of *Truth*, Brandeis no longer felt really at home. For the first time, he began to realize what a homeland for persecuted people might mean, and he was ready to understand Zionism as a nationalist, not simply a missionist, movement. Bernard Rosenblatt of the Federation of American Zionists, who sat on the platform, records that "as he [Sokolow] finished, Brandeis jumped to his feet, came forward and turned to Sokolow, saying: 'Thank you, Dr. Sokolow—you have brought me back to my people.' " Then came his own turn to speak. The *Advocate* reporter wrote that "Mr. Brandeis began by saying that he was present in order to evidence his personal affiliation with the Zionist movement, which he recognized as a great ideal attempt to accomplish what had become the greatest Jewish need." By adding to Zionism the concept of need, Brandeis aligned himself with European Zionist thinking.[32]

An American Zionist

Nahum Sokolow's Zionism was nevertheless not identical to Brandeis's. Brandeis's most basic attitude did not change, and he managed to integrate classical Zionism into his former philosophy:

> The Jewish people have a great vision. In every land they are struggling for social rights. They are trying to relieve the burden of their friends and relatives in Russia and to lessen the toil of the

poor. The true happiness in life is not to donate, but to serve. The great message that Mr. Sokolow brought to Boston may sometime become a reality, and the Jewish people may establish the national state that they have aspired for and longed for so long.

Brandeis's Jews were the American Jews. He felt that because they possessed the ability to see "a great vision," because "they are struggling for social rights" and "trying to . . . lessen the toil of the poor," they also "are trying to relieve the burden of their friends and relatives in Russia." The Progressive in him did not allow him to commit himself to Zionism that did not include foremost a social rationale. [33]

"We Cannot Afford to Do a Mean Thing" was the title of his speech to the Young Men's Hebrew Association of Chelsea in May 1913, delivered two weeks after his meeting with Aaron Aaronsohn. In it Brandeis stressed the creativity and purity of the Zionist pioneers rather than the idea of a national revival. Neither the renaissance of the Jewish culture and language nor the goal of political sovereignty was his main concern. He said that Zionism's reason for existing lay in utilizing the Jewish talent for bettering society: the enterprise in Palestine had become dear to him because there, more than in any other place, the Jews could demonstrate their skills.

> Now what is going on in Palestine can perhaps go on only there in the fullest degree, but it is a lesson which must apply to the Jews all over the world. We have our obligations, we have the same 'noblesse oblige.' Our traditions are the same . . . in order that the world may gain from what is choice in us and so that the effort of the 150,000 Jews in Palestine may spread its spirit all over the world and have its effect, we should all support the Zionist movement, whether you or I are interested or never think of going to Palestine . . . If we aid that effort the Jew will be brought to the full development . . . and thus be enabled to do his full duty to his race and his country. [34]

Where and how would Brandeis himself work in the ranks of missionist Zionists? The answer was evident: chiefly by being a good American Progressive. Indeed despite his failure to obtain a cabinet post, the way soon seemed clear for him to carry on his work in Washington. On March 10, 1913, he informed his brother from the capital: "Had a good private talk with the President this evening for an hour—and with Lane, Redfield, Bryan, and McReynolds today—inter alia pushing along New Haven and Shoe Machinery matters—& spent this morning at the I.C.C. on New Haven matters. There is no lack of occupation." He was in fact very busy, and his relations with Woodrow Wilson were excellent. Later in the spring, according to a history of Wilson's administration, Brandeis "had a decisive hand in shaping the Federal Reserve bill and almost single-handedly persuaded the President to adopt an anti-trust program that ran counter to Wilson's original plan."[35]

Even in New England, avenues for political action remained open to Brandeis. The United Shoe Machinery Company was undefeated, but the New Haven had run into financial difficulties. And even more encouraging to Brandeis was the fact that, during the course of his efforts to bring the Grand Trunk Railroad into Massachusetts, his old allies—merchants and shoe manufacturers—had accepted his leadership. The Boston Chamber of Commerce worked closely with him in this endeavor, and the New England Shoe and Leather Association passed a resolution favoring the admission of the Grand Trunk to the state. After he was eliminated from the cabinet list, seven important Boston businessmen sent an indignant telegram to Wilson. Though almost all of them were his clients and were confined to the fields of commerce and shoemaking, their action demonstrated that Brandeis still had friends in Boston. In April the Interstate Commerce Commission reopened the New Haven hearings, with Brandeis representing the Chamber of Commerce.[36]

Brandeis could not spare much time now for the Zionist movement. He joined the Zion Association of greater Boston on April 17, 1913, by filling out an application and sending annual dues, but he declined to become the president of the association and was made an honorary president instead. The Zion Associations had been founded in 1911 by the Federation of American Zionists to provide a source of affiliation for people who considered themselves Zionists but did not intend to be active in the movement. By joining the Zion Association and not the Zionist Federation itself, Brandeis demonstrated that his quest for Zion would best be pursued through Progressive activities in America, linked with a token connection to the Zionist movement.[37]

Also reflecting the weakness of the nationalist aspect of Brandeis's Zionism was his slight interest in Jewish history and culture. Although, according to Jacob De Haas, Brandeis "studied the footnotes as well as the printed page of Jewish history and made the Zionist idea his own . . . he snatched odd hours in which he gave close application to Jewish matters," there is little to suggest that this was in fact the case. On his way to visit Palestine in 1919, Brandeis wrote to his wife: "I have read again Paul Goodman's little history of the Jews, which accompanied us to Quebec in 1913 and yesterday the Book of Daniel in which I found some acquaintances." De Haas's comment that "of all the post-Biblical books the wisdom of Ben Sira has appealed most to him" probably refers to some time after 1913. It is instructive, however, that this book attracted Brandeis; it is rather general in character, directing men to the love of wisdom and ethical conduct, virtue and good deeds, and proper behavior. Though in the mainstream of the religious Jewish tradition, its contents hardly render a sense of the landscape of Palestine, its history, or the flavor of its society. The Wisdom of Ben Sira, like the book of Daniel, was also well known in the non-Jewish world.[38]

That Brandeis's Zionism was not chiefly cultural or nationalist in orientation was demonstrated in the conclusion of his address at the meeting in honor of Sokolow in 1913: "We have listened to the unfolding of a wonderful dream," he said. "The great quality of the Jews is that they have been able to dream through all the long and dreary centuries; that mankind has credited them with another quality—the power to realize their dreams. The task ahead of them is to make this Zionist ideal a living fact." He then quoted "a Greek philosopher, a representative of that other great race that has done so much for mankind," who said " 'If they wish it, they can by service bring it about.' " It seems significant that even with a glorious gallery of Jewish wise men, and a rich Jewish literature thousands of years old, from which to pick an appropriate conclusion to his speech (Herzl himself had said, "If you will it, it is no legend"), Brandeis chose to speak in the name of an ancient Greek. In his view it seemed important that Jewish civilization, like that of classical Greece, had much to contribute to the spiritual and political development of mankind.[39]

August 1914 signaled the beginning of the First World War; Progressives in America were shocked, and Jews were anxious about their brethren caught up in the European catastrophe and the menace to the small and aspiring Jewish community in Palestine. Brandeis warned that "the achievements of a generation are imperilled. The young Jewish Renaissance in the Holy Land, the child of pain and sacrifice, faces death from starvation." Along with these fears there were hopes that Jewish Palestine would gain from the negotiations for peace that would eventually follow. But the European Zionist movement was paralyzed by war and its political complexities; the American Zionists were expected to take over.[40]

Brandeis responded to the call for an emergency meeting of American Zionists in New York on August 30, 1914. At this meeting Jacob De Haas proposed that Brandeis be elected chairman of the temporary conference, and Brandeis accepted the nomination of what would be called the Provisional Executive Committee for General Zionist Affairs. With this step he actually assumed the leadership of American Zionism. In his speech of acceptance he said:

> Throughout long years which represent my own life, I have been to a great extent separated from Jews. I am very ignorant in things Jewish. But experiences, public and professional, have taught me this: I find Jews possessed of those qualities which we of the twentieth century seek to develop in our struggle for justice and democracy; a deep moral feeling which makes them capable of noble acts; a deep sense of brotherhood of man; and a high intelligence, the fruit of three thousand years of civilization.

He went on to explain the raison d'être for the survival of the Jewish people: "These experiences have made me feel that the

Jewish people have something which should be saved for the world; that the Jewish people should be preserved; and that it is our duty to pursue that method of saving which most promises success." In Brandeis's philosophy, Zionism was chiefly the best method for preserving the most noble accomplishments of Jewish civilization.[41]

Primary Sources

Manuscripts and Scrapbooks

Aaron Aaronsohn MSS. Aaronsohn House's Archives, Zikhron Ya'aqov, Israel.

Meyer Bloomfield Scrapbook. In the possession of Lincoln Bloomfield, Cohasset, Mass.

Louis D. Brandeis MSS. University of Louisville Law School Library, Louisville, Ky.

Louis D. Brandeis's Office Diary; Brandeis's personal correspondence; case files. Archives of Nutter, McClennen and Fish (previously Brandeis, Dunbar and Nutter), Boston.

Dedham Country and Polo Club Scrapbook. Dedham Historical Society, Dedham, Mass.

Lewis N. Dembitz Scrapbook. Kentucky Authors Scrapbook, Louisville Free Public Library, Louisville, Ky.

Lewis N. Dembitz Scrapbook. In possession of Lewis N. Dembitz (grandson), Washington, D.C.

Herbert B. Ehrman, "Louis D. Brandeis." In Herbert B. Ehrman MSS, Harvard Law School Archives, Cambridge, Mass.

Charles W. Eliot MSS. Harvard University Archives, Cambridge, Mass.

Elizabeth G. Evans MSS. Schlesinger Library, Radcliffe College, Cambridge, Mass.

Bernard Flexner Scrapbook. Kentucky Authors Scrapbook, Louisville Free Public Library, Louisville, Ky.

Felix Frankfurter MSS. Harvard Law School Archives, Cambridge, Mass.

Charles Hamlin File. Harvard University Archives, Cambridge, Mass.

Harvard Menorah Society File. Harvard University Archives, Cambridge, Mass.

Henry Lee Higginson MSS. Harvard Business School Archives, Cambridge, Mass.

Henry Lee Higginson Papers. Massachusetts Historical Society, Boston.

Immigration Restriction League MSS. Houghton Library, Harvard University, Cambridge, Mass.

Louis E. Kirstein MSS. Harvard Business School Archives, Cambridge, Mass.

Massachusetts Savings Bank Insurance League MSS. Savings Bank Life Insurance Division Archives, Boston.

George R. Nutter MSS. Massachusetts Historical Society, Boston.

Good Government Association Collection. Massachusetts Historical Society, Boston.

Mary Kenney O'Sullivan MSS. Schlesinger Library, Radcliffe College, Cambridge, Mass.

Henry H. Putnam File. Harvard University Archives, Cambridge, Mass.

James J. Storrow File. Harvard University Archives, Cambridge, Mass.

Samuel D. Warren File. Harvard University Archives, Cambridge, Mass.

Samuel D. Warren MSS. Massachusetts Historical Society, Boston.

Interviews

Barnet, Carl (in the leather business), Boston, October 23, 1973.

Bernkopf, Elizabeth (friend of the Hecht family), Brookline, Mass., October 14, 1973.

Bloomfield, Dorothy Dreyfus (widow of Daniel Bloomfield, brother of Meyer), Brookline, Mass., October 21, 1973.

Bloomfield, Lincoln (son of Meyer Bloomfield), Cohasset, Mass., November 6, 1973.

Buxton, Frank (*Boston Herald* reporter), Brighton, Mass., November 9, 1973.

Cohen, Jacob (Zionist activist in Boston), Brookline, Mass., July 13, 1975.

Dietz, Ernest F. (son of Myer Dana of Beth Israel Hospital and son-in-law of Abraham Pinansky), Newton, Mass., November 17, 1973.

Ehrlich, Louis (son of adopted child of Jacob and Lina Hecht), New York, October 23, 1973.

Ehrlich, Richard (nephew of Abraham C. Ratshesky), Brookline, Mass., February 16, 1974.

Fisher, Elizabeth E. (childhood friend of Elizabeth Brandeis in Dedham), Wellesley, Mass., October 4, 1973.

Freund, Paul A. (law clerk to Justice Brandeis, 1932-33; later Harvard Professor), Cambridge, Mass., November 13, 1973.

Gorfinkle, Bernard L. (Member of the New Century Club since 1911), Boston, August 14, 1973.

Gottlieb, Arthur (friend of William Blatt of the New Century Club), Boston, March 18, 1975.

Harris, Nathaniel (senior citizen of Dedham), Dedham, Mass., September 18, 1973.

Hecht, Ida (daughter of Solomon Friedman; widow of Simon E. Hecht), Boston, October 21, 1973.

Kaplan, Leonard (of Nutter, McClennen and Fish; son of Jacob Kaplan), Boston, July 2, 1973.

Ladd, Helen Filene, Jr. (daughter of A. Lincoln Filene), Wayne, Me., September 3, 1974.

McDonald, Edward (son of undertaker of the Brandeis Dedham estate ca. 1904-14), Dedham, February 9, 1974.

Markell, Samuel (of Goulston and Storrs), Boston, October 23, 1973.

Perkins, Elliott (son of Thomas N. Perkins, Ropes, Gray partner, of Westwood), Cambridge, Mass., December 18, 1973.

Pinanski, Abraham E., Mrs. (widow of Abraham E. Pinanski), Brookline, Mass., November 4, 1973.

Rabb, Sidney (merchant), Boston, February 3, 1974.

Shapiro, Hester (daughter of William Blatt), Schenectady, N.Y., April 16, 1975.

Silberman, Dorothy Conrad (daughter of Sidney S. Conrad), Cambridge, Mass., July 4, 1973.

Silbert, Coleman (lawyer), Brookline, Mass., January 12, 1974.

Silverman, Arnold P. (son of Jacob J. Silverman of the New Century Club), Boston, September 6, 1973.

Solomon, Maida Herman (member of leading Boston Jewish family), Boston, July 16, 1973.

Sullivan, Daniel M. (caddie at Dedham Country and Polo Club), Dedham, Mass., November 30, 1973.

Tachau, Charles G., Mrs. (daughter of Alfred Brandeis), Louisville, Ky., January 23, 1974.

Taussig, Helen (daughter of Frank W. Taussig), Cotuit, Mass., July 15, 1973.

Vorenberg, Frank (son of Felix and Rose Frankenstein Vorenberg), Cambridge, Mass., November 25, 1973.

Wakefield, Lothrop (born in Dedham in 1895), Dover, Mass., December 10, 1973.

Warren, Samuel D. (grandson of Brandeis's partner), Boston, October 19, 1973.

Whitcomb, John (senior citizen of Dedham), Cambridge, Mass., December 5, 1973.

Whitehill, Walter M. (member of established Boston clubs and associations), Andover, Mass., February 1, 1974.

Wolfson, Harry (early member of Harvard Menorah Society; later Harvard Professor), Cambridge, Mass., March 11, 1974.

Newspapers and Magazines

The American Art Review, Boston, 1878-98.

Boston Advocate (changed to *Jewish Advocate*, May 28, 1909), 1905-13.

Journal of American Irish Historical Society, Boston, 1898.

Menorah Journal, New York, 1915.

Present Problems, New York, 1895-97.

Truth, Boston, 1912-14.

  Occasional issues of the following periodicals were considered for the 1884-1914 period: *Boston American; Boston Daily Advertiser; Boston Evening Transcript; Boston Globe; Boston Herald; Boston Journal; Boston News Bureau; Boston Post; Boston Traveler; Courier Journal*, Louisville, Ky.; *Dedham Transcript; New York Evening Post; New York Times*.

Government and Organization Documents

Boston Athletic Association, Constitution, By-Laws . . . Boston, 1890-97, 1918.

Boston Blue Book. 1876-1913.

Annual Report of the Boston Chamber of Commerce (changed to *Report of the* . . . , 1910). 1886-1913.

The Boston Directory. 1879-1913.

By-Laws of the Boston Merchants Association . . . (title varies). 1876, 1880, 1889, 1897, 1902.

Boston Merchants Association Bulletin. 1901-9.

City Affairs. Published by the Good Government Association.

Curtiss, Frederic F. and John Heard, *The Country Club, 1882-1932*. Brookline, Mass., 1932.

Resident and Business Directory of Dedham, Massachusetts (changed to . . . *Directory of Dedham and Westwood* . . . , 1899). 1893-1913.

Report of Boston Equal Suffrage Association for Good Government. Boston, 1901-12.

The Curtis Club, an Account of its 50th Anniversary, November 18, 1930, Together with List of Members . . . Boston, 1930.

List of Persons Assessed for Poll Tax in Dedham. 1890-1913.

Annual Reports of Denison House, The College Settlement. Boston, 1904-5, 1910-12.

The Economic Club of Boston, Constitution and List of Members. December 1907.

Charter and By-Laws of the Exchange Club . . . Boston 1896.

Facts about the Filipinos (changed to *The Philippine Review*). Boston, May 1901-May 1902.

First Annual Report of the Federation of Jewish Charities of Boston, 1896.

Second Annual Report of the Federation of Jewish Charities of Boston . . . *July 1, 1896 to May 1, 1897*. Boston, 1897.

Ninth Annual Report of the Federation of Jewish Charities of Boston . . . *May 1st, 1904 to May 1st, 1905*. Boston, 1905.

The Federated Jewish Charities of Boston, Subscription to October First, 1909.

Eighteenth Annual Report, Federated Jewish Charities of Boston and Constituent Societies. 1912.

Federated Jewish Charities of Boston, Its Officers, Members and Subscribers. 1913-14.

Annual Report of the Germanic Museum Association, 1901-1902. Cambridge, Mass., 1903.

Report for 1901-1902, Hebrew Industrial School. Boston, 1902.

1906, Annual Report, Hebrew Industrial School. [Boston, 1906].

Home Market Club (changed to *The Protectionist*, 1900). Boston, 1891-1912.

Insurance Yearbook. Philadelphia, 1911.

Annual Report of the Louisville Board of Trade (changed to *Minutes of the . . .* , 1892). Louisville, Ky., 1880-1913.

Massachusetts Reform Club . . . Secretary's Report (title varies). Boston, 1885-1913.

Constitution and By-Laws, Massachusetts State Board of Trade . . . Boston, 1896.

Massachusetts State Board of Trade, Annual Reports . . . Boston, 1900-14.

Bulletin of the National Association of Wool Manufacturers. Boston, 1884-1913.

Proceedings of the National Conference of Charities and Correction at the Thirty-Eighth Annual Session, Held in Boston, Mass., June 7-14, 1911.

The National Economic League Quarterly. Boston, May 1915.

Membership List of the National Council of the National Economic League. Boston [1915?].

New Century Club, Boston, Mass., A Brief History, By-Laws, List of Members. Boston, 1926.

New Century Club, A Brief History. Boston, 1947.

The New Century Club, 1900-1950. [Boston], 1950.

New England Shoe and Leather Association Gazette (changed to *New England Shoe and Leather Industry,* June 1910). Boston, 1902-13.

Proceedings of The New England Cotton Manufacturers' Association (changed to *Transaction of . . .* , 1894; later changed to *. . . of the National Association of Cotton Manufacturers,* 1906). Boston, 1884-1913.

New York State 4th Report of the Factory Investigating Commission, 1915. 5 vols. Albany, N.Y., 1915.

Social Register, Boston. 1890-1913.

Textile World (changed to *Textile World Record,* 1904). Boston, 1885-1913.

Sixty Years of the Union Boat Club . . . Boston, 1913.

The Union Club of Boston, 1863-1893. Boston, 1893.

Union Club of Boston Fiftieth Anniversary. Boston, 1913.

Annual Report of the United Hebrew Benevolent Association 1894. Boston, 1895.

U.S. Department of Commerce and Labor, Bureau of Census, *Manufacturers 1905, Pt. 1*. Washington, D.C., 1907.

U.S. Department of Commerce and Labor, Bureau of Census, *Manufacturers 1905, Pt. 2, States and Territories*. Washington, D.C., 1907.

U.S. Congress, House, *Tariff Hearings before the Committee on Ways and Means*, 54th Cong., 2d sess., 1897, 2 vols.

U.S. Congress, House, *Pulp and Paper Investigation*, 60th Cong., 2d sess., 1909, 6 vols.

U.S. Congress, House, *Hearings before the Committee on Investigation of United States Steel Corporation*, 62d Cong., 2d sess., 1912, 8 vols.

U.S. Congress, Senate, *Hearings before the Committee on Interstate Commerce . . . to Investigate and Report Desirable Changes in the Laws Regulating and Controlling Corporations, Persons, and Firms Engaged in Interstate Commerce*, 62d Cong., 2d sess., 1912, 3 vols.

U.S. Congress, Senate, *Nomination of Louis D. Brandeis. Hearings before the Subcommittee of the Committee on the Judiciary United States Senate, on the Nomination of Louis D. Brandeis to be an Associate Justice of the Supreme Court of the United States . . .* 64th Cong., 1st sess., 1916, 2 vols.

White, James C., *A Brief History of the Somerset Club . . . 1852-1913*. Boston, 1913.

Constitution, By-Laws, and Declaration of Principles of the Young Men's Democratic Club of Massachusetts . . . Boston, March 1888.

Books and Articles

Aaronsohn, Aaron. *Aaron Aaronsohn's Diary (1916-1919)* [in Hebrew]. Ed. Yoram Ephrati. Tel-Aviv, 1970.

Acheson, Dean, *Morning and Noon*. Boston, 1965.

Barron, Clarence W. *More They Told Barron: The Notes of the Late Clarence W. Barron*. Ed. Arthur Pound and Samuel T. Moore. New York, 1931.

Old Testament Apocrypha . . . Ben Sira [In Hebrew]. Interpreted with preface by E. S. Artom. Tel-Aviv, Israel, 1963.

Brandeis, Frederika Dembitz. *Reminiscences of Frederika Dembitz Brandeis, Written for Her Son, Louis, in 1880 to 1886*. Translated by Alice G. Brandeis for her grandchildren in 1943. Privately printed. In Goldfarb Library, Brandeis University, Waltham, Mass.

Brandeis, Louis D. *Business—A Profession*. 1914. Enlarged ed. Boston, 1933.

———. *The Curse of Bigness: Miscellaneous Papers of Louis D. Brandeis*. Ed. Osmond K. Fraenkel. New York, 1934.

———. *Letters of Louis D. Brandeis*. Ed. Melvin I. Urofsky and David W. Levy. 4 vols. Albany, N.Y., 1971-1975.

———. *Other People's Money, and How the Bankers Use It*. 1914. Ed. with an introduction and notes by Richard M. Abrams. New York, 1967.

Bridgman, Raymond L. *The Independents of Massachusetts in 1884.* Boston, 1885.

De Haas, Jacob. *Louis D. Brandeis: A Biographical Sketch, with Special Reference to His Contributions to Jewish and Zionist History.* New York, 1929.

Dembitz, Lewis N. "The Advent of the Australian Ballot," *Nation,* 54 (January 14, 1892), 32.

———. "Results of Bad Teaching," *Nation,* 43 (October 14, 1886), 306.

———. "The Navigation Laws," *Nation,* 84 (February 28, 1907), 197.

———. Scattered reviews and so on in the *Nation* for the period 1881-1907.

Dunbar, Charles F. *C. F. Dunbar: Economic Essays.* Ed. O. M. W. Sprague. New York, 1904.

Dunham, Allison, and Philip B. Kurland, eds. *Mr. Justice.* Revised and enlarged ed. Chicago, 1964.

Eliot, Charles W. "Political Principles and Tendencies," *Outlook,* 66, no. 8 (October 20, 1900), 457-460.

Fels, Mary. *Joseph Fels: His Life-Work.* New York, 1916.

Filene, A. Lincoln. *A Merchant's Horizon.* Boston, 1924.

Filene, Edward A. *The Way Out.* New York, 1924.

Flexner, Abraham. *An Autobiography.* A revision of the author's *I Remember* (New York, 1940). New York, 1960.

Forbes, John M. *Letters and Recollections of John M. Forbes.* Ed. Sarah F. Hughes. 2 vols. Boston, 1899.

Francke, Kuno. *Deutsche Arbeit in Amerika.* Leipzig, 1930.

Frankfurter, Felix. *Felix Frankfurter Reminisces: Recorded in Talks with Harlan B. Phillips.* Ed. H. B. Phillips. New York, 1960.

George, Henry. *Protection or Free Trade* [New York?], 1886.

Godkin, Edwin L. *Problems of Modern Democracy: Political and Economic Essays by Edwin Lawrence Godkin.* Ed. with an introduction by Morton Keller. Cambridge, Mass., 1966.

Goldmark, Josephine. *Pilgrims of '48: One Man's Part in the Austrian Revolution of 1848 and a Family Migration of America.* New Haven, 1930.

———. *Impatient Crusader: Florence Kelley's Life Story.* Urbana, Ill., 1953.

Hapgood, Hutchins. *The Spirit of the Ghetto.* 1902. With introduction by Moses Rischin; ed. of John Harvard Library. Cambridge, Mass., 1967.

Hapgood, Norman. *The Changing Years: Reminiscences of Norman Hapgood.* New York, 1930.

Harris, Barbara Ann. "Zionist Speeches of Louis Dembitz Brandeis: A Critical Edition." Ph.D. dissertation, University of California, 1967.

Harvard College Yearbooks, *Classes of 1875, 1876, 1885.* Cambridge, Mass.

Hulbert, Edmund D. "Some Points in Opposition to the Aldrich Plan." *Journal of Political Economy* (January 1912), pp. 25-32.

[Hurwitz, Henry, and I. Leo Sharfman, eds.]. *The Menorah Movement, for the Study and Advancement of Jewish Culture and Ideals.* Ann Arbor,

Mich., 1914.

James, William. *The Letters of William James.* Ed. Henry James. 2 vols. Boston, 1920.

————. *The Philosophy of William James, Selected from His Chief Works.* With an introduction by Horace M. Kallen. New York, 1953.

Kallen, Horace M. "The Ethics of Zionism." *The Maccabaean,* 11, no. 2 (August 1906), 61-71.

————. *Culture and Democracy in the United States: Studies in the Group Psychology of the American Peoples.* New York, 1924.

Kohut, George, ed. *The Standard Book of Jewish Verse.* New York, 1917.

La Follette, Robert M. *La Follette's Autobiography: A Personal Narrative of Political Experiences.* Madison, Wisc., 1960.

Lee, Henry, *Memoir of Colonel Henry Lee.* Ed. John T. Morse. Boston, 1905.

Marquand, John P. *The Late George Apley: A Novel in the Form of a Memoir.* New York, 1936.

Mendelson, Wallace, ed. *Felix Frankfurter: A Tribute.* New York, 1964.

Poole, Ernest. "Brandeis," *American Magazine,* 71 (February 1911), 481-493.

Porter, Robert P. *Protection and Free Trade.* Boston, 1884.

Putnam, George H. *Memoirs of a Publisher, 1865-1915.* New York, 1915.

Richard, Livy S. "Up From Aristocracy," *Independent* (Cleveland, July 27, 1914), pp. 130-32.

Richards, Bernard G. "First Steps in Zionism." In *Herzl Year Book,* vol. 5. New York, 1963.

Rosenblatt, Bernard A. *Two Generations of Zionism: Historical Recollections of an American Zionist.* New York, 1967.

Russell, Francis. "The Coming of the Jews." *Antioch Review* (Yellow Springs, Ohio) 15, no. 1 (March 1955), 19-38.

Santayana, George. *The Last Puritan: A Memoir, in the Form of a Novel.* New York, 1936.

————. *Persons and Places.* 3 vols. New York, 1945.

Schindler, Solomon. *Israelites in Boston: A Tale Describing Development of Judaism in Boston.* Boston, 1889.

Schoenhof, Jacob. *A History of Money and Prices.* New York, 1896.

Schurz, Carl. *Reminiscences of Carl Schurz.* 3 vols. New York, 1908.

Scudder, Vida D. *A Listener in Babel.* Boston, 1903.

————. *On Journey.* New York, 1937.

Shaler, Nathaniel S. *Nature and Man in America.* New York, 1891.

————. *The Neighbor: The Natural History of Human Contacts.* Boston, 1904.

————. *The Autobiography of Nathaniel Southgate Shaler.* Boston, 1909.

Steffens, Lincoln. *The Autobiography of Lincoln Steffens.* 1931. 2 vols. New York, 1958.

Welliver, Judson C. "Sidney W. Winslow, Czar of Footwear." *Hampton's Magazine* (September 1910), pp. 326-39.

Woods, Robert A. *The Neighborhood in Nation-Building.* Boston, 1923.

————, ed., *Americans in Process: North and West Ends.* Boston, 1902.

————, and Albert J. Kennedy. *The Settlement Horizon.* New York, 1922.

————, and Albert J. Kennedy, *The Zone of Emergence: Observations of the Lower Middle and Upper Working Class Communities of Boston, 1905-1914.* Ed. and abridged with a preface by Sam Bass Warner, Jr. 2d ed. Boston, 1969.

"The Growth of Zionism in Boston." *The Maccabaean*, 2, no. 5 (May, 1902), 241-243.

Notes

Abbreviations

AJYB	*American Jewish Year Book*
BDN	Archives of Nutter, McClennen and Fish (previously Brandeis, Dunbar and Nutter), Boston.
BL	Louis D. Brandeis, *Letters of Louis D. Brandeis*, ed. Melvin I. Urofsky and David W. Levy, 4 vols. (Albany, N.Y., 1971-75).
BCC	Boston Chamber of Commerce
BD	Brandeis Office Diary (in BDN)
BMA	Boston Merchants Association
FCA	Filene Cooperative Association
GGA	Good Government Association
HLS	Harvard Law School
HMC	Home Market Club
IRL	Immigration Restriction League
LDB	Louis Dembitz Brandeis
LU	Louis D. Brandeis's MSS, University of Louisville Law School Library, Louisville, Kentucky
MRC	Massachusetts Reform Club
NACM	National Association of Cotton Manufacturers
NESLA	New England Shoe and Leather Association
NECMA	New England Cotton Manufacturers' Association
PAJHS	*Publications of American Jewish Historical Society*
PFL	Public Franchise League
SBLI	Savings Bank Life Insurance Division Archives, Boston

1. Brandeis the Liberal

1. Alpheus T. Mason, *Brandeis: A Free Man's Life* (New York, 1946), chs. 1, 2.

2. Herbert B. Ehrman, "Louis Dembitz Brandeis," Ehrman MSS, Harvard Law School Archives, Cambridge, Mass.

3. Clippings in Kentucky Authors Scrapbook, Louisville Free Public Library, Louisville, Ky.; Mason, *Brandeis*, p. 27. For Brandeis's admiration of Dembitz, LDB to Otto Wehle, August 3, 1879, *BL*, I, 47; LDB to Theodore Roosevelt, February 21, 1903, BDN #12075; quot., Bernard Flexner, *Mr. Justice Brandeis and the University of Louisville* (Louisville, Ky., 1938), pp. 36-37.

4. Corresp. of LDB and Lewis N. Dembitz in BDN ##123, 358, 1717, 1860, 4704, 12230, 12352, 13812, 14370.

5. Biographical account based on sources edited by Carolyn Helm for master's thesis, University of Louisville, Ky. For background, Rogers Hollingsworth, *The Whirligig of Politics: The Democracy of Cleveland and Bryan* (Chicago, 1963), ch. 1; Lewis N. Dembitz, "The Free Coinage Problem," *Present Problems* (New York), 1, no. 1 (March 1, 1895); for the journal's policy see also J. D. Warner, "Free Coinage Dissected," 1, no. 3 (September 1, 1896); "Wages vs. 16 to 1," 1, no. 4 (September 15, 1896); John R. Procter, "The Dollar of the Fathers," 1, no. 6 (October 16, 1896); Fred P. Powers, "Jefferson and Jackson on Present Problems," 1, no. 15 (March 1, 1897). Most of Dembitz's contributions to the *Nation* were published as book reviews and letters to the editor; his first traceable article is "The Story of Troy," 32 (March 31, 1881), 218; just two weeks before he died, the *Nation*, 84 (March 11, 1907), 197, published his argument against a specific feature of the protective system. Richard Hofstadter, *The Age of Reform: From Bryan to F.D.R.* (New York, 1955), pp. 131-148; Morton Keller, "Introduction," in Keller, ed., *Problems of Modern Democracy: Political and Economic Essays by Edwin Lawrence Godkin* (Cambridge, Mass., 1966), pp. vii-xii.

6. *Courier Journal*, March 12, 1907; Lewis N. Dembitz, "The Advent of the Australian Ballot," *Nation*, 54 (January 14, 1892), 32; Arthur M. Wallace, "The Advent of the Australian Ballot," ibid., 54 (February 4, 1892), 87.

7. Mason, *Brandeis*, pp. 26-27; Abraham Flexner, *I Remember* (New York, 1940), pp. 31-32. LDB to Alfred Brandeis, May 27, 1906, *BL*, I, 438; Abraham Flexner to LDB, October 26, 1902, and LDB to A. Flexner, November 3, 1902, BDN #11915.

8. Clippings in Kentucky Authors Scrapbook; Mrs. Charles G. Tachau to Gal, October 15, 1973.

9. Mason, *Brandeis*, p. 25; Earle D. Ross, *The Liberal Republican Movement* (Ithaca, N.Y., 1910), passim; William Taussig to LDB, November 4, 1905, and LDB to W. Taussig, November 7, 1905, BDN #15795; LDB to Alfred Brandeis, July 13, 1907, May 18, 1908, *BL*, II, 12, 156; LDB to W. Taussig, June 18, 1908, ibid., 187; LDB to W. Taussig [June 1908], BDN #16712; LDB to Alfred Brandeis, June 14, 1910, *BL*, II, 349; LDB to Alfred Brandeis, July 9, 1913, ibid., III, 127.

10. Josephine Goldmark, *Pilgrims of '48: One Man's Part in the Austrian Revolution of 1848 and a Family Migration to America* (New Haven, Conn.,

1930), pp. 172-173; LDB to Alfred Brandeis, January 30, 1884, *BL*, I, 66; LDB to Amy F. Acton, February 1, 1905, ibid., 280; *Sixth Report of Boston Equal Suffrage Association for Good Government, 1910-1912* (Boston, 1912), pp. 1-5; on LDB's change of attitude, ibid., pp. 11-12. Claude M. Fuess, *Carl Schurz, Reformer* (Port Washington, N.Y., 1963), p. 381; George H. Putnam, *Memoirs of a Publisher, 1865-1915* (New York, 1915), pp. 13-21, 344-351.

11. On the culture of Bohemian Jews, Prof. Sarah Landau and Dr. Louis Gottschalk to Gal, August 2, 20, 1974; on LDB's home, Elizabeth B. Raushenbush to Gal, August 3, 1974, and Mrs. Charles G. Tachau to Gal, August 2, 1974; for Germans in Louisville, Albert B. Faust, *The German Element in the United States*, 2 vols. (Boston, 1909), I, 579. For LDB's education, e.g., LDB to Alfred Brandeis, March 20, 1888, *BL*, I, 74.

12. Cf. Mason, *Brandeis*, pp. 29-31. German expressions and appreciative references to Germany are in abundance in *BL*, esp. I, e.g., 22, 45, 245; also, LDB to Adolph Brandeis, July 9, 28, 1905, ibid., 334, 352-353; LDB to Walter Wright, December 29, 1905, ibid., 394-395; LDB to Pierre Jay, January 4, 1909, ibid., II, 215; LDB to Norman Hapgood, June 9, 1911, ibid., 451.

13. For relations with people of German background: with P. B. Marcou, see *BL*, I, 14-62; with E. Emerton, see Mason, *Brandeis*, pp. 42, 48, and *BL*, I, passim; LDB to Alfred Brandeis, June 22, 1910, ibid., II, 356; LDB to Amy Wehle, November 25, 1880, ibid., I, 59. For connections with organizations, LDB to Amy Wehle, January 2, 1881, ibid., 61; G. J. Walther to LDB, June 1, 1891, BDN #7263. For the Germanic Museum, Kuno Francke to LDB, April 23, 1901; LDB to K. Francke, April 26, 1901; K. Francke to LDB, April 27, 1901; — in BDN #10836; Frederic S. Goodwin to LDB, November 11, 1901, BDN #11606; quot., *Annual Report of the Germanic Museum Association, 1901-1902* (Cambridge, Mass., 1903); Kuno Francke, "The Germanic Museum, 1903-1928," in Samuel E. Morison, ed., *The Development of Harvard University . . . , 1869-1929* (Cambridge, Mass., 1930), pp. 146-149.

14. Faust, *German Element*, II, 200; Oscar Handlin, *Boston's Immigrants: A Study in Acculturation*, revised and enlarged ed. (Cambridge, Mass., 1959), pp. 136, 205. Kuno Francke, *Deutsche Arbeit in Amerika* (Leipzig, 1930), pp. 2-19, 25-26, 51; Carl Schurz, *Reminiscences of Carl Schurz*, 3 vols. (New York, 1908), II, 118-119; Geoffrey Blodgett, *The Gentle Reformers: Massachusetts Democrats in the Cleveland Era* (Cambridge, Mass., 1966), pp. 20, 62, 80-83, and passim; Henry H. Putnam File, Harvard University Archives, Cambridge, Mass.

15. Fuess, *Carl Schurz*, p. 172; LDB to Alice Goldmark, October 20, 1890, *BL*, I, 93.

16. LDB to Jacob Schoenhof, September 25, 1902, BDN #11915; for Carl Schoenhof, #1712 and other files in BDN.

17. For Harvard milieu, Blodgett, *Gentle Reformers*, pp. 20-21 and pas-

sim; Hugh Hawkins, *Between Harvard and America: The Educational Leadership of Charles W. Eliot* (New York, 1972), pp. 139-143, 217; Daniel B. Schirmer, *Republic or Empire: American Resistance to the Philippine War* (Cambridge, Mass., 1972), p. 15. Quot., LDB to Alice Goldmark, October 13, 1890, *BL*, I, 92-93; Harvard Law School Association, *The Centennial History of the Harvard Law School, 1817-1917* ([Cambridge, Mass.], 1918), pp. 267-276, 276-283; *Boston Daily Advertiser*, June 13, 1884; Raymond L. Bridgman, *The Independents of Massachusetts in 1884* (Boston, 1885), pp. 6, 10, 11.

18. Quot., LDB to Otto Wehle, March 12, 1876, *BL*, I, 8; Mason, *Brandeis*, p. 65; LDB-Ames corresp. in BDN ##10311, 10836, 11606, 11850, 11915; Harvard Law School Association, *Centennial History*, pp. 175-189.

19. *Boston Daily Advertiser*, June 13, 1884; LDB to Charles Nagel, November 19, 1900, *BL*, I, 147; LDB to J. Ames, December 21, 1900, ibid., 152.

20. Morison, *Harvard*, pp. 150-159; Nathaniel S. Shaler, *The Autobiography of Nathaniel Southgate Shaler* (Boston, 1909), pp. 378, 384; Mason, *Brandeis*, pp. 42-43, 63, 117; Alpheus T. Mason to Gal, August 16, 1974.

21. Morison, *Harvard*, pp. 310-321; Mason, *Brandeis*, p. 43; Blodgett, *Gentle Reformers*, pp. 12, 14, 58, 89, 105, 119; N[athaniel] S. Shaler, *The Neighbor: The Natural History of Human Contacts* (Boston, 1904), pp. 326-328.

22. Interview with Helen Taussig; Elizabeth G. Evans, "Memoirs," Evans MSS, Schlesinger Library, Radcliffe College, Cambridge, Mass., pp. 3-4; Mason, *Brandeis*, pp. 50-58; for Frank W. Taussig's influence, LDB to E. G. Evans, August 6, 1896, *BL*, I, 123; F. W. Taussig to LDB, May 25, 1901, LU, NMF 3-1.

23. Evans, "Memoirs"; Alfred Lief, *Brandeis: The Personal History of an American Ideal* (1936; New York, 1964), p. 469 and passim; William James to Elizabeth G. Evans, January 17, 1900, in Henry James, ed., *The Letters of William James*, 2 vols. (Boston, 1920) II, 112-115; Ralph B. Perry, *The Thought and Character of William James* (New York, 1954), pp. 209, 231, 248, 272, 366, chs. 16, 17; *Facts About the Filipinos* [biweekly] (Boston), May-September, 1901; Lief, *Brandeis*, p. 320.

24. Mason, *Brandeis*, pp. 48, 65; Alice H. Grady, "Boyhood of Brandeis," *Boston American*, June 4, 1916.

25. "Secretary's Report, December 1884," *Massachusetts Reform Club, Constitution, List of Members* . . . (Boston, 1885), pp. 2, 3; pamphlets of the Massachusetts Reform Club in Boston Public Library; Bridgman, *Independents*, pp. 10, 11, 17; Hawkins, *Eliot*, ch. 5; Blodgett, *Gentle Reformers*, passim; quots., Hawkins, *Eliot*, pp. 140-141, 142; and see Charles W. Eliot, "Political Principles and Tendencies," *Outlook*, 66, no. 8 (October 20, 1900), 457-460.

26. Mason, *Brandeis*, p. 150; Alpheus T. Mason, *The Brandeis Way: A Case Study in the Working of Democracy* (Princeton, N.J., 1938), p. 159;

quots., LDB to Charles W. Eliot, May 14, 1908, Eliot MSS, Harvard University Archives, Cambridge, Mass.

27. Mason, *Brandeis*, chs. 3-5; quot., p. 95.

28. Samuel D. Warren File, Harvard University Archives, Cambridge, Mass.; *Dedham Transcript*, February 26, 1910; LDB to Arthur A. Maxwell, April 24, 1900, *BL*, I, 143; LDB to S. D. Warren, April 11, 1904, and ed. note 1, ibid., 248; LDB to S. D. Warren, February 12, 1909, ibid., II, 219; *Boston Daily Advertiser*, June 13, 1884. For background of Warren's paper interests, Lyman H. Weeks, *A History of Paper-Making in the United States, 1690-1916* (New York, 1916), ch. 11; Charles W. Huntington, *The Warren-Clarke Genealogy* (Cambridge, Mass., 1894), p. 169; Cumberland Institute for Paper Perfection, *Records and Proceedings* (Westbrook, Me., 1912), 1, no. 1 (September 1912), 18-20.

29. Mason, *Brandeis*, pp. 238-241; LDB to Alfred Brandeis, March 20, 1889, March 20, 1886, February 12, 1908, *BL*, I, 77, 67-68 and ed. notes 68, 78, II, 68; S. D. Warren and Company to G. W. Wheelwright Paper Company, November 20, 1908, in U. S., Congress, House, *Pulp and Paper Investigation*, 60th Cong., 2d sess., 1909, vol. vi of 6, 3208-3209; and see F[rank] W. Taussig, *The Tariff History of the United States*, 8th revised ed. (New York, 1931), ch. 8.

30. Letters of LDB to Fiske Warren, November 20, 28, December 14, 26, 1900, *BL*, I, 148, 150, 151, 153; corresp. of F. Warren and LDB, February-March 1902, BDN #11622.

31. Frank W. Taussig, "Economics, 1871-1929," in Morison, *Harvard*, pp. 187-191; F[rank] W. Taussig, "Introduction," in O. M. W. Sprague, ed., *C. F. Dunbar: Economic Essays* (New York, 1904), pp. vii-xvii.

32. Hawkins, *Eliot*, pp. 63, 149, 217, 326 (note 33); quot., Henry James, *Charles W. Eliot: President of Harvard University, 1869-1909* (Boston, 1930), pp. 121-123; quot., Charles F. Dunbar to Gal, March 20, 1974.

33. Charles F. Dunbar to Gal, March 20, 1974; Mason, *Brandeis*, pp. 87, 221.

34. Quot., Mason, *Brandeis*, p. 82; *Class of 1885, Harvard College* (Cambridge, Mass., 1940), pp. 63-69; George R. Nutter to Charles W. Eliot, April 4, 1911; C. W. Eliot to G. R. Nutter, April 5, 1911; G. R. Nutter to C. W. Eliot, June 15, 1911; — in BDN #20389.

35. For history of the GGA and quot., *City Affairs* (Boston), 1, no. 1 (March 1905), in the Good Government Association Collection, Mass. Historical Society, Boston. Richard M. Abrams, *Conservatism in a Progressive Era: Massachusetts Politics, 1900-1912* (Cambridge, Mass., 1964), pp. 143-150; *Boston Daily Advertiser,* February 28, 1903; George R. Nutter MSS, Mass. Historical Society, Boston; Nutter Diary, years 1905-36, Nutter MSS.

36. *Class of 1876, Harvard College* (Cambridge, Mass., 1929), pp. 82-83; *Boston Evening Transcript,* March 9, 1923; *Constitution . . . Young Men's Democratic Club of Massachusetts* (March 1888), p. 17; Blodgett,

Gentle Reformers, pp. 84-86.

37. Mason, *Brandeis,* pp. 86-87.
38. Hofstadter, *The Age of Reform,* pp. 137, 142.
39. The conclusions as to the nature of the firm's clientele are based on my research in the Archives of Nutter, McClennen and Fish, and on interviews with George P. Davis of the same firm. Mr. Davis, a member of the firm since 1917, is currently writing its offical history. Discussions also took place with other senior partners of the law firm. The guideline for the conclusion regarding size was the average number of wage earners per manufacturing establishment in Massachusetts in 1905, which was about sixty; see "Comparative Summary for Forty-Two Leading Industries: 1905 and 1900," in Department of Commerce and Labor, Bureau of the Census, *Manufacturers 1905, Pt.2, States and Territories* (Washington, D.C., 1907), p. 418; for data on specific industries, ibid., pp. 418-419; importance of clients' groups was determined chiefly according to number of files devoted to each client.
40. Samuel D. Warren to LDB inviting him to found a copartnership in Boston, October 21, 1878-June 18, 1879, in the Felix Frankfurter MSS, Harvard Law School Archives, Cambridge, Mass., esp. letters of January 30 and May 5, 1879; LDB to S. D. Warren, May 30, 1879, *BL*, I, 34-35; for the firm's clientele, note 39, *supra.*
41. Lief, *Brandeis,* p. 24; the information on Hecht's support was confirmed by members of both families: interview with Louis Ehrlich of New York City (related to Hecht); Prof. Ben Halpern interview with Frank B. Gilbert of New York City (LDB's son-in-law); Mason, *Brandeis,* p. 45.
42. Barbara M. Solomon, *Pioneers in Service: The History of the Associated Jewish Philanthropies of Boston* (Boston, 1956), pp. 10-11 and passim.
43. Mason, *Brandeis,* pp. 54, 61; Lief, *Brandeis,* p. 24; *Germanic Museum Association* (1903); Solomon, *Pioneers in Service,* chs. 1-3; Alfred J. Kutzik, "The Social Basis of American Jewish Philanthropy," Ph.D. diss. (Brandeis University, 1967), pp. 443-491; Solomon Schindler, *Israelites in Boston: A Tale Describing Development of Judaism in Boston* (Boston, 1889), chs. 3, 5; Albert Ehrenfried, *A Chronicle of Boston Jewry: From the Colonial Settlement to 1900* ([Boston], 1963), chs. 14-27; note 39, *supra.*
44. Note 39, *supra; By-Laws of the Boston Merchants Association* (Boston, 1876); see the BMA's annuals and *Bulletins,* Boston Public Library; Boston Tercentenary Committee, *Fifty Years of Boston,* 1880-1930 (Boston, 1932), pp. 162-163. For the law firm's role in the merger, corresp. and documents in LU, NMF 15-2; BMA, *Bulletin,* no. 67 (January-February 1908), pp. 1-2; conclusions on the new BCC based on BCC, *Report for 1909* (Boston, 1910), pp. 16-18, 197; BMA *Bulletin,* no. 70 (December 5, 1908), 3-8; no. 74 (February 10, 1909), passim; BD, October 1908-July 1909; see also Lincoln Steffens, *The Autobiography of Lincoln Steffens,* 2 vols. (New York, 1958), II, 600-601; Gerald W. Johnson, *Liberal's Progress* (New York, 1948), p. 91; Nutter became vice president of BCC in 1918 and president in 1920.

45. Blodgett, *Gentle Reformers,* ch. 4 and passim; for Hamlin see ibid., pp. 83-84 and passim; Charles Hamlin File, Harvard University Archives, Cambridge, Mass. BMA, *Bulletin,* no. 70 (December 5, 1908), p. 4.

46. For details on the firm's clientele, see note 39, *supra;* BD, October-December 1911; cf. Mason, *Brandeis,* pp. 351-352; on S. Conrad, *Boston Globe,* July 11, 1947; on B. Conrad, ibid, January 25, 1943; interview with Dorothy Conrad Silberman.

47. M. J. Fox to LDB, January 29, 1915; LDB to M. J. Fox and to W. C. Redfield, February 8, 1915; W. C. Redfield to LDB, February 11, 1915; — in LU, NMF 63-3, and see note 39, *supra.*

48. George R. Nutter MSS; LDB to William H. Lincoln, April 28, 1903, *BL,* I, 234; LDB to Samuel D. Warren, April 11, 1904, ibid., 248; BMA, *Bulletin,* no. 23 (April 1903), p. 8; no. 36 (June 1904), p. 2; no. 39 (December 1904), pp. 9-10; the *Bulletin* also published reports designed to promote the GGA's activities.

49. George R. Nutter MSS; *New England Shoe and Leather Industry,* 10, no. 1 (January 1912), 7-8; U.S. Congress, House, *Tariff Hearings Before the Committee on Ways and Means,* 54th Cong., 2nd sess., 1897, vol. II of 2, 2081; Taussig, *Tarriff History,* pp. 332-333, 378-379, 442-443; quot., *New England Shoe and Leather Industry.* 10, no. 1 (January 1912), 7; on Charles H. Jones, *Boston Evening Transcript,* January 4, 1933; quot., LDB to C. H. Jones, August 9, 1909, *BL,* II, 286, and see note 39, *supra.*

50. Blodgett, *Gentle Reformers,* p. 78; on the Arkwright Club see also Melvin T. Copeland, *The Cotton Manufacturing Industry of the United States* (Cambridge, Mass., 1912), pp. 157-159; Robert P. Porter, *Protection and Free Trade* (Boston, 1884); *Textile World* (Boston), 11, no. 3 (September 1896), 19-20; ibid., 11, no. 5 (November 1896), 19-20; 19, no. 3 (September 1900), 408-409; 19, no. 5 (November 1900), 32; *Textile World Record* (Boston), 28, no. 2 (November 1904); 36, no. 2 (November 1908); 44, no. 2 (November 1912).

51. NECMA, *Proceedings . . . Semi-Annual Meeting . . . , 1887,* no. 43 (Boston, 1887), pp. 4-6; *. . . Annual Meeting . . . ,1898,* no. 64 (Boston, 1898), pp. 82-88. Conclusions about the Home Market Club are based on the *Home Market Bulletin* (Boston), vols. 3-10, years 1891-99, and *The Protectionist* (Boston) vols. 11-24, years 1900-12, in Boston Public Library. For articles against the BCC, *The Protectionist,* 13, no. 153 (January 1902), 600-601; 17, no. 195 (July 1905), 113-116, 17, no. 196 (August 1905), 207-208; 17, no. 201 (January 1906), 462-463; 18, no. 215 (March 1907), 526; for a late attack on the BMA, 20, no. 236 (December 1908), 446-448. For criticism of Harvard people, *Home Market Bulletin,* 5, no. 15 (April 1894), 8, 9; *The Protectionist,* 11, no. 121 (May 1899), 65; 16, no. 190 (February 1905), 505; 20, no. 236 (December 1908), 408-411.

52. Schirmer, *Republic or Empire,* pp. 8-10, 38, 52, 100, 158, and passim; for shoe manufacturers, cf. pp. 21, 185, and passim.

53. Positive interest in bimetalism was occasionally expressed on the

pages of the *Home Market Bulletin* during 1893-96; an official resolution for bimetalism was adopted in the club's annual meeting of 1894, 6, no. 8 (December 1894), 12-13; for mercantile criticism on the HMC monetary laxity, see 5, no. 5 (September 1893), 15. Boston's *Textile World* supported the gold standard during the 1890s; New England's textile industrialists took this position in earlier decades as well: see Irwin Unger, *The Greenback Era: A Social Political History of American Finance, 1865-1879* (Princeton, N.J., 1964), pp. 144-147.

54. Conclusions about the policy of the *Bulletin of the National Association of Wool Manufacturers* based on vols. 14 (1884) — 43 (1913), in Baker Library, Harvard Business School, Cambridge, Mass.; testimony of William Whitman (March 4, 1916) in U.S. Congress, Senate, *Nomination of Louis D. Brandeis,* 64th Cong., 1st sess., 1916, vol. I of 2, p. 973; Arthur H. Cole, *The American Wool Manufacture,* 2 vols. (Cambridge, Mass., 1926), II, 36; *Bulletin of . . . Wool Manufacturers,* 42, no. 3 (September 1912), 191-218; LDB to Robert La Follette, July 26, 1912, *BL,* II, 652; LDB to William C. Redfield, February 8, 1915, LU, NMF 63-3.

55. Quot., LDB to Alfred Brandeis, November 4, 1908, *BL,* II, 213; quot., Mason, *Brandeis,* p. 621.

56. Alice H. Grady, "Boyhood of Brandeis," *Boston American,* June 4, 1916; Mason, *Brandeis,* pp. 88-89, 118; W. W. Vaughan to LDB, March 29, 1902, BDN #11850.

57. Mason, *Brandeis,* pp. 89-90, 106-116, ch. 17; LDB to Edmund Billings, *BL,* I, II, passim.

58. LDB to Adolph Brandeis, November 21, 1889, *BL,* I, 82; Henry George, *Protection or Free Trade* ([New York?] 1886). LDB to Alice Goldmark, October 20, 1890, *BL,* I, 93; quot., Lief, *Brandeis,* p. 63.

59. Louis D. Brandeis, "Tariff Legislation Not Needed," in U.S. Congress, *Tariff Hearings,* II, 2081-2084; after his testimony the chairman of the Free Trade League wanted to promote Brandeis to the executive committee of the organization: Samuel W. Mendum to LDB, April 24, 1897, BDN #6638. Receipts for membership dues in BDN, and see note 61, *infra.* Hazard Stevens to LDB, June 13, 1901, and LDB to H. Stevens, June 14, 1901, BDN #10836; LDB to Henry L. Gantt, September 16, 1912, *BL,* II, 674; LDB to Alfred Brandeis, June 20, 1908, ibid., I, 191; LDB to Adolph Goldmark, April 14, 1909, BDN #17740. Quot., LDB to American Free Trade League, January 31, 1914, BDN #21571.

60. LDB to Woodrow Wilson, August 1, 1912, *BL,* II, 658; LDB to William C. Redfield, August 1, 1912, ibid.; LDB to Norman Hapgood, August 1, 1912, ibid., 657.

61. Blodgett, *Gentle Reformers,* pp. 224-226; quot., LDB to Elizabeth G. Evans, August 6, 1896, *BL,* I, 123-124.

62. Everett V. Abbot to LDB, October 6, 1904, and LDB to E. V. Abbot, October 8, 1904, BDN #13258; Hollingsworth, *Whirligig of Politics,* pp. 218-221; LDB to Alfred Brandeis, November 4, 1908, *BL,* II, 213.

63. LDB to Woodrow Wilson, June 14, 1913, *BL*, III, 114. LDB's opposition to Keynes and Franklin D. Roosevelt, interview with Paul A. Freund; for background, William E. Leuchtenburg, *Franklin D. Roosevelt and the New Deal, 1932-1940* (New York, 1963), pp. 50-51, 79-82.

64. LDB to Alfred Brandeis, July 8, 1903, BDN #12846; LDB to Alfred Brandeis, July 28, 1904, *BL*, I, 262; June 28, 1878, ibid., 23; ed. note 5, ibid., 263; Lief, *Brandeis*, p. 29.

65. LDB to Alfred Brandeis, March 20, 1886, *BL*, I, 68; LDB to Adolph Brandeis, July 11, 1905, ibid., 335. For Brandeis and Denmark, Paul A. Freund, "Mr. Justice Brandeis," in Allison Dunham and Philip B. Kurland, eds., *Mr. Justice*, revised and enlarged ed. (Chicago, 1964), p. 178.

66. Lief, *Brandeis*, 320; *BL*, I, 147-159.

67. [Fiske Warren?] to LDB, November 23, 1900, and draft of a letter from LDB to F. Warren, December 26, 1900; F. Warren to LDB, February 15, March 8, 1902; memo of John G. Palfrey, February 28, 1902; LDB to William H. Dunbar, December 17, 1902—in BDN #10987.

68. Erving Winslow to LDB, December 11, 1903; quot., LDB to E. Winslow, December 12, 1903—in BDN #12352; LDB to Adolph Brandeis, July 14, 1905, *BL*, I, 337.

69. LDB to Adolph Brandeis, July 14, 1905, September 14, 1905, *BL*, I, 337, 359.

70. LDB to Adolph Brandeis, August 29, September 3, July 11, 1905, *BL*, I, 354, 356, 335. See also LDB to Alfred Brandeis, September 6, 1905, ibid., 358, and note 65, *supra*.

71. Benjamin F. Trueblood to LDB, April 8, 1909, and LDB to B. F. Trueblood, April 9, 1909, BDN #17740.

72. Fuess, *Carl Schurz*, pp. 370-371; Schurz, *Reminiscences*, III, 449; Blodgett, *Gentle Reformers*, pp. 3-4 and passim; "Secretary's Report," *Massachusetts Reform Club* (1885), p. 8; pamphlets of the Massachusetts Reform Club in Boston Public Library. Brandeis is listed as member in the earliest available annual report of the MRC, *Massachusetts Reform Club* (1885), p. 14, and in all subsequent issues until 1903; he is not listed in the issues of 1905 on; although the issue of 1904 has not been available, it seems that he was still a member then: see corresp. with E. V. Abbot, note 62, *supra*.

2. From Mugwump to Progressive

1. Stephan Thernstrom, *The Other Bostonians: Poverty and Progress in the American Metropolis, 1880-1970* (Cambridge, Mass., 1973), p. 113; for the distinction between "acculturation" and "assimilation," see Michael Parenti, "Ethnic Politics and the Persistence of Ethnic Identification," in Brett W. Hawkins and Robert A. Lorinskas, eds., *The Ethnic Factor in American Politics* (Columbus, Ohio, 1970), pp. 66-68.

2. Geoffrey Blodgett, *The Gentle Reformers: Massachusetts in the*

Cleveland Era (Cambridge, Mass., 1966), ch. 6 and passim; Arthur Mann, *Yankee Reformers in the Urban Age: Social Reform in Boston, 1880-1900* (Boston, 1954), pp. 3-7 and passim; Richard M. Abrams, *Conservatism in a Progressive Era: Massachusetts Politics, 1900-1912* (Cambridge, Mass., 1964), ch. 2 and passim; see also J. Joseph Huthmacher, *Massachusetts People and Politics, 1919-1933* (Cambridge, Mass., 1959). Robert A. Woods, ed., *Americans in Process: North and West Ends* (Boston, 1902), esp. Frederick A. Bushée, "The Invading Host," p. 69, and Woods, "Assimilation: A Two-Edged Sword," pp. 379-380. In *Streetcar Suburbs: The Process of Growth in Boston, 1870-1900* (Boston, 1962), p. 80, Sam B. Warner, Jr., terms the ethnic concentrations "temporary and subsidiary to the main integrating flow of ethnically mixed income groups." At the same time he explains how the fragmentation of suburban life encouraged ethnic and church groupings. Robert A. Woods and Albert J. Kennedy, *The Zone of Emergence*, originally written in 1905-14, abridged and edited by Sam B. Warner, Jr., 2d ed. (Boston, 1969); autonomous life and activities along ethnic lines are depicted in practically all the book's chapters. For admiration of the achievements of highly ethnically organized communities, see, e.g., Albert J. Kennedy, "East Boston," ibid., p. 193; Warner, "Preface to the First Edition," ibid., pp. 14-15.

3. Oscar Handlin, *Boston's Immigrants: A Study in Acculturation*, revised and enlarged ed. (Cambridge, Mass., 1959), pp. 25, 51-52, 176-177; quots., pp. 191, 215-216; William V. Shannon, *The American Irish* (New York, 1963), ch. 11; see Thernstrom, *Other Bostonians*, pp. 130-144, 149-175.

4. George W. Pierson, "The Obstinate Concept of New England: A Study of Denudation," *New England Quarterly*, 28 (March 1955), esp. 13-15; Cleveland Amory, *The Proper Bostonians* (New York, 1947), passim; Oliver Alden and his milieu in George Santayana, *The Last Puritan: A Memoir, in the Form of a Novel* (New York, 1936); George Santayana, *Persons and Places*, 3 vols. (New York, 1945), II, ch. 6, esp. 112-113; John P. Marquand, *The Late George Apley* (New York, 1936), in its entirety; Nathaniel S. Shaler, *The Autobiography of Nathaniel Southgate Shaler* (Boston, 1909), p. 378. Nathan C. Shiverick, "The Social Reorganization of Boston," in Alexander W. Williams, *Social History of the Greater Boston Clubs* (Boston, 1970), pp. 128-129; quot., pp. 129-130.

5. Frederic C. Jaher, "The Boston Brahmins in the Age of Industrial Capitalism," in Jaher, ed., *The Age of Industrialism in America: Essays in Social Structure and Social Values* (New York, 1968), pp. 197, 227-229, 235-237; quot., p. 228.

6. Barbara M. Solomon, *Ancestors and Immigrants: A Changing New England Tradition* (Chicago, 1956), chs. 5-7; John Higham, "Origins of Immigration Restriction, 1882-1897: A Social Analysis," *Mississippi Valley Historical Review*, 39 (June 1952), 77-88.

7. Handlin, *Boston's Immigrants*, p. 219; Bushée, "Invading Host,"

pp. 53-58; William Cole and Rufus Miles, "Community of Interest," in Woods, *Americans in Process,* p. 331; Barbara M. Solomon, *Pioneers in Service: The History of the Associated Jewish Philanthropies of Boston* (Boston, 1956), pp. 33-43. The Jewish population in the nineties was estimated at 20,000; it expanded from about 10,000 in the early eighties to 40,000 by 1902 and 60,000 by 1907; the total population of Boston in 1900 was about 600,000. See Albert Ehrenfried, *A Chronicle Boston Jewry: From the Colonial Settlement to 1900* ([Boston], 1963), p. 545; Mann, *Yankee Reformers,* p. 3; Solomon, *Pioneers in Service,* p. 36.

8. Solomon, *Ancestors and Immigrants,* p. 17 and passim; for anti-Semitism of dispirited Brahmins, ibid., ch. 2; Alfred J. Kutzik, "The Social Basis of American Jewish Philanthropy," Ph.D. diss. (Brandeis University, 1967), pp. 446-447; Higham, "Social Discrimination," p. 18; Francis Russell, "The Coming of the Jews," *Antioch Review,* 15, no. 1 (March 1955), 20-22. Cf. Oscar Handlin, "American Views of the Jew at the Opening of the Twentieth Century," in Leonard Dinnerstein, ed., *Antisemitism in the United States* (New York, 1971), pp. 48-57; John Higham, "American Anti-semitism Historically Reconsidered," ibid., p. 75; John Higham, *Strangers in the Land: Patterns of American Nativism, 1860-1925* (New York, 1971), pp. 94, 160-161, 183. Jacob Neusner, "Politics, Anti-Semitism and the Jewish Community of Boston, 1880-1914," paper at the American Jewish Historical Society (Waltham, Mass.), p. 258 and passim. Mann, *Yankee Reformers,* p. 53; interview with Elliott Perkins.

9. Arthur Mann, ed., *Growth and Achievement: Temple Israel, 1854-1954* (Cambridge, Mass., 1954), pp. 46, 60, 70, 98; Solomon, *Pioneers in Service,* p. 8; Ehrenfried, *Chronicle of Boston Jewry,* chs. 18, 24, and passim; Kutzik, "Social Basis," pp. 443-476, passim. Ehrenfried, *Chronicle of Boston Jewry,* pp. 573-575; cf. Solomon, *Pioneers in Service,* p. 89; interviews with Richard Ehrlich and other Boston German Jews; Kutzik, "Social Basis," pp. 475-476.

10. Kutzik, "Social Basis," pp. 446-447, 451-455, 461-463, 469; Jacob Neusner, "The Impact of Immigration and Philanthropy upon the Boston Jewish Community (1880-1914)," *PAJHS,* 46 (December 1956), 81-82, 85; interviews with Mrs. Abraham E. Pinanski and other Boston Jews; for Max Mitchell see Solomon, *Pioneers in Service,* pp. 42-45 and passim.

11. *New Century Club, Boston, Mass.: A Brief History, By-Laws, List of Members* ([Boston], 1926), p. 3; interview with Arthur Gottlieb; poem, *The New Century Club, 1900-1950* ([Boston], 1950).

12. Interviews with Samuel Markell and Coleman Silbert.

13. Interviews with Arnold P. Silverman and Bernard L. Gorfinkle.

14. Solomon, *Pioneers in Service,* pp. 55-64; Ehrenfried, *Chronicle of Boston Jewry,* pp. 753-754; Kutzik, "Social Basis," pp. 460-470; interview with Ernest F. Dietz.

15. See ch. 1, note 41, *supra;* interviews with Ida Hecht and Maida H. Solomon.

16. *Annual Report of the United Hebrew Benevolent Association, 1894* (Boston, 1895); *First Annual Report of the Federation . . . , 1896*, p. 92, and subsequent issues.

17. Alpheus T. Mason, *Brandeis: A Free Man's Life* (New York, 1946), p. 63; social acquaintances of LDB also in *BL*, I, 5-25.

18. *Class of 1875, Harvard College*, Secretary's Reports nos. 1-6; Williams, *Greater Boston Clubs*, pp. 5-6, 87-102; interview with Walter M. Whitehill; Marquand, *The Late George Apley*, pp. 73-74, 80; Amory, *Proper Bostonians*, pp. 291-310.

19. Burton C. Bernard, "Brandeis in St. Louis," *The St. Louis Bar Journal*, 77, no. 2 (Winter 1964), 53-68.

20. Ibid.

21. Ibid., 57.

22. Mason, *Brandeis*, pp. 63-64, 103; "Marriage Certificate" in Samuel D. Warren MSS, Mass. Historical Society, Boston; Dixon Wecter, *The Saga of American Society: A Record of Social Aspirations, 1607-1937* (New York, 1937), ch. 8. Interview with Samuel D. Warren: this grandson of Brandeis's partner recalls that his grandmother did not like Brandeis and, after her husband's death, probably burned the letters of Brandeis to him.

23. Mason, *Brandeis*, pp. 75-77, 86; Elizabeth B. Raushenbush to Gal, August 21, 1973.

24. Elizabeth G. Evans, "Memoirs," Evans MSS, Schlesinger Library, Radcliffe College, Cambridge, Mass.; *New York Times*, May 13, 1917, p. 15 and January 14, 1945, p. 40; Mason, *Brandeis*, p. 435 and passim.

25. Allan Forbes, *Sport in Norfolk County* (Boston, 1938), chs. 1, 2; *Resident and Business Directory of Dedham, Massachusetts*, 1893 on; Elizabeth B. Raushenbush to Gal, August 21, 1973; Susan Brandeis Gilbert to John M. Whitcomb, October 22, 1957, letter in the latter's possession. Interviews with Nathaniel Harris, Edward McDonald, Daniel M. Sullivan, Lothrop Wakefield, and John M. Whitcomb. Mr. Whitcomb, whose family bought the house of Samuel D. Warren in Dedham, was intrigued by the fact he learned as secretary of Dedham Historical Society, i.e., that Brandeis's life and activities were not recorded by the local historical society; Whitcomb's observations led him to conclude that the Brandeises were socially isolated in Dedham.

26. Forbes's *Sport in Norfolk County*, which recounts in detail the history of the Dedham Polo Club, mentions Brandeis briefly for the years 1887-88, pp. 14, 15, and for 1895, pp. 39, 155; LDB to Alfred Brandeis, August 11, 1878, *BL*, I, 27; Susan Brandeis Gilbert to John M. Whitcomb, October 22, 1957; for this letter and Elizabeth B. Raushenbush, see note 25, *supra*; John T. Morse to Henry Cabot Lodge in 1916, A. L. Todd, *Justice on Trial: The Case of Louis D. Brandeis* (Chicago, 1964), pp. 129-130.

27. See interviews in note 25, *supra*; interview with Elizabeth E. Fisher. LDB to Alfred Brandeis, October 13, 1889, *BL*, I, 79-80.

28. Interviews, note 25, *supra*; *List of Persons Assessed for Poll Tax in*

Dedham, years 1890-1913; receipt for membership dues to the Dedham Historical Society, February 7, 1905, BDN #13812; Frank Smith, *A History of Dedham, Massachusetts* (Dedham, Mass., 1936); on the Brandeises' daughters: Melvin I. Urofsky, *A Mind of One Piece: Brandeis and American Reform* (New York, 1971), p. 11; interview with Elliott Perkins.

29. Shiverick, "Social Reorganization of Boston," pp. 136-141; Wecter, *Saga of American Society*, p. 271; Frederic F. Curtiss and John Heard, *The Country Club, 1882-1932* (Brookline, Mass., 1932), pp. 7, 19, 44-46; Forbes, *Sport in Norfolk County*, p. 14.

30. LDB to Adolph Brandeis, November 1, 1889, *BL*, I, 81; interview with Elliott Perkins; Urofsky, *Mind of One Piece*, p. 10.

31. *Sixty Years of the Union Boat Club* . . . (Boston, 1913); *Boston Athletic Association, Constitution* . . . (Boston, June 1890) and subsequent issues; Williams, *Greater Boston Clubs*, pp. 28, 70-76, 126; interview with Walter M. Whitehill. *The Union Club of Boston, 1863-1893* [Boston, 1893]; interview with Elliott Perkins. *The American Art Review* (Boston, 1878) and issues of subsequent twenty years, including annual reports of the Art Club; LDB's pocket appointment books in LU. *Charter and By-Laws of the Exchange Club* . . . (Boston, 1896); Alexander Williams to Gal, February 4, 1974; interviews with Walter M. Whitehill and Elliott Perkins; quot., LDB to Alfred Brandeis, October 10, 1914, LU, M 4-1.

32. Mason, *Brandeis*, p. 481; *The Curtis Club: An Account of its 50th Anniversary, Nov. 18, 1930, together with List of Members* . . . [Boston, 1930], pp. 14, 18, 38; LDB to Alice Goldmark, October 17, 1890, *BL*, I, 93.

33. LDB to Edward F. McClennen, February 17, 1916, *BL*, IV, 67, 68; U.S. Congress, House, *Nomination of Louis D. Brandeis*, 64th Cong., 1st sess., 1916 [hereafter *Nomination*], vol. II of 2, 614-615; ibid., 618.

34. Quots., *Nomination*, 271-272, 618; long quot., 305-306.

35. Arthur D. Hill to George W. Anderson, February 24, 1916, *Nomination*, I, 620.

36. Conclusions are based on Samuel D. Warren to LDB, January 30, May 5, 14, 22, 1879, Felix Frankfurter MSS, Harvard Law School Archives, Cambridge, Mass.; LDB to S. D. Warren, May 30, 1879, *BL*, I, 34-35; S. D. Warren to LDB, June 4, 18, 1879, Frankfurter MSS; Mason, *Brandeis*, pp. 54-55; quot., p. 55.

37. See note 36, *supra*; for Morse and Friedman, Ehrenfried, *Chronicle of Boston Jewry*, pp. 624-626, 661-662; on the firm's clientele, ch. 1, note 39, *supra*.

38. Ch. 1, note 39, *supra*.

39. Ibid.

40. *First Annual Report of the Federation* . . . , *1896* [Boston, 1896], pp. 92-97; *Ninth Annual Report of the Federation* . . . , *1904-1905* (Boston, 1905), pp. 42-49; for wills, ch. 1, note 39, *supra*; all these and Solomon's *Pioneers in Service* are also the sources of the ensuing discussion.

41. The firm's Jewish clientele up to 1906 has been computed as a per-

centage of the names listed in the *First Annual Report of the Federation . . . , 1896*, pp. 92-97. Subscribers of less than twenty-five dollars were, in general, outside of the market for legal services and therefore are not included in this computation.

42. *Boston Evening Transcript*, July 27, 1929; Ehrenfried, *Chronicle of Boston Jewry*, p. 639; corresp. of LDB and David A. Ellis in 1905-7 in BDN ##14370, 15589.

43. LDB's letter of March 11, 1903, BDN #12075; Jacob Heilborn to LDB, August 31, 1908, and LDB to J. Heilborn, September 4, 1908, BDN #16388.

44. Mason, *Brandeis*, p. 640; ch. 1, note 39, *supra*; cf. Edward F. McClennen, "Louis D. Brandeis as a Lawyer," *Massachusetts Law Quarterly*, 33 no. 3 (September 1948), 23. For Yankees' dominance: in finance, Jaher, "Boston Brahmins," pp. 191-193, 230, 232, and passim; in railroads, Edward C. Kirkland, *Men, Cities and Transportation: A Study of New England History, 1820-1900*, 2 vols. (Cambridge, Mass., 1948), II, 467-468; in textiles, Melvin T. Copeland, *The Cotton Manufacturing Industry of the United States* (Cambridge, Mass., 1912), pp. 159-160.

45. LDB to Norman Hapgood, March 17, 1913, *BL*, III, 47.

46. Blodgett, *Gentle Reformers*, pp. 276, 11-12, 109-111, 78-79; Abrams, *Conservatism in a Progressive Era*, p. 170. Henry G. Pearson, *An American Railroad Builder: John Murray Forbes* (Boston, 1911), pp. 144-151, 182-183; Sarah F. Hughes, ed., *Letters and Recollections of John M. Forbes*, 2 vols. (Boston, 1899), II, 184-210. Edward C. Kirkland, *Charles Francis Adams Jr., 1835-1915: The Patrician at Bay* (Cambridge, Mass., 1965), pp. 65-129, 173-182; M. A. DeWolfe Howe, *Portrait of an Independent: Moorfield Storey, 1845-1929* (Boston, 1932), pp. 164-165, 183-186.

47. McClennen, "Brandeis," p. 23; cf. Mason, *Brandeis*, pp. 70-71; ch. 1, note 39, *supra*.

48. Alice H. Grady, "Boyhood of Brandeis," *Boston American*, June 4, 1916; Mason, *Brandeis*, pp. 24, 33, and passim; quot., Mrs. Charles G. Tachau to Gal, October 10, 1973; see also LDB to Charles H. Davis, April 29, 1908, BDN #16931; LDB to William G. McAdoo, November 6, 1915, BDN #22217.

49. LDB to Alfred Brandeis, January 15, 1887, *BL*, I, 72; for the Brandeises and Louisville Board of Trade, *Annual Report of . . .* , 1880-91, *Minutes of . . .* , 1892-1913, in Louisville Free Public Library, Louisville, Ky.; *The Courier-Journal*, August 9, 1928; interview with Mrs. Charles G. Tachau. Alfred Kelly, "A History of Illinois Manufacturers' Association," Ph.D. diss. (University of Chicago, 1938), ch. 12, esp. pp. 110-111; LDB to Alfred Brandeis, January 3, 1910, ed. note 1, *BL*, II, 306; interview with Mrs. C. G. Tachau.

50. Interview with Mrs. Charles G. Tachau; LDB to Alfred Brandeis, July 26, December 10, 1906, *BL*, I, 459, 511, and passim; J. M. Glenn to LDB, November 7, 1906, LDB to J. M. Glenn, November 28, 1906, BDN

#15589; LDB to Alfred Brandeis, July 17, 20, 1908, January 3, 8, 1910, *BL*, II, 200, 201, 306, 307; LDB to Alfred Brandeis, July 14, 1912, LU, M-3. *The Ashland Gazette* (Nebraska), November 27, 1913; Mrs. Charles G. Tachau to Gal, October 15, 1973; LDB to Alfred Brandeis, March 27, 1910, *BL*, II, 327; LDB to J. H. Marble, March 4, 1913, ibid., III, 38; LDB to Franklin K. Lane, March 5, 1913, ibid., 40.

51. Blodgett, *Gentle Reformers*, pp. 109-113, 225-226, 212.

52. Ibid., p. 226; *BL*, I, 145-224; Mason, *Brandeis*, pp. 106-117; Alfred Lief, *Brandeis: The Personal History of American Ideal* (1936; New York, 1964), pp. 64-69; for M. Prince's role see *BL*, I, 143-200, passim.

53. Lief, *Brandeis*, pp. 65-67; Gerald W. Johnson, *Liberal's Progress* (New York, 1948), p. 90; LDB to Edward A. Filene, June 1, 1901, *BL*, I, 169; E. A. Filene to LDB, July 29, 1903, LU, NMF 8-1.

54. BMA, *Bulletin*, no. 1 (March 16, 1901), 1; no. 18 (November 1902), 2-3; no. 19 (December 1902), 6. R. A. Boit to LDB, March 21, 1900, LU, NMF 3-1; Mason, *Brandeis*, p. 109; J. T. Boyd to LDB, October 21, 1902, LU, NMF 4-2.

55. LDB to Adolph Brandeis, November 21, 1889, *BL*, I, 82; LDB to E. D. Mead, November 9, 1895, ibid., 121.

56. Mason, *Brandeis*, ch. 9.

57. Quot., *Constitution and By-Laws, Massachusetts State Board of Trade* . . . (Boston, 1896), p. 5; for constituency, ibid. and *Annual Reports*, 1900-14.

58. Abrams, *Conservatism in a Progressive Era*, pp. 59-62; for contributors, corresp. and reports for 1903-12, LU, NMF 8-1.

59. Mason, *Brandeis*, chs. 7, 9; McClennen, "Brandeis," pp. 22-23.

60. Note 61, *infra*.

61. Lief, *Brandeis*, p. 56; Vincent P. Carosso, *Investment Banking in America: A History* (Cambridge, Mass., 1970), p. 311; Mason, *Brandeis*, p. 115; Lief, *Brandeis*, p. 56; LDB to Albert E. Pillsbury, May 20, 1897, *BL*, I, 131.

62. LDB to J. Richard Carter, March 24, 1900, *BL*, I, 138; LDB to Lawrence Minot, April 16, 1900, ibid., 141; LDB to Arthur A. Maxwell, April 24, 1900, ibid., 143; LDB to Henry Lee Higginson, April 28, 1900, Higginson MSS, Harvard Business School Archives, Cambridge, Mass.; see also LDB to Morton Prince, May 18, 1900, *BL*, I, 145.

63. LDB to Arthur A. Maxwell, *BL*, I, 143 and ed. note 8, 144; quot., Mason, *Brandeis*, p. 115.

64. Mason, *Brandeis*, pp. 127, 109; Joseph Lee's contribution probably began some years before 1907, the first year for which we have a full financial statement of the PFL, LU, NMF 8-1.

65. Corresp. of Henry L. Higginson and Joseph Lee, 1896-1919, in Higginson MSS; Bliss Perry, *Life and Letters of Henry Lee Higginson* (Boston, 1921), pp. 432-433; for antiimperialism, ibid., pp. 425-429 and H. L. Higginson to John D. Long, April 4, 11, 16, 1898, Higginson Papers, Mass. His-

torical Society, Boston; Higginson was often successfully appealed to for help by various peace societies, see Higginson MSS; John T. Morse, Jr., ed., *Memoir of Colonel Henry Lee* (Boston, 1905), pp. 218-219; J. Lee to H. L. Higginson, April 4, 1911, November 22, 1912, Higginson MSS; Blodgett, *Gentle Reformers*, passim. Daniel B. Schirmer, *Republic or Empire: American Resistance to the Philippine War* (Cambridge, Mass., 1972), pp. 39-40, 52; Charles C. Jackson, e.g., was the treasurer of the Mass. Civil Service Reform Assn. and of the Citizens Municipal League, and secretary of Boston Charter Assn.

66. Mrs. Charles G. Tachau to Gal, December 5, 1974.

67. Lewis N. Dembitz, "The Free Coinage Problem," *Present Problems* (New York), 1, no. 1 (August 1, 1896), 22-29; Lewis N. Dembitz, "Results of Bad Teaching," *Nation*, 43, no. 4 (October 14, 1886), 306.

68. LDB to Adolph Brandeis, November 21, 1889, *BL*, I, 82; LDB to Edwin D. Mead, November 9, 1895, ibid., 121. Quot., Mason, *Brandeis*, p. 141; Brandeis's memoirs in Livy S. Richard, "Up from Aristocracy," *The Independent*, July 27, 1914, p. 130; Josephine Goldmark, *Impatient Crusader: Florence Kelley's Life Story* (Urbana, Ill., 1953), pp. 152-153; Lief, *Brandeis*, pp. 39-40.

69. Lief, *Brandeis*, pp. 33-34.

70. Mary Kenney O'Sullivan, "Autobiography," O'Sullivan MSS in Radcliffe College, Schlesinger Library, Cambridge, Mass., pp. 84-85, 124-25; quots., p. 156; *Boston Globe*, September 23, 1902, p. 14.

71. LDB to Elizabeth G. Evans, August 6, 1896, *BL*, I, 123-124; Lief, *Brandeis*, p. 33; notwithstanding other indications in his own book, Lief suggests that the influence of the O'Sullivans began around 1896.

72. Louis M. Lyons, *Newspaper Story: One Hundred Years of the Boston Globe* (Cambridge, Mass., 1971), p. 82; O'Sullivan, "Autobiography," ch. 10; Mann, *Yankee Reformers*, pp. 187-188; LDB to Philip Cabot, September 19, 1904, *BL*, I, 263.

73. Vida D. Scudder, *On Journey* (New York, 1937), pp. 111, 297; LDB to Cornelia L. Warren, March 10, April 21, June 11, 1900, *BL*, I, 137, 142, 146; LDB to Helena S. Dudley, October 26, 1900, ibid., 146; LDB to Mary Kehew, December 4, 1900, ibid., 151; LDB to Katherine Coman, December 14, 1900, ibid., 151; LDB to Boston City Council, February [9], 1901, ibid., 160; *Annual Reports of Denison House: The College Settlement*, 1904-5, 1910-12.

74. Goldmark, *Impatient Crusader*, pp. 70, 136-38, 153; O'Sullivan, "Autobiography," pp. 62-74, 115, 159-171; Scudder, *On Journey*, pt. 2, ch. 4; quot., pp. 154-155.

75. O'Sullivan, "Autobiography," ch. 9, pp. 200-201; quot., p. 155.

76. This passage relies on a close study by Mary La Dame, *The Filene Store: A Study of Employees' Relations to Management in a Retail Store* (New York, 1930); cf. Tom Mahoney and Leonard Sloane, *The Great Merchants* (New York, 1966), ch. 6.

77. La Dame, *Filene Store*, "Introduction," ch. 1, p. 214. Edward A. Filene, *The Way Out* (New York, 1924), chs. 2, 9, 11, 14; A. Lincoln Filene, *A Merchant's Horizon* (Boston, 1924); Mason, *Brandeis*, pp. 146-147; quot., LDB to E. A. Filene, June 25, 1906, *BL*, I, 447.

78. Alice H. Grady to LDB, July 18, 1903; quot. on league's purpose, "Certificate of Organization"; — these and reports of meetings in LU, NMF 7-2.

79. Note 78, *supra*; LDB to William H. Dunbar, July 21, 1903, *BL*, I, 236. For LDB's role see, e.g., the report of the meeting of January 24, 1905, LU, NMF 7-2; LDB to W. H. Dunbar, July 22, 1903, and to James P. Munroe, March 2, 1905, *BL*, I, 238, 286; conclusions on the Filenes' role based on reports and corresp. in LU, NMF 7-2.

80. LDB, "Business — a Profession" (from address of October 1912), in his *Business — a Profession* (Boston, 1933), pp. 9-12.

81. LDB, "The Incorporation of Trade Unions," (from address of December 4, 1902), ibid., pp. 88-98; on the value of trade unions, ibid., pp. 88-90; H. D. Lloyd to LDB, March 4, 1902, and LDB to H. D. Lloyd, March 5, 1902, BDN #11606; Lief, *Brandeis*, pp. 39, 87; Mason, *Brandeis*, p. 143; quot., LDB to Cearo Lloyd Withington, June 23, 1906, BDN #15589.

82. Conclusion based on table 19, Bureau of Census, *Manufacturers 1905, Pt. 2, States and Territories*, pp. 462-467; cf. Abrams, *Conservatism in a Progressive Era*, pp. 274-276; labor force's composition based on table 30, Bureau of Census, *Manufacturers 1905, Pt. 1*, p. lxxxi; Frederick J. Allen, *The Shoe Industry* (Boston, 1916), pp. 261-295, esp. pp. 264-271; Copeland, *Cotton Manufacturing*, pp. 123-128, 157; data, p. 126; quot., LDB to Philip Cabot, September 19, 1904, *BL*, I, 263.

83. LDB, "Business — a Profession," pp. 5-12; Mason, *Brandeis*, pp. 145-146; in addition to William McElwain, Charles H. Jones also highly appreciated LDB's position in labor matters: see, e.g., Charles H. Jones to LDB, February 6, 1905, LU, NMF 12-1. Lief, *Brandeis*, pp. 40-41; quot., p. 41; LDB to John F. Tobin, March 28, 1905, *BL*, I, 298.

84. LDB, "The Employer and Trade Unions" (from an address of April 21, 1904), in LDB, *Business*, pp. 18-21; LDB, "Hours of Labor" (from an address of January 11, 1906), ibid., p. 28. Robert H. Wiebe, *Business and Reform: A Study of the Progressive Movement* (Cambridge, Mass., 1962), pp. 20, 169, and passim; James Weinstein, *The Corporate Ideal in the Liberal State, 1900-1918* (Boston, 1968), p. 11. For Higginson in labor matters, LDB to Henry Lee Higginson, April 26, 1905, *BL*, I, 309, and see LDB to H. Robbins, June 19, 1905, ibid., 328 and ed. annotations; R. N. Turner (secretary of Mass. Assn. for Labor Legislation) to H. L. Higginson, February 17, 1913, and H. L. Higginson to Turner, February 13, 27, 1913, Higginson MSS. For Lee in labor matters, Frank L. Mott, *A History of American Magazines, 1885-1905* (Cambridge, Mass., 1957), p. 744; Clarke A. Chambers, *Paul U. Kellogg and the Survey* (Minneapolis, 1971), pp. 18-32; quot., Joseph Lee to H. L. Higginson, September 5, 1912, Higginson MSS.

85. Solomon, *Ancestors and Immigrants*, p. 104; Wiebe, *Businessmen and Reform*, pp. 182-184; Maldwyn A. Jones, *American Immigration* (Chicago, 1960), pp. 218, 247-265; quot., LDB to Prestcott F. Hall, November 8, 1904, BDN #13258; Richard Hofstadter, *The Age of Reform: From Bryan to F.D.R.* (New York, 1955), p. 178; Abrams, *Conservatism in a Progressive Era*, p. 143.

86. For the date of Brandeis's departure from the MRC, see ch. 1, note 73, *supra*; LDB to Everett V. Abbot, October 8, 1904, BDN #13258; quot., *The Economic Club of Boston, Constitution . . .* (December 1907), p. 3; LDB to William H. Lincoln, April 28, 1903, *BL*, I, 234; *Membership List of the National Council of the National Economic League* (Boston, [1915?]); for Brandeis's addressing the club see Mason, *Brandeis*, passim and Alpheus T. Mason, *The Brandeis Way: A Case Study in the Workings of Democracy* (Princeton, N.J., 1938), p. 127.

3. The Claims of Ethnicity

1. Frederika Brandeis to LDB, November 2, 1884, *Reminiscences of Frederika Dembitz Brandeis Written for Her Son, Louis, in 1880 to 1886*, translated by Alice G. Brandeis for her grandchildren in 1943 (privately printed), pp. 32-34, in Goldfarb Library, Brandeis University, Waltham, Mass.

2. Gershom Scholem, "A Sabbathaian Will from New York," in *The Jewish Historical Society of England, Miscellanies, Part V* (London, 1948), p. 193; Josephine Goldmark, *Pilgrims of '48: One Man's Part in the Austrian Revolution of 1848 and a Family Migration to America* (New Haven, 1930), pp. 191-194; Frederika Brandeis to LDB, January 1, 1881, F. Brandeis, *Reminiscences*, pp. 8-9; quot., F. Brandeis to LDB, November 2, 1884, pp. 32-33.

3. Quot., Frederika Brandeis to LDB, September 25, November 2, 1884, F. Brandeis, *Reminiscences*, pp. 32, 33.

4. Gershom Scholem, "Jacob Frank," in *Encyclopedia Judaica* (Jerusalem, 1971), VII, 55-72; Gershom Scholem, *Studies and Texts Concerning the History of Sabbatianism and its Metamorphoses* [in Hebrew] (Jerusalem, 1974), pp. 47-67.

5. F. Brandeis, *Reminiscences*, passim; quot., "An interview with Louis Dembitz Brandeis," *American Hebrew*, 88, no. 5 (December 2, 1910), 135.

6. Moshe Davis, *The Emergence of Conservative Judaism: The Historical School in 19th Century America* (Philadelphia, 1963), pp. 333-335 and passim. Note of Lewis N. Dembitz (grandson of Brandeis's uncle), August 16, 1905, in possession of the former; L. N. Dembitz to Gal, March 20, 1974.

7. Frederika Brandeis to LDB, August 7, 1886, F. Brandeis, *Reminiscences*, p. 47; and see possession of Lewis N. Dembitz, note 6, *supra*; for Dembitz's philosophy see his address before the Jewish Theological Seminary, *The American Hebrew*, 75, no. 4 (June 10, 1904), 109 and "Editorial Notes," 101; for Dembitz's opposition to Yiddish and separatism, ibid., 109

and Davis, *Conservative Judaism*, p. 320; see also Dembitz, "The Future of Zionism," *The Maccabaean*, 7, no. 2 (August 1904), 84.

8. A dozen letters from Lewis N. Dembitz to LDB from November 10, 1881-June 6, 1882, were connected with the former's financial and legal problems in his capacity as leader of the Jewish congregation in Louisville, Ky., BDN #123; LDB to L. N. Dembitz, April 23, 1903, BDN #12230.

9. LDB to Arthur A. Dembitz, September 28, 1905, BDN #14370; David W. Amram, *Leading Cases in the Bible* (Philadelphia, 1905).

10. Mrs. Charles G. Tachau to Gal, October 15, 1973; interview with Mrs. C. G. Tachau; LDB to Adolph Brandeis, December 1, 1905, *BL*, I, 387; the obit. in the local *Courier-Journal*, August 29, 1928, does not indicate any Jewish affiliation.

11. Alpheus T. Mason, *Brandeis: A Free Man's Life* (New York, 1946), pp. 75-76; LDB to Walter B. Douglas, October 1, 1890, *BL*, I, 91; Benny Kraut, "Felix Adler's Emergence Out of Judaism," Ph.D. diss. (Brandeis University, 1975), ch. 4.

12. Kraut, "Felix Adler," pp. 182-183, 257-275, 301-319; *New York Evening Post*, November 25, 1905, p. 4.

13. LDB to Alice Goldmark, February 2, 1891, *BL*, I, 99; Felix Adler to LDB, December 21, 1904, and LDB to F. Adler, December 27, 1904, BDN #13812. Alfred Lief, *Brandeis: The Personal History of an American Ideal* (1936; Freeport, N.Y., 1964), p. 31; Mason, *Brandeis*, p. 103.

14. For admiration of Adler, Brandeis's letter to Alice Goldmark, note 13, *supra*; background, note 13, *supra*, and ch. 1, note 10, *supra*.

15. Quots., Elizabeth B. Raushenbush to Gal, August 21, 1973, and LDB to Amy B. Wehle, January 8, 1881, *BL*, I, 61; LDB to Adolph Brandeis, November 1, 1889, ibid., 81; LDB to Alice Goldmark, December 22, 1890, ibid., 96; quot., LDB to Otto A. Wehle, January 11, 1880, ibid., 50.

16. *Annual Report of the United Hebrew Benevolent Association, 1894* (Boston, 1895); *Ninth Annual Report of the Federation . . . , May 1st 1904 to May 1st 1905*, p. 5. Harry Liebmann to LDB, December 8, 1905; quot., LDB to H. Liebmann, December 26, 1905; H. Liebmann to LDB, December 27, 1905; — in BDN #15589.

17. *First Annual Report of the Federation . . . , 1896*, p. 92; *Second Annual Report of the Federation . . . , July 1, 1896 to May 1, 1897; Ninth Annual Report of the Federation*, p. 43; receipts and acknowledgements in BDN, for 1902 — #11606, 1903 — #11915, 1904 — #12532, 1906 — #15589, 1907 — #16598; the amount of the donation in 1905 is questionable: according to the *Ninth Annual Report* it was ninety dollars, while a draft in BDN #15589 indicated only thirty. For Brandeis's income, Mason, *Brandeis*, p. 640.

18. First letter of Jacob H. Hecht to LDB, February 17, 1880; last letter in the corresp. is of Hecht to Warren and Brandeis firm, December 1, 1880; also, relevant documents in BDN #17; interview with Louis Ehrlich.

19. Jacob Neusner, "The Impact of Immigration and Philanthropy

Upon the Boston Jewish Community (1880-1914)," *PAJHS*, 46 (December 1956), 72-74; Barbara M. Solomon, *Pioneers in Service: The History of the Associated Jewish Philanthropies of Boston* (Boston, 1956), p. 13; quots., Jacob H. Hecht to LDB, February 2, 4, 1885, BDN #394.

20. Solomon, *Pioneers in Service*, pp. 22-25, Lina Hecht to LDB [?], 1898, BDN #7515; incorporation in BDN #11591; *Report for 1901-1902, Hebrew Industrial School* [Boston, 1906], p. 14; Brandeis's annual donation during 1903-7 was twenty-five dollars: drafts and receipts in BDN ##15589, 19732; Solomon, *Pioneers in Service*, pp. 52-53; Golde Bamber to LDB [n.d., received by LDB on November 16, 1912], BDN #20256.

21. Jacob H. Hecht to LDB, October 22, 1902; LDB to Richard Olney, October 24, 1902; Nissim Behar to LDB, November 4, 1902; quots., revised appeal attached to LDB to N. Behar, November 4, 1902; — in BDN #11915.

22. For Brandeis and the federation's Purim Balls, Harry Liebmann to LDB, December 1, 1900, and LDB to H. Liebmann, December 7, 1900; LDB to Summit L. Hecht, January 3, 1904; S. L. Hecht to LDB, February 2, 1906, and LDB to S. L. Hecht, February 9, 1906; — in BDN ##10311, 12352, 15589. For Brandeis and Jacob H. Hecht Club, Alice H. Grady and LDB to Harry S. Bernstein, January 6, 23, 1904; LDB to J. Walelstein, February 27, 1904; LDB's secretary to H. Stern, December 23, 1904; — in BDN ##12352, 12812. For Brandeis and the Young Men's Hebrew Association, David A. Ellis to LDB, February 15, 1905, and LDB to D. A. Ellis, February 17, 1905; Max Goldberg to LDB, March 10, 1905, and LDB to M. Goldberg, March 13, 1905; J. H. Landau to LDB, April 6, 1905, and LDB to J. H. Landau, April 7, 1905; David A. Lorie to LDB, November 2, 1905, and LDB to D. A. Lorie, November 3, 1905; — in BDN ##13812, 14370. For Brandeis and the Council of Jewish Women, Minnie E. Lauferty to LDB, August 20, 1903, and LDB to M. E. Lauferty, September 10, 1903; M. E. Lauferty to LDB, September 18, 1903; Summit L. Hecht to LDB, August 17, 1904; Alice H. Grady to S. L. Hecht, August 22, 1904, and S. L. Hecht to LDB, August 23, 1904; M. E. Lauferty to LDB, September 27, 1904, and LDB to M. E. Lauferty, September 28, 1904; — in BDN ##12486, 13258; and see notes 23, 24, *infra*.

23. Solomon, *Pioneers in Service*, p. 59; cf. *Boston Globe*, November 23, 1903, p. 11; Joseph L. Bergman to LDB, November 18, 1903, LDB to J. L. Bergman, November 20, 1903, and J. L. Bergman to LDB, November 23, 1903, BDN #12352.

24. Edward J. Bromberg to LDB, February 10, 1905, and LDB to E. J. Bromberg, February 14, 1905, LU, Z1-2.

25. Jacob De Haas, *Louis D. Brandeis: A Biographical Sketch . . .* (New York, 1929), p. 51; De Haas (who came to the United States in 1902 and to Boston in 1906) tended to ignore the Jewish image of Brandeis in order to underscore his own role in Brandeis's conversion to Zionism; see relevant discussion and notes, ch. 5, *infra*.

26. For background, Solomon, *Pioneers in Service*, p. 36; LDB to Leh-

man Pickert, May 21, 1903, and L. Pickert to LDB, May 21, 1903, BDN #12230; Isaac Frothingham to LDB, November 19, 1905; LDB to I. Frothingham and to Joseph Koshland, November 20, 1905, BDN #14370.

27. Rudolf Glanz, *Jews in Relation to the Cultural Milieu of the Germans in America up to the Eighteen Eighties* (New York, 1947), p. 6; Oscar Handlin, *Boston's Immigrants: A Study in Acculturation*, revised and enlarged ed. (Cambridge, Mass., 1959), p. 156; *Annual Report of the Germanic Museum Association, 1901-1902* (Cambridge, Mass., 1903).

28. Interview with Richard Ehrlich; the liberal or Progressive opinions of the two famous rabbis of Temple Israel, Solomon Schindler (1874-93) and Charles Fleischer (1894-1911), were by no means supported by the bulk of their constituency, see Arthur Mann, ed., *Growth and Achievement: Temple Israel, 1854-1954* (Cambridge, Mass., 1954), pp. 45, 63; quots., LDB to Alice G. Brandeis, June 18, 1919, *BL*, IV, 401. Interview with Maida Herman Solomon.

29. Solomon, *Pioneers in Service*, pp. 176-179; the sisters-in-law of A. Lincoln Filene were married to Sidney Dreyfus and Ludwig Eisemann, both of the local German Jewish community; interviews with Dorothy Dreyfus Bloomfield, Carl Barnet, and Helen Filene Ladd, Jr.

30. Geoffrey Blodgett, *The Gentle Reformers: Massachusetts Democrats in the Cleveland Era* (Cambridge, Mass., 1966), pp. 168, 242; Jacob Neusner, "Politics, Anti-Semitism and the Jewish Community of Boston, 1880-1914," paper at the American Jewish Historical Society (Waltham, Mass.), p. 259.

31. For Abrahams, *Jewish Advocate*, December 10, 24, 1909, pp. 3, 8; Arthur Mann, *Yankee Reformers in the Urban Age: Social Reform in Boston, 1880-1900* (Boston, 1954), pp. 187-198; Albert Ehrenfried, *Chronicle of Boston Jewry: From the Colonial Settlement to 1900* ([Boston], 1963), p. 513; cf. Moses Rischin, *The Promised City: New York's Jews, 1870-1914* (New York, 1962), pp. 53-75, esp. pp. 61-68.

32. Interview with Maida Herman Solomon; Ehrenfried, *Chronicle of Boston Jewry*, pp. 515-516.

33. Handlin, *Boston's Immigrants*, pp. 52-91 and passim; last communication inviting Brandeis to a directors' meeting is of December 27, 1906, in BDN #16123.

34. Handlin, *Boston's Immigrants*. For Brandeis and Collins, *BL*, I, 203 and passim; corresp. in BDN #11915. Mann, *Yankee Reformers*, ch. 2; Donna Merwick, *Boston Priests, 1848-1910: A Study of Social and Intellectual Change* (Cambridge, Mass., 1973), pp. 147-177.

35. Merwick, *Boston Priests*, pp. 161-177, 177-192; Blodgett, *Gentle Reformers*; Abrams, *Conservatism in a Progressive Era*. For the law firm, ch. 1, note 39, *supra*; quot., LDB to Alice Goldmark, October 28, 1890, *BL*, I, 94.

36. Obituaries in the *Boston Globe* of John F. O'Sullivan, John F. Tobin, and Mary K. O'Sullivan, September 23, 1902, pp. 1, 14, April 15, 1919, p.

12, and January 19, 1943, p. 13; Thomas N. Brown, *Irish-American Nationalism: Eighteen Seventy to Eighteen Ninety* (New York, 1966), p. 155. For Patrick Collins see Blodgett, *Gentle Reformers*, pp. 53-55 and passim. Daniel B. Schirmer, *Republic or Empire: American Resistance to the Philippine War* (Cambridge, Mass., 1972), pp. 14, 15-16, and passim; Grozier's obit., *Boston Globe*, May 10, 1924, pp. 1, 2; Report of the *Post*'s manager, December 31, 1890, and subsequent documents and corresp., BDN #1586; LDB to Samuel D. Warren, January 16, 1891; LDB to Edwin Grozier re "Plan for Reorganization Post Pub. Co.," July 16, 1906; E. Grozier to LDB and LDB's reply, August 29 and September 3, 1907; — in BDN #1586; see also LDB to E. Grozier, June 27, 1901, *BL*, I, 173. And see ch. 1, note 39, *supra*.

37. Richard Abrams, "Introduction . . . Torchbook edition," in LDB, *Other People's Money and How the Bankers Use It* (1914; New York, 1967), pp. xxiv-xxvi; Melvin I. Urofsky, *A Mind of One Piece: Brandeis and American Reform* (New York, 1971), pp. 4-9; LDB to Frederika Brandeis, November 12, 1888, Mason, *Brandeis*, pp. 93-94; quot., LDB to Amy B. Wehle, November 19, 1898, *BL*, I, 135.

38. Mason, *Brandeis*, pp. 33-38; James M. Landis, "Mr. Justice Brandeis and the Harvard Law School," *Harvard Law Review*, 55 (1941-42), 184-188.

39. LDB to Alfred Brandeis, June 28, 1878, *BL*, I, 24; LDB to Frederika Brandeis, July 20, 1879, ibid., 43. LDB to Otto A. Wehle, November 12, 1876, ibid., 12; Mason, *Brandeis*, pp. 38-40; quot., LDB to Alice Goldmark, October 13, 1890, *BL*, I, 93.

40. LDB, "Duty of Educated Jews" (address of November 8, 1914), in Barbara Harris, "Zionist Speeches of Louis Dembitz Brandeis: A Critical Edition," Ph.D. diss. (University of California, 1967), pp. 142-143.

41. Quots., "Hearings of the New York State Factory Investigating Commission, Held in . . . New York City, Jan. 22, 1915," *New York State 4th Report of the Factory Investigating Commission, 1915*, 5 vols. (Albany, N.Y., 1915), V, 2895-2896.

42. *BL*, I, 84-88, 113-118; quots., LDB to Christopher C. Langdell, December 30, 1889, ibid., 88; LDB to Charles W. Eliot, April 25, 1893, ibid., 114.

43. Samuel D. Warren to LDB, September 7, 1901, Mason, *Brandeis*, p. 389; Dean Acheson, *Morning and Noon* (Boston, 1965), pp. 57-58, 63, 78-79, 83; Paul A. Freund, "Mr. Justice Brandeis," in Allison Dunham and Philip B. Kurland, eds., *Mr. Justice*, revised and enlarged ed. (Chicago, 1964), pp. 187-189; Gal's notes of Paul A. Freund's lecture before Hillel of Harvard University, March 2, 1973. See also LDB to Alice Goldmark, December 10, 1890, Mason, *Brandeis*, p. 481; quot., Freund, "Mr. Justice Brandeis," p. 181.

44. Mason, *Brandeis*, pp. 119-121; "Corruption at City Hall, Says Brandeis," *Boston Post*, March 19, 1903; ibid., April 9, 1903. For the Irish and for Brandeis and Collins, see notes 35, 34, *supra*.

45. *Boston Herald*, April 14, 1903.

46. *Roxbury Gazette*, April 25, 1903. Elizabeth G. Evans, "Memoirs," Evans MSS, Radcliffe College, Schlesinger Library, Cambridge, Mass., folder #2, p. 3.

47. LDB's memo, September 8, 1905; Robert Silverman's statement (submitted to Brandeis sometime between September 8 and 14, 1905); Edward F. McClennen to David A. Ellis, September 14, 1905;—in BDN #14846.

48. Frederick A. Bushée, "The Invading Host," in Robert A. Woods, ed., *Americans in Process: North and West Ends* (Boston, 1902), pp. 57-58; Stephan Thernstrom, *The Other Bostonians: Poverty and Progress in the American Metropolis, 1880-1970* (Cambridge, Mass. 1973), pp. 135-138.

49. Ehrenfried, *Chronicle of Boston Jewry*, p. 545; Thernstrom, *Other Bostonians,* p. 135; Neusner, "Politics, Anti-Semitism," p. 260.

50. Quot., William Blatt, in *New Century Club: A Brief History* (Boston, 1947), p. 1; poem, William Blatt, in *The New Century Club: 1900-1950* ([Boston], 1950).

51. The role of Lomasney, *Boston Traveler,* October 11, 1905; quot., *Boston Advocate,* November 17, 1905.

52. Bushée, "The Invading Host," pp. 40-53.

53. Quots., *Boston Advocate,* September 29, 1905, p. 8.

54. Quots., *Boston Advocate,* September 29, 1905, p. 8.

55. Abrams, *Conservatism in a Progressive Era,* pp. 143-147; quot., *Boston Transcript.,* December 4, 1905.

56. *Boston Advocate,* October 20, 1905, p. 5; *Boston Transcript,* December 2, 1905.

57. Quots., *Boston Advocate,* October 20, 1905, p. 1; and see ibid., November 3, 1905, p. 8, November 24, 1905, pp. 3, 8, December 8, 1905, pp. 2, 8.

58. Documents in BDN #14846; quots., Edward F. McClennen to Robert Silverman, January 22, 1906, and R. Silverman to LDB, January 31, 1906, ibid.

59. Mason, *Brandeis,* p. 125; LDB to Mary Kehew, January 20, 1902, *BL,* I, 178; LDB to Edmund Billings, December 6, 1903; E. Billings to LDB, November 4, 1905; LDB to E. Billings, November 18, 1905;—in *BL,* I, 238, 368, 375.

60. *Boston Transcript*, November 14, 1905; quot., LDB to Henry Dewey, November 13, 1905, *BL,* I, 372.

61. *BL,* I, 371-390; LDB to Edmund Billings, November 21, 23, 1905, ibid., 376-377; LDB to John F. Fitzgerald, March 21, 1906; ibid., 414; LDB to George Hibbard, December 11, 1907, ibid., II, 60; *Boston Transcript,* December 8, 1905.

62. Jacob Silverman to LDB, October 26, 1905; LDB to J. Silverman, October 27, 1905; J. Silverman to LDB, November 6, 1905; J. Silverman to LDB, November 8, 1905;—in LU, NMF 12-6. Previous invitations, J. Silverman to LDB, September 5, 1901; LDB to J. Silverman, September 10, 1901;

LDB to William Blatt, October 8, 1904; — in BDN #13258.

63. LDB to Jacob Silverman, November 14, 1905, LU, NMF 12-6. *Boston Advocate*, November 24, 1905, p. 1; quots., "What Loyalty Demands," 5 pp. typescript in LU, NMF 12-6, pp. 1-5.

64. "What Loyalty Demands," p. 5.

65. Notes 53, 54, 57, *supra*; quot., *Boston Advocate*, October 20, 1905, p. 1.

66. LDB to Adolph Brandeis, December 1, 1905, *BL*, I, 387; LDB to Adolph Brandeis, November 29, 1905, ibid., 386.

67. Ch. 2, note 9, *supra*; *Boston Advocate*, December 1, 1905, p. 1, and see Rabbi Fleisher's speech on p. 4.

68. *Boston Transcript,* December 13, 1905; *Boston Advocate,* December 22, 1905, p. 8.

4. Daniel in the Lions' Den

1. Alpheus T. Mason, *The Brandeis Way: A Case Study in the Workings of Democracy* (Princeton, N.J., 1938), p. 88. This book is the major source for general information on Brandeis's activity in the field of life insurance.

2. LDB, "Life Insurance: The Abuses and Remedies," in his *Business —A Profession* (1914; Boston, 1933), p. 132; Donald R. Johnson, *Savings Bank Life Insurance* (Homewood, Ill., 1963), pp. 7-9. LDB to Walter C. Wright, November 3, 1905, *BL*, I, 367, and see 381-384, 393-395; LDB to Norman Hapgood, June 25, 1906, *BL*, I, 449; quot., LDB, "The Greatest Life Insurance Wrong" (*Independent* article of December 20, 1906), in Osmond K. Fraenkel, ed., *The Curse of Bigness: Miscellaneous Papers of Louis D. Brandeis* (New York, 1934), p. 24; see also "Massachusetts' Substitute for Old-Age Pensions," ibid., 26 and LDB, "Massachusetts' Savings-Bank Insurance and Pension System," *Quarterly Publications of the American Statistical Association* (Boston), 9, no. 85 (March 1909), 410.

3. Quot., Mason, *Brandeis Way*, p. 179; ibid., pp. 179-180 and passim; quot., LDB to Pierre Jay, November 1, 1907, *BL*, II, 43.

4. Mason, *Brandeis Way*, pp. 181-223; LDB to Alfred Brandeis, March 2, 1906, *BL*, I, 408.

5. LDB to William McElwain, May 1, 1907, *BL*, I, 563.

6. LDB to John Golden, May 2, 1907, *BL*, I, 566; Norman White to Alice H. Grady, May 11, 1907, SBLI; BD, January 1, 1907; BMA, *Bulletin*, no. 59 (January-February 1907), 3, 11; more on Brandeis's cooperation with the BMA, S. McVeigh (secretary of the association) to LDB, and LDB to S. McVeigh, April 4, 15, 1907, SBLI.

7. BD, December 3, 1906, and subsequent entries; Bernard Rothwell to LDB, November 28, 1906, LDB to B. Rothwell, November 30, 1906, and B. Rothwell to LDB, December 27, 1906, SBLI; quot., BCC, *Report of . . . for 1909* (Boston, 1910), p. 33.

8. Edward A. Filene to LDB, June 27, 1906, and later corresp.; Alice

H. Grady to A. Lincoln Filene, November 15, 1906; LDB to Henry Morgenthau, November 22, 1906, SBLI.

9. "Savings Insurance . . . Letters to Young Men's Hebrew Association and Fedn. of Jewish Charities," in BD, December 19, 1906; The Committee of One Hundred, letters of Norman White to LDB, March 18, 19, 20, 21, 1907; — all corresp. in SBLI.

10. Note 9, *supra*; for Mitchell's reputation beyond the Jewish community, see *Boston Transcript*, April 1, 1929, p. 12. *New York Times*, March 15, 1938, p. 23; interview with Lincoln Bloomfield; scrapbook in the possession of Lincoln Bloomfield. Interview with Jacob Cohen.

11. BD, December 26, 1906, January 25, March 14, 19, 1907; *Boston Advocate*, February 22, 1907, p. 8.

12. BD, May 16, 24, June 3, 1907; *Boston Advocate*, June 14, 1907, p. 8.

13. LDB to Lehman Pickert, December 17, 1907, BDN #16598. Brandeis explained that his charity in the future would go to the federation rather than to a variety of lesser organizations. Even so, the increase — from $105 to $175 — was very sharp. Brandeis's contribution to the federation itself for 1907 was $75, see ch. 3, note 17, *supra*.

14. Albert Ehrenfried, *A Chronicle of Boston Jewry from the Colonial Settlement to 1900* (Boston, 1963), pp. 684-685. The conclusions about the *Advocate* are based on a screening of the 1905-13 issues at the American Jewish Historical Society, Waltham, Mass.

15. *Insurance Yearbook* (Philadelphia, 1911), pp. 192-193.

16. Note 1, *supra*.

17. Ehrenfried, *Chronicle of Boston Jewry,* pp. 670-671, 684-688; *Boston Advocate,* July 16, 1943, p. 1; recollections of De Haas by Bernard Richards, ibid., April 16, 1937, p. 9.

18. BD, January 15, 22, 1909; following the publication Brandeis wrote on February 16 a "Lr. to Boston Advocate," in BD; *Boston Advocate,* February 5, 26, 1909, May 7, 14, 1909, pp. 6, 8, 6, 3; BD, March 13, 1909.

19. LDB to Norman Hapgood, September 23, 1908; Alice H. Grady to Robertson Hunter, September 28, 1908; LDB to R. Hunter, September 30, 1908; — in SBLI.

20. Susan B. Gilbert and Elizabeth B. Raushenbush to L. Kirstein, October 6, 1941; Louis E. Kirstein's necrology in *New Palestine,* November 14, 1941, p. 13; LDB to L. E. Kirstein, September 7, 1912; L. E. Kirstein and Nathan Pinanski in file "Old Friends"; — in Louis E. Kirstein MSS, Harvard Business School Archives, Cambridge, Mass.

21. Interview with Mrs. Abraham Pinanski; LDB to Abraham Pinanski, March 12, 1909, *BL*, II, 228.

22. Richard M. Abrams, *Conservatism in a Progressive Era: Massachusetts Politics, 1900-1912* (Cambridge, Mass., 1964), chs. 1, 5, 8 and Henry L. Staples and Alpheus T. Mason, *The Fall of a Railroad Empire: Brandeis and the New Haven Merger Battle* (Syracuse, N.Y., 1947) are the general sources of this discussion; quot., ibid., p. 15.

23. LDB to Edward A. Filene, June 29, 1907, *BL*, I, 592.

24. Quots., LDB, "The New England Transportation Monopoly" (address given February 11, 1908), in his *Business—A Profession,* pp. 265, 273-274, 282-283, 285; there was not much truth in any of Brandeis's contentions regarding the Boston and Maine, see Abrams, *Conservatism in a Progressive Era,* pp. 211-213.

25. Abrams, *Conservatism in a Progressive Era,* pp. 275-281.

26. LDB to Edward A. Filene, June 29, 1907, *BL*, I, 593; LDB to George Barnes, March 26, 1908, ibid., II, 109.

27. LDB to George Barnes, note 26, *supra* and May 25, 1908, *BL*, II, 167. Henry Lee Higginson to Henry Cabot Lodge, April 24, 28, 1908, Higginson MSS, Harvard Business School Archives, Cambridge, Mass.; cf. Irving Katz, "Henry Lee Higginson vs. Louis D. Brandeis," *New England Quarterly,* 41 (November 1968), 75 and passim.

28. Henry Lee Higginson to Eben S. Draper, June 30, 1908; H. L. Higginson to Henry Cabot Lodge, May 25, 1909; — in Higginson MSS.

29. Abrams, *Conservatism in a Progressive Era,* ch. 8.

30. "Hearings of the New York State Factory Investigating Commission, Held in . . . New York City, Jan. 22, 1915," *New York State 4th Report of the Factory Investigating Commission, 1915,* 5 vols. (Albany, N.Y., 1915), V, 2895-2896; quot., 2896; Staples and Mason, *Fall of a Railroad Empire,* pp. 141-142.

31. LDB to Alfred Brandeis, June 15, 1909, July 19, 1913, *BL*, II, 282, III, 143; LDB to Alfred Brandeis, August 19, 1909, LU, M 2-4. LDB to Edward A. Filene, June 29, 1907, *BL*, I, 592-593. On the growing cooperation of Lee, Higginson and Co. and J. P. Morgan's interests with regard to New England railroads, see Arthur Pound and Samuel T. Moore, eds., *More They Told Barron: The Notes of the Late Clarence W. Barron* (New York, 1931), pp. 153-154. On the growing involvement of the banking house in corporation consolidation, see Marshall W. Stevens, "History of Lee, Higginson and Company" (Boston, 1927), typescript at Harvard Business School Library, Cambridge, Mass., pp. 22-40.

32. NACM, *Transaction of . . . April 1909* (Boston 1909), p. 325; "Address by Col. Albert Clarke before the Boston Central Labor Union, March 1, 1908," in LU, NMF 1-D-1; NESLA, *Gazette,* Boston, January 15, 1907, March 15, 1908, January 15, 1909, pp. 7, 3-5, 10; LDB to Edward A. Filene, June 29, 1907, *BL*, I, 593; BMA, *Bulletin,* June 1907, pp. 6-7. BCC, *Annual Report of . . . for the Year . . . 1908* (Boston, 1909), pp. 33-35; the report for 1909 ignores the merger issue, cf. memos in LU, NMF 1-D-3, list of members in LU, NMF 1-F-2.

33. Abrams, *Conservatism in a Progressive Era,* pp. 71-79, 211, and passim; quot., NESLA, *Gazette,* March 15, 1908, p. 4; note 32, *supra.*

34. Brandeis's first letters to these labor leaders in *BL*, I: to Tobin, April 21, 1904, 248; to Golden, May 2, 1907, 566; to Abrahams, December 3, 1906, 503; Cohen is first mentioned in a letter to Golden, June 24, 1907, 587.

LDB to Henry Abrahams, June 5, 1909, LU, NMF 1-K-1; LDB to H. Abrahams, December 6, 1907, *BL*, II, 59.

35. Mason, *Brandeis Way,* pp. 156-170 and passim; notes 8, 9, *supra*; LDB to Edmund Grozier, May 6, 1907, *BL*, I, 569; LDB to David F. Tilley, February 5, 1909, ibid., II, 218.

36. LDB to George Barnes, March 26, 1908, *BL*, II, 109 and passim; memos of LDB and Alice H. Grady in LU, NMF 1-D-3; Rothwell to LDB, May 21, 1909, ibid.; LDB to Rothwell, May 18, 1908, *BL*, II, 156.

37. Donna Merwick, *Boston Priests, 1848-1910: A Study of Social and Intellectual Change* (Cambridge, Mass., 1973), ch. 4; John H. Cutler, *"Honey Fitz"* . . . *The Life and Times of John F. (Honey Fitz) Fitzgerald* (Indianapolis, 1962), pp. 179, 191; Abrams, *Conservatism in a Progressive Era,* p. 146.

38. Merwick, *Boston Priests,* pp. 183-191; for Catholic anti-Semitism see ibid., pp. 185-186. Vested interests' anti-Semitism: Alpheus T. Mason, *Brandeis: A Free Man's Life* (New York, 1946), quot., p. 486; Jacob De Haas, *Louis D. Brandeis: A Biographical Sketch* . . . (New York, 1929), pp. 50-51.

39. List of members of the Mass. Anti-Merger League, LU, NMF 1 F-2; the league's letterhead, LU, NMF 1-D-2; interviews with Frank Vorenberg and Dorothy Conrad Silberman. Memo from Meyer Bloomfield, May 27, 1909, LU, NMF 1-K-1; BD, March-May 1909; LDB to Max Mitchell, May 24, 1909, *BL*, II, 265.

40. Notes 31, ch. 3, and 34, this ch., *supra*.

41. Alice H. Grady to George Barnes, April 22, 1908; Walter Harstone to LDB, April 24, 1908; A. H. Grady to Edward Bromberg, April 25, 1908; —in LU, NMF 1-D-1; quot., LDB to Alfred Brandeis, May 3, 1908, *BL*, II, 140.

42. Alfred Lief, *Brandeis: The Personal History of an American Ideal* (1936; New York, 1964), p. 151; Mason, *Brandeis,* p. 95; LDB to Edward A. Filene, March 22, 1909, *BL*, II, 236 and passim to p. 296; BD, April 3-30, 1909; quot., April 30; corresp. and documents for the period April 12, 1909-January 4, 1910, BDN #19714.

43. Note 42, *supra*.

44. *Boston Advocate* for May-June; see esp. May 21, 1909, p. 3, June 11, 1909, p. 7, June 25, 1909, p. 1.

45. LDB to A. Lincoln Filene, May 26, 1909, *BL*, II, 269, Lief, *Brandeis,* p. 137.

46. James J. Storrow File, Harvard University Archives, Cambridge, Mass.; LDB to Edmund Grozier, May 10, 1907, *BL*, I, 571; LDB to Edward A. Filene, May 24, 1909, ibid., II, 262-263; LDB to Charles Hamlin, November 11, 1909, ibid., 295.

47. This and following discussion are based on the *Jewish Advocate*, September 3, 1909-January 21, 1910; Robert and Jacob Silverman were active, ibid., November 26, 1909, p. 1; for Mitchell, ibid., October 8, 1909, p. 3.

48. Ibid., October 15, 22, 29, 1909, p. 3; for Brandeis's being mentioned see, e.g., October 22, 1909, p. 3.

49. Quots., Elizabeth G. Evans, "Memoirs," Evans MSS, Radcliffe College, Schlesinger Library, Cambridge, Mass., folder #2, bundle 9, p. 1 and folder #2, bundle 11, pp. 5-6.

50. *Jewish Advocate*, June 11, 1909, p. 3.

51. LDB to Alfred Brandeis, November 5, 7, 1909, *BL*, II, 292, 294.

52. Evans MSS, folder #2, bundle 11, pp. 6-10; quots., pp. 8-9; Mary K. O'Sullivan, "Autobiography," (1943), O'Sullivan MSS at Schlesinger Library, Radcliffe College, Cambridge, Mass., chs. 10-12; Belle C. La Follette and Fola La Follette, *Robert M. La Follette*, 2 vols. (New York, 1953), I, 288-298; Lief, *Brandeis*, pp. 153-155.

53. *Boston American*, February 21, 1910; interview with Samuel D. Warren (grandson of Brandeis's partner).

54. Mason, *Brandeis*, pp. 238-240; quot., p. 240.

55. Quot., LDB to Samuel D. Warren, November 1, 1905, *BL*, I, 366. S. D. Warren's connections with State Street, note 53, *supra*; S. D. Warren in his interview indicates financier Allan Forbes as his grandfather's very close friend in Dedham; on Forbes, *Dedham Transcript*, July 15, 1955, p. 1.

56. The general sources for this and the ensuing discussion are Mason, *Brandeis*, ch. 19 and BD, July 14, 1910, and subsequent entries.

57. LDB to Alfred Brandeis, July 24, 1910, *BL*, II, 365; quots. from documents of the Coop. League, December 8, 1906, and June 1, 1910, in BDN #15599.

58. See note 56, *supra*.

59. Moses Rischin, *The Promised City: New York Jews, 1870-1914* (New York, 1964), pp. 46-47, 164-168, 192-194, 244; Ronald Sandres, *The Downtown Jews: Portraits of an Immigrant Generation* (New York, 1969): quot., Milton R. Konvitz, "Louis D. Brandeis," in Simon Noveck, ed., *Great Jewish Personalities in Modern Times* (New York, 1960), p. 300.

60. Quots., LDB, "Why I am a Zionist" (address given October 25, 1914), in Barbara Harris, "Zionist Speeches of Louis Dembitz Brandeis: A Critical Edition," Ph.D. diss. (University of California, 1967), p. 125; see also Mason, *Brandeis*, p. 672, note 9 and interview with LDB, *Boston American*, July 4, 1915.

61. LDB to John A. Dyche, February 11, 1915, *BL*, III, 428.

62. Quot., De Haas, *Brandeis*, p. 51; LDB to Max Meyer, September 6, 1910, ibid., p. 373.

63. LDB to Jane Adams, November 26, 1910, *BL*, II, 387; Benny Kraut, "Felix Adler's Emergence Out of Judaism," Ph.D. diss. (Brandeis University, 1975), pp. 267-278; the officers of New York Down Town Ethical Society were: directors—H. Moscowitz and Henry Neuman; secretary—Walter Leo Solomon; trustee—Max Meyer; LDB to L. F. Abbott, September 6, 1910, *BL*, II, 372.

64. *Jewish Advocate*, July 29, 1910, p. 8; August 5, 1910, p. 4; August

19, 26, 1910, p. 4. Unfortunately missing issues of the weekly prevent a closer account of its report of Brandeis's efforts. For critical comment on De Haas's account, see ch. 5, note 98, *infra*; the meeting of 1910 is not recorded in BD; quot., De Haas, *Brandeis*, pp. 51-52; *Jewish Advocate*, September 30, 1910, p. 2.

65. BD, October 4, 1910.

66. For Brandeis and midwestern Progressives, Mason, *Brandeis*, ch. 17; and see LDB to Norman Hapgood, April 21, 1908, *BL*, I, 130; LDB to Alfred Brandeis, May 3, 1908, ibid., 140; Norman Hapgood, *The Changing Years: Reminiscences of Norman Hapgood* (New York, 1930), p. 185; Elizabeth B. Raushenbush to Gal, August 21, 1973; LDB to Alfred Brandeis, October 5, 1909, *BL*, II, 289; LDB to N. Hapgood, March 31, 1908, BDN #16931; for LDB-Crane relations, corresp. in ibid. and ##17341, 18077, 19350, 21573 and *BL*, I, II, passim; La Follette and La Follette, *La Follette*, I, 265 and passim. For LDB and Amos and Gifford Pinchot, *BL*, II, 309-310 and passim; for important contacts between LDB and Theodore Roosevelt, see letters and ed. annotations in ibid., I, 502-520, II, 68, 99, 124, 168, 186, 355. For Roosevelt's maneuvers, George E. Mowry, *Theodore Roosevelt and the Progressive Movement* (New York, 1946), chs. 4, 5; La Follette and La Follette, *La Follette*, I, 301-304. For Brandeis and Roosevelt, LDB to Mark Sullivan, June 4, 1910, *BL*, II, 341-342; LDB to Gifford Pinchot, June 18, and LDB to Alfred Brandeis, June 22, 25, 1910, ibid., 355-359; LDB to R. Collier, June 30, 1910, ibid., 363; LDB to Alfred Brandeis, August 21, 1910, ibid., 370; LDB to Judson Welliver, September 23, 1910, ibid., 376.

67. *New York Times*, September 29, 1910, p. 10; ibid., p. 5; Mowry, *Roosevelt*, p. 150; *New York Times*, September 30, 1910, p. 1; see also Robert M. La Follette, *La Follette's Autobiography* (Madison, Wisc., 1960), pp. 210-211. For midwestern Progressives' course, La Follette and La Follette, *La Follette*, I, ch. 28; Mowry, *Roosevelt*, pp. 171-174.

68. For Brandeis's attitude, LDB to Alfred Brandeis, April 13, 1910, *BL*, II, 329; quot., LDB to Norman Hapgood, October 2, 1912, ibid., 695; La Follette and La Follette, *La Follette*, I, 308; Mason, *Brandeis*, p. 368; LDB to Gifford Pinchot, February 27, 1911, *BL*, II, 413. BD, October 15, 1910, and subsequent entries; La Follette and La Follette, *La Follette*, I, 265, 308, 341, and passim; Ernest Poole, "Brandeis," *American Magazine*, 71 (February 1911), 481.

69. *Jewish Advocate*, June 3, 1910, p. 8; ibid., September 2, 1910, p. 8.

70. Criticism of J. P. Morgan, ibid., September 30, 1910, pp. 1, 4 and October 28, 1910, p. 4; criticism of Lodge, November 11, 1910, p. 8.

71. Ibid., November 18, 1910, p. 4; ibid., November 11, 1910, pp. 1, 4; Lodge was endorsed by Roosevelt, Mowry, *Roosevelt*, pp. 148, 152.

72. The publication of the interview with LDB in the *American Hebrew* and the *Jewish Advocate* was mentioned in BD on December 7, 1910, "Lr. from De Haas," December 10, 1910, "Lr. to Jewish Advocate," and December 12, 1910, "Lr. to Amer. Hebrew"; there is no record of these letters in

BDN. See notes 73, 78, *infra*; quot., note 65, *supra*.

73. Attacks on Roosevelt, *Jewish Advocate*, November 11, 1910, p. 1; ibid., December 16, 1910, p. 1. L. H. Semonoff, who had interviewed Brandeis for the *Jewish Advocate*, became a leader of the Menorah Society at Yale University. See ch. 5, note 49, *infra*; cf. De Haas, *Brandeis*, p. 151; quots., *American Hebrew*, 88, no. 5 (December 2, 1910), 135.

74. Ibid.

75. Ibid.

76. *Jewish Advocate*, December 2, 1910, p. 8; *American Hebrew*, 88, no. 5 (December 2, 1910), p. 135.

77. Mason, *Brandeis*, ch. 20; Albro Martin, *Enterprise Denied: Origins of the Decline of the American Railroads, 1897-1917* (New York, 1971), chs. 7, 8; *Boston Transcript*, November 12, 1910; *New England Shoe and Leather Industry*, 9, no. 1 (January 1911), 15; "Speech of William Sulzer in the House of Representatives," June 29, 1906, in BDN #19618.

78. *Jewish Advocate*, December 9, 1910, pp. 1, 8.

79. Ibid.

80. Ibid.; and see Jehoshua M. Grintz, "Daniel," *Hebrew Encyclopedia* [in Hebrew] (Jerusalem, 1959), XII, 867-874.

81. Notes 73, 78, *supra*; for the eliminated sections see "What Loyalty Demands," typescript in LU, NMF 12-6, pp. 1, 5.

82. *Jewish Advocate*, December 9, 1910, p. 8. The features of Brandeis's attitude, detailed above, perhaps account for the fact that the whole paragraph of his 1905 address censuring hyphenated-Americanism remained intact.

5. The New Zion

1. Quots., LDB to George Wigglesworth, February 11, 1907, BDN #16123; LDB to Jocelyn P. Yoder, February 26, 1912, *BL*, II, 563; LDB to Ray S. Baker, February 26, 1912, ibid., 563.

2. Alpheus T. Mason, *Brandeis: A Free Man's Life* (New York, 1946), pp. 301-304; LDB to Paul U. Kellogg, January 24, 1911, and P. U. Kellogg to LDB, February 1, 1911, BDN #18930; LDB to Meyer Bloomfield, March 11, 1911, BDN #19223; Henry Moskowitz to LDB, January 6, 1911, BDN #18930; BD, September 16, 1911 — end of January 1912; LDB to H. Moskowitz, September 29, 1911, *BL*, II, 502; LDB to Roy Painter, March 31, 1913, ibid., III, 55.

3. Mason, *Brandeis*, pp. 248-251; see corresp. of LDB and Josephine Goldmark on *Muller* v. *Oregon* from November 14, 1907, to June 3, 1913. BDN #16712.

4. Josephine Goldmark to LDB, December 11, 1907, BDN #16712. Maurice Wertheim to LDB, November 3, 1911, and LDB to M. Wertheim, November 7, 1911, LU, NMF 41-1; Brandeis's statement quoted in Stephen S. Wise to LDB, December 15, 1911, LU, NMF 43-44; LDB to William H. Taft, December 30, 1911, *BL*, II, 531 and ed. annotations.

5. Stephen S. Wise to LDB, September 25, 1912; LDB to S. S. Wise, September 28, 1912; S. S. Wise to LDB, September 30, 1912; — in BDN #20111.

6. Abraham Flexner to LDB, February 25, 1908; LDB to A. Flexner, February 26, 1908; A. Flexner to LDB, February 28, 1908; — in BDN #16712; A. Flexner to LDB, December 24, 1912; LDB to A. Flexner, December 26, 1912; — in BDN #20204; Abraham Flexner, *An Autobiography* (New York, 1960), pp. 244, 278-279.

7. Bernard Flexner to LDB, February 14, 1908, and LDB to B. Flexner, February 17, 1908; B. Flexner to LDB, December 13, 1909, and LDB to B. Flexner, December 16, 1909; B. Flexner to LDB, February 24, 1911, and LDB to B. Flexner, February 27, 1911; — in BDN ##16712, 18206, and 19223.

8. Bernard Flexner to LDB, February 12, 1912, and LDB to B. Flexner, February 15, 1912, LU, NMF 40-10.

9. For the beginning of Ernst Freund-Brandeis cooperation, Clarence Goodwin to LDB, October 13, 1909; Josephine Goldmark to LDB, October 13, 1909, and later corresp.; LDB to E. Freund, November 8, 1909; LDB to E. Freund, December 1, 1909; corresp. between LDB and E. Freund from November 8, 1909 to February 7, 1910; — in BDN #18206; for December 1911-June 1912 see BDN #22408; E. Freund to LDB, October 27, 1913, Mason, *Brandeis*, p. 337. See also Oscar Kraines, *The World and Ideas of Ernst Freund* . . . (University, Ala., 1974), pp. 5, 52.

10. Ernst Freund to LDB, December 4, 1909; quot., LDB to Levy Mayer, December 9, 1909; L. Mayer to LDB, December 11, 15, 1909; LDB to L. Mayer, December 18, 1909; — in BDN #18206; for Chicago's Jewish community, Edward H. Mazur, "Minyans for a Prairie City: The Politics of Chicago Jewry, 1850-1940" Phd. diss. (University of Chicago, 1974), chs. 3-5.

11. For the Rosenthals, Harry Barnard, *The Forging of an American Jew: The Life and Times of Judge Julian W. Mack* (New York, 1974), chs. 6-8, p. 57, and passim; LDB and Lessing Rosenthal, LDB to Josephine Goldmark, December 30, 1909, BDN #18206; first acquaintance of LDB and J. Mack, Barnard, *Mack*, p. 25; later connection: J. Mack to LDB, January 13, 1894, BDN #4266; J. Mack to LDB, September 6, 1901; LDB to J. Mack, September 10, 1901; J. Mack to LDB, September 12, 1901; — in BDN #11606; see also LDB to Felix Frankfurter, April 9, 1912, *BL*, II, 577.

12. LDB to Felix Frankfurter, March 14, 1910, BDN #18206; Liva Baker, *Felix Frankfurter* (New York, 1969), p. 17; H. B. Phillips, ed., *Felix Frankfurter Reminisces: Recorded in Talks with Harlan B. Phillips* (New York, 1960), ch. 5; on F. Frankfurter as LDB's follower, see ibid., ch. 11; quot., F. Frankfurter to LDB, March 15, 1910, BDN #18206.

13. Quot., LDB to Felix Frankfurter, June 14, 1910, *BL*, II, 350; quot., F. Frankfurter to LDB, February 25, 1911; LDB to F. Frankfurter, February 27, 1911; F. Frankfurter to LDB, March 2, 1911; — in BDN #19223; F.

Frankfurter to LDB, November 21, 1911, LU, NMF 43-4; quot., F. Frankfurter to LDB, April 5, 1912; LDB to F. Frankfurter, April 9, 1912; F. Frankfurter to LDB, April 12, 1912; — in BDN #19844; corresp. of August-September 1912, LU, NMF 50-3; Phillips, *Frankfurter*, ch. 6; LDB to F. Frankfurter, January 28, 1913; F. Frankfurter to LDB, January 30, 1913; — in LU, NMF 53-2.

14. Ohio case, Josephine Goldmark to LDB, December 2, 1908, and LDB to J. Goldmark, December 3, 1908, BDN #16712; secretary of Ohio Fed. of Labor to LDB, July 20, 1911, and LDB's reply, July 21, 1911; more corresp. and documents in BDN #20252. For Illinois case, see J. Goldmark to LDB, July 13, 1909, and LDB to J. Goldmark, July 16, 1909; more corresp. in BDN #18206; corresp. for December 1911-June 1912 in BDN #22408. For California case, G. S. Arnold to LDB, January 9, 1911; J. Goldmark to LDB, June 14, 1912; LDB to J. Goldmark, July 2, 1912; — in BDN #22625. Corresp. between J. Goldmark and LDB beginning in December 1910 regarding general trends and many small cases in BDN #22624.

15. Mary Fels, *Joseph Fels: His Life-Work* (New York, 1916); Alfred Lief, *Brandeis: The Personal History of an American Ideal* (1936; Freeport, N.Y., 1964), p. 300; Daniel Kiefer to LDB, October 19, 1912, LU, NMF 53-2; Mason, *Brandeis*, p. 420.

16. For Brandeis and the *Survey*, Clarke A. Chambers, *Paul U. Kellogg and the Survey* (Minneapolis, 1971), chs. 2-4; Alpheus T. Mason, *The Brandeis Way: A Case Study in the Workings of Democracy* (Princeton, N.J., 1938), pp. 249-250; *BL*, II, 267-272 and passim; LDB to Arthur P. Kellogg, November 7, 1912, BDN #20256; "Will of Louis D. Brandeis," BDN #59815. For Jews named and the *Survey*, Chambers, *Kellogg* and notes 2-15, *supra*.

17. LDB to David F. Tilley, February 5, 1909, *BL*, II, 218; *Boston Advocate*, February 26, 1909, p. 8; LDB to Henry C. Metcalf, July 29, 1909, *BL*, II, 284; quot., LDB to Alice G. Brandeis, December 30, 1913, ibid., III, 228.

18. See letters, circulars, and documents in LU, NMF 21-2; for LDB's enrollment, Alice H. Grady to Adna F. Weber, October 19, 1907; for LDB's election to vice presidency and to the Committee on Woman's Work, John B. Andrews to LDB, January 11, 1910; — in ibid.

19. See sources in notes 6-15, *supra*; for LDB's interview, *American Hebrew*, 88, no. 5 (December 2, 1910), 135.

20. Yonathan Shapiro, *Leadership of the American Zionist Organization, 1897-1930* (Urbana, Ill., 1971), pp. 53-54, 105.

21. Quot., Horace M. Kallen, "Democracy *Versus* the Melting-Pot" (*Nation*, February 18, 25, 1915), in his *Culture and Democracy in the United States* (New York, 1924), p. 116; cf. an historical sketch by Milton M. Gordon, *Assimilation in American Life: The Role of Race, Religion and National Origins* (New York, 1964), pp. 137-144. John Higham, *Strangers in the Land: Patterns of American Nativism, 1860-1925* (New York, 1971), pp. 121, 236; quot., Robert A. Woods, "University Settlements: Their Point and

Drift" (address given in 1899), in his *The Neighborhood in Nation-Building* (Boston, 1923), pp. 57-59; Robert A. Woods, "Assimilation: A Two-Edged Sword," in Woods, ed., *Americans in Process: North and West Ends* (Boston, 1902), pp. 356-383; quot., pp. 382-383.

22. Quots., Robert A. Woods, "Social Work: A New Profession" (address given in 1905) and "The Neighborhood in Social Reconstruction" (address given in 1909), in his *Neighborhood*, pp. 93-94, 158-159.

23. Forward and preface by Sam B. Warner, Jr., to Robert Woods and Albert Kennedy, *The Zone of Emergence: Observations of the Lower Middle and Upper Working Class Communities of Boston, 1905-1914* (Boston, 1969), iv, 14-15; quots., 198. See also Robert Woods and Albert Kennedy, *The Settlement Horizon* (New York, 1922), p. 328.

24. Eleanor H. Woods, *Robert A. Woods: Champion of Democracy* (Boston, 1929), ch. 15; *BL*, I, 210 and passim; Claude M. Fuess, *Joseph B. Eastman: Servant of the People* (New York, 1952), introduction and ch. 4; E. H. Woods, *Woods*, ch. 26.

25. *Annual Report of Denison House, The College Settlement*, 1904-05, 1910-12; LDB to Cornelia L. Warren, August 29, 1911, *BL*, II, 482; Vida D. Scudder, *On Journey* (New York, 1937), p. 150; Vida D. Scudder, *A Listener in Babel* (Boston, 1903), ch. 4; Scudder, *On Journey*, ch. 9; ibid., p. 262; see also pp. 266-267.

26. Alpheus T. Mason to Gal, August 16, 1974; Mason, *Brandeis*, pp. 42-43, 63, 117; quots., N[athaniel] S. Shaler, *Nature and Man in America* (New York, 1891), p. 229 and Mason, *Brandeis*, p. 43.

27. William James, *The Philosophy of William James, Selected from his Chief Works*, with an introduction by Horace M. Kallen (New York, 1953), pp. 242-254, 334-358; ibid., p. 310.

28. Sarah L. Schmidt, "Horace M. Kallen and the Americanization of Zionism," Ph.D. diss. (University of Maryland, 1973), ch. 2; quot., p. 36.

29. Ibid., p. 48; [Henry Hurwitz and I. Leo Sharfman], *The Menorah Movement, for the Study and Advancement of Jewish Culture and Ideals* (Ann Arbor, Mich., 1914), pp. 1-9.

30. Quots., ibid., pp. 103, 99, 12, 13-14. Both Hurwitz and Sharfman were among the founders of the Harvard Menorah Society, addressed its public dedication exercises, and served as presidents in the 1907-10 period.

31. Quots., ibid., pp. 13-14.

32. Horace M. Kallen in interview with Sarah L. Schmidt, July 1972, attached to Schmidt thesis on Kallen, on deposit in the Dept. of Near Eastern and Judaic Studies, Brandeis University, p. 3; *Jewish Advocate*, May 13, 1910, p. 1.

33. Schmidt, "Kallen," p. 48; ibid., pp. 46-47; quots., Horace M. Kallen, "The Ethics of Zionism," *The Maccabaen*, 11, no. 2 (August 1906), 61-62.

34. Horace M. Kallen interview with Sarah L. Schmidt, pp. 3-4.

35. LDB to Charles W. Eliot, May 14, 1908; J. Warren (Eliot's secretary)

to LDB, May 16, 1908; — Eliot MSS, Harvard University Archives, Cambridge, Mass.; Charles Birtwell to LDB, January 29, 1912, and LDB's assistant secretary to C. Birtwell, February 8, 1912, LU, NMF 40-10; Hugh Hawkins, *Between Harvard and America: The Educational Leadership of Charles W. Eliot* (New York, 1972), ch. 5, esp. pp. 148-152; quots., Norman Hapgood, *The Changing Years: Reminiscences of Norman Hapgood* (New York, 1930), pp. 49-50 and C. W. Eliot to Charles A. Culberson, May 17, 1916, Eliot MSS.

36. Hawkins, *Eliot*, pp. 180-193; Eliot's address, *Boston Advocate*, December 1, 1905, and in full in *PAJHS*, no. 14 (1906), 78-83; quots., 79, 83.

37. [Hurwitz and Sharfman], *Menorah*, pp. 2, 6-8; quots., pp. 30, 31; see also pp. 28-29.

38. Hawkins, *Eliot*, p. 183; quots., *Jewish Advocate*, March 12, 1909, p. 8; Hawkins, *Eliot*, pp. 183-184; Barbara M. Solomon, *Ancestors and Immigrants: A Changing New England Tradition* (Chicago, 1956), p. 183.

39. Hapgood, *Changing Years*, chs. 5, 6, and passim; for Norman Hapgood with the *Commercial Advertiser*, ibid., ch. 10, esp. p. 127; Gordon, *Assimilation in American Life*, p. 140; discussion based on Moses Rischin's introduction to Hutchins Hapgood, *The Spirit of the Ghetto*, ed. of John Harvard Library (Cambridge, Mass., 1967); quots., pp. ix, xxii.

40. Herbert B. Ehrmann to LDB, April 15, 1910; LDB to H. B. Ehrmann, April 18, 1910; — in BDN #18650. Herbert B. Ehrmann, "Felix," in Wallace Mendelson, ed., *Felix Frankfurter: A Tribute* (New York, 1964), p. 90; BD, March 10, 13, April 21, 1911; quots., Ehrmann, "Felix," pp. 80, 90.

41. Ehrmann, "Felix," p. 90.

42. Alexander Johnson, ed., *Proceedings of the National Conference of Charities and Correction at the Thirty-Eighth Annual Session, Held in Boston, Mass., June 7-14, 1911* (1911), pp. 156, 488-489.

43. Quots., LDB's address [n.d.] 3 pp. typescript in Harvard Menorah Society File, Harvard University Archives, pp. 1, 2; date — May 8, 1911 — is determined according to BD, May 8, 1911, and *American Hebrew*, May 12, 1911, p. 46.

44. Ehrmann, "Felix," pp. 90-91; interview with Harry Wolfson; H. Wolfson, "The Spirit of Hebraism," in George Kohut, ed., *The Standard Book of Jewish Verse* (New York, 1917), p. 538.

45. Interview with Harry Wolfson.

46. BD, May 9, 1911; quots., Barnard, *Mack*, p. 179 and Johnson, *Proceedings of the National Conference*, p. 489.

47. Johnson, *Proceedings of the National Conference*, p. 162; H. L. Sabsovich to LDB, August 16, 1911, and LDB to H. L. Sabsovich, September 2, 1911, BDN #19363; corresp. of David M. Bressler and LDB in the period August 11-November 2, 1911, LU, NMF 41-4; *Jewish Advocate*, June 9, 1911, p. 8; another editorial June 16, 1911, p. 8; Herman D. Stein, "Jew-

ish Social Work in the United States (1654-1954)," *AJYB*, 57 (1956), esp. 51-56.

48. Alex Kanter to LDB, February 27, 1912, and LDB to A. Kanter, March 8, 1912, LU, NMF 40-10; A. Kanter to LDB, December 31, 1912, and LDB to A. Kanter, December 31, 1912, BDN #20256.

49. Aaron Horvitz to LDB, December 24, 1912, and LDB to A. Horvitz, December 31, 1912; Henry Hurwitz to LDB, March 10, 1913, and LDB to H. Hurwitz, March 12, 1913, BDN #18650. L. H. Semonoff to LDB, March 29, 1913, and LDB to L. H. Semonoff, March 31, 1913, BDN #29814.

50. Circular of April 25, 1913, and LDB to Harvard Menorah Society, May 24, 1913; communication of May 23, 1913 (Intercollegiate Menorah Association), and LDB to I. Lehman, May 24, 1913; — in BDN #20814; for Mack see also Barnard, *Mack*, ch. 13 and esp. ch. 14.

51. Quots., *Menorah Journal* (New York), 1, no. 1 (January 1915), 13; for Kallen, Sarah Schmidt, "The Zionist Conversion of Louis D. Brandeis," *Jewish Social Studies*, 37, no. 1 (January 1975), 26-27.

52. Bernard Richards to LDB, February 1, 1911, LU, NMF 41-2; LDB to B. Richards, February 2, 1911, *BL*, II, 402.

53. "The Growth of Zionism in Boston," *The Maccabaean*, 2, no. 5 (May 1902), 241-243; Avyatar Friesel, *The Zionist Movement in the United States, 1897-1914* [in Hebrew], ([Tel-Aviv], Israel, 1970), p. 40.

54. Isadore Kronstein to LDB, June 22, 1911, and LDB to I. Kronstein, June 23, 1911, BDN #19152.

55. Israel Friedlander to Judah Magnes, June 22, 1911, Magnes MSS, Hebrew University Archives, Jerusalem, P3-870; I am indebted to Prof. Arthur A. Goren (Hebrew University, Jerusalem) for this letter.

56. Arthur A. Goren, *New York Jews and the Quest for Community: The Kehilla Experiment, 1908-1922* (New York, 1970), chs. 3, 4, and passim; Friesel, *Zionist Movement*, pp. 143-157; Melvin I. Urofsky, *American Zionism from Herzl to the Holocaust* (New York, 1975), pp. 117, 118; Bernard G. Richards, "First Steps in Zionism," in *Herzl Year Book* (New York, 1963), V, 351-380.

57. Richards, "First Steps in Zionism," pp. 361-380; Friesel, *Zionist Movement*, pp. 143-144; Naomi W. Cohen, *Not Free to Desist: The American Jewish Committee, 1906-1966* (Philadelphia, 1972), chs. 1, 2.

58. LDB to Adolph Brandeis, July 13, 14, 15, 1905, *BL*, I, 336, 337, 338; Cyrus Adler, *Jacob H. Schiff: His Life and Letters*, 2 vols. (New York, 1929), I, 131-144 and passim; Stephen Birmingham, *"Our Crowd": The Great Jewish Families of New York* (New York, 1967), ch. 21 and passim; LDB's criticism of the Union Pacific, "The New England Transportation Monopoly" (address given in 1908), in his *Business—A Profession* (1914; Boston, 1933), pp. 280-281. Mason, *Brandeis*, pp. 254-282; LDB to Robert La Follette, July 29, 1911, *BL*, II, 467-472. LDB to Norman Hapgood, September 7, 1911, ibid., 487; Birmingham, *"Our Crowd,"* p. 8 and throughout

the book; LDB to Alfred Brandeis, July 28, 1904, *BL*, I, 262; LDB to Adolph Brandeis, November 29, 1905, ibid., 386. Lawrence H. Fuchs, *The Political Behavior of American Jews* (Glencoe, Ill., 1956), pp. 52-55, 57-58; Arthur S. Link, *Wilson: The Road to the White House* (Princeton, N.J., 1947), pp. 201, 338, 479, 485.

59. Bernard Richards to LDB, April 21, 1912, LU, NMF 40-10; LDB to B. Richards, April 26, 1912, *BL*, II, 611; B. Richards to LDB, May 1, 1912; Louis Lipsky to LDB, May 13, 1912; — in LU, NMF 40-10. For meeting with Rosenblatt see note 62, *infra*.

60. Quot., LDB to A. Lincoln Filene, June 1911, *BL*, II, 444.

61. BD, May 3, 1912; LDB to Bernard A. Rosenblatt, May 3, 1912, *BL*, II, 614; Bernard A. Rosenblatt, *Two Generations of Zionism: Historical Recollections of an American Zionist* (New York, 1967), p. 55.

62. After May 3, the first time LDB was in New York was on May 14; he left Boston at noon after reading Lipsky's letter: see BD; the corresp. between the two was resumed on June 17, 1912. Quot., Rosenblatt, *Two Generations of Zionism*, p. 55.

63. *Jewish Advocate*, May 17, 1912, p. 2; ibid., July 5, 1912, p. 1. According to Jacob De Haas "His [LDB's] affiliation with the Zionist Organization was reported at the Cleveland convention of 1912 but the announcement created no great stir": see his *Louis D. Brandeis: A Biographical Sketch* . . . (New York, 1929), p. 54. By minimizing the importance of the event, De Haas exaggerated his own later role in the Zionization of Brandeis. He was also interested in minimizing the part of Richards with whom he was at political odds when he wrote this book.

64. *Jewish Advocate*, August 5, 1910; Francis Russell, "The Coming of the Jews," *Antioch Review* (Ohio), 15, no. 1 (March, 1955), 28.

65. Russell, "The Coming of the Jews," 31; N[athaniel] S. Shaler, *The Neighbor: The Natural History of Human Contacts* (Boston, 1904), pp. 113, 114; see also *Jewish Advocate*, July 26, 1912, p. 1.

66. *Boston Traveler*, January 20, December 1, 1911; papers filed in the case of Blanche M. Powers [Welch's adopted daughter], p.p.a. (As Amended) v. Joseph L. Bergman, Suffolk County, Mass. Superior Court, 210, Mass. 346 (1911).

67. Note 66, *supra*; *Jewish Advocate*, May 17, 1912, p. 8.

68. Lincoln Steffens, *The Autobiography of Lincoln Steffens*, 2 vols. (1931; New York, 1958), II, 599; documents in LU, NMF 16-3.

69. On Kernwood Country Club, Adolph Ehrlich to Louis E. Kirstein, November 28, 1914, Kirstein MSS, Harvard Business School Archives, Cambridge, Mass.; *Boston American*, August 29, 1915, sec. 3, p. 3.

70. George Santayana, *The Last Puritan: A Memoir, in the Form of a Novel* (New York, 1936), ch. 6; quots., pp. 433-434.

71. Allan Forbes, *Sport in Norfolk County* (Boston, 1938), ch. 21, esp. pp. 118-119; *Dedham Transcript*, March 5, 1910, p. 3. Joshua Crane to

LDB, March 11, 1910; LDB to J. Crane, March 14, 1910; Herbert Maynard to LDB, March 15, 1910; Alice H. Grady to H. Maynard, March 17, 1910; — in BDN #18015; H. Maynard to LDB, May 3, 1910; communications of the Norfolk Country Club and the Dedham Country and Polo Club, April-September 1910; H. Maynard to LDB, September 12, 1910; — BDN #18650; LDB to secretary of Dedham Country and Polo Club (letter of resignation), November 9, 1911, and secretary to LDB, February 1, 1912, BDN ##19363, 19844.

72. Note 71, *supra*; Dedham Country and Polo Club Scrapbook, Dedham Historical Society, Dedham, Mass. In a way, Brandeis's social position in Dedham paralleled the one in Boston. In the city he was excluded from the Somerset Club (and the Country Club of Brookline) and now he was outside of "the Somerset" of Dedham and Westwood; see ch. 2, note 31, *supra*. The Boston *Social Register* reveals that, indeed, most of Westwood's society people were members in the Somerset Club as well.

73. Marjory R. Fenerty, *West Dedham and Westwood: 300 Years* [Westwood, Mass., 1972], pp. 29-31; interviews with Lothrop Wakefield and Elliott Perkins. When years later the secretary of the Dedham Polo Club published a book recounting the history of sport (and therefore of society) in Norfolk County, Brandeis was perhaps unique among the old-timers in that he did not subscribe in advance to this nostalgic book, see Forbes, *Sport in Norfolk County*, pp. 267-274.

74. Mason, *Brandeis*, ch. 14; Judson C. Welliver, "Sidney W. Winslow, Czar of Footwear," *Hampton's Magazine*, September 1910, pp. 326-339; Edward F. McClennen's testimony in U.S. Congress, Senate, *Nomination of Louis D. Brandeis, Hearings before the Subcommittee of the Committee on the Judiciary* [Hereafter *Nomination*], 64th Cong., 2d sess., 1916, vol. I of 2, 702-705, 713-714.

75. Quots., LDB to Moses E. Clapp, February 24, 1912, *BL*, II, 557.

76. U.S. Congress, Senate, *Hearings Before the Committee on Interstate Commerce* [Hereafter *Hearings* (1912)], 62d Cong., 2d sess., 1912, vol. I of 3, 1189; LDB to Robert La Follette, May 5, 1911, *BL*, II, 429; *Hearings* (1912), I, 1188.

77. Quots., *BL*, II, 557-558; Charles H. Jones to Alice H. Grady (and an attached list of "Members of the Shoe Manufacturers Alliance"), September 28, 1911, BDN #20854; *New England Shoe and Leather Industry*, 10, no. 1 (January 1912) and 11, no. 1 (January 1913), 5-11, 7-14; quot., *Hearings* (1912), I, 1189; *The Weekly Bulletin* (Boston), 16, no. 23 (January 20, 1912), 1-2; documents in BDN #20854.

78. *Boston Transcript*, September 19, 1911.

79. *BL*, II, 435-721, passim; see esp. LDB to James B. Studley, January 22, 1912, ibid., 540-541.

80. LDB to Moses E. Clapp, February 24, 1912, ibid., 556-557, 558; *Hearings* (1912), I, 1160-1161; LDB to Judson C. Welliver, September 23,

1910, and to Robert M. La Follette, May 5, 1911, *BL*, II, 376, 428; quot., Welliver, "Winslow," p. 333.

81. Albro Martin, *Enterprise Denied: Origins of the Decline of American Railroads, 1897-1917* (New York, 1971), chs. 7, 8; and see also Samuel Haber, *Efficiency and Uplift: Science Management in the Progressive Era, 1890-1920* (Chicago, 1964), pp. 51-57 and ch. 5. Richard M. Abrams, "Introduction . . . Torchbook edition," in LDB, *Other People's Money and How the Bankers Use It* (1914; New York, 1967), pp. xxxvi-xxxvii; Melvin I. Urofsky, *A Mind of One Piece: Brandeis and American Reform* (New York, 1971), pp. 55-56. For the firm's clientele see discussions in chs. 1 and 2, *supra*. LDB's testimony, *Hearings* (1912), I, 1147; and see ibid., 1168, 1174.

82. *Hearings* (1912), I, 1155; U.S., Congress, House, *Hearings before the Committee on Investigation of United States Steel Corporation*, 62d Cong., 2d sess., 1912, vol. IV of 8, 2872; *BL*, II, 544-545.

83. BD, January 5-7, 1912.

84. LDB to Alfred Brandeis, January 7, 1912, *BL*, II, 537.

85. M. R. Werner, *Julius Rosenwald* (New York, 1939), pp. 98-99; Barnard, *Mack*, ch. 15 and passim; Eliezer Livneh, *Aaron Aaronsohn: His Life and Times* [in Hebrew] (Jerusalem, 1969), ch. 5, esp. pp. 134-135, 137.

86. For Mrs. Julius Rosenwald's account, Aaron Aaronsohn to Mack, October 9, 1916, Aaronsohn MSS, Aaronsohn House's Archives, Zikhron Ya'aquov, Israel, Aaron division, 29/2 (letter has been published in Yoram Ephrati, ed., *Aaron Aaronsohn's Diary (1916-1919)* [in Hebrew], Tel-Aviv, 1970, pp. 101-113); Mrs. Rosenwald's account is again mentioned — and more emphatically — in A. Aaronsohn to Felix Frankfurter, March 25, 1917, Aaronsohn MSS, Aaron division, 15/1. Hapgood, *Changing Years*, 197-199. According to p. 197, and to Lief, *Brandeis*, p. 278, Brandeis first heard of the wild-wheat discovery from Aaronsohn himself. This could not in fact have happened, as Aaronsohn had first visited America from June 1909 to April 1910, when he did not meet Brandeis. Aaronsohn's second visit to America began in October, 1912, some months after Brandeis had heard the talk on the wild-wheat discovery. See Livneh, *Aaronsohn*, ch. 5 and p. 154.

87. Aaron Aaronsohn to LDB, April 19, 1913, and LDB to Aaronsohn, April 21 and May 1, 1913, BDN #20814. Lief, *Brandeis*, p. 278.

88. Quots., *Jewish Advocate*, May 23, 1913, p. 1; Brandeis's letter to his brother, note 84, *supra*.

89. See Welliver, "Winslow," p. 333; Hapgood, *Changing Years*, pp. 197-199.

90. Quots., LDB, "The Rebirth of the Jewish Nation" (address given September 27, 1914), in Harris, "Zionist Speeches," p. 103 and LDB "[The Jewish Future Can be as Secure as the Jewish Past]" (address given November 1914), ibid., p. 158; ibid., p. 164; *Boston American*, July 4, 1915; in the interview LDB very illustratively equated the Pilgrims' striving with Zionism.

91. For Mitchell, *Boston Transcript*, April 1, 1929, p. 12; Mitchell and Brandeis cooperated also in the labor issue, BD, January 19-March 15, 1912; cf. LDB to Marlen E. Pew, March 13, 1912, *BL*, II, 568. For the bank, interview with Sidney Rabb; BD, September 19, 1911, and subsequently; LDB's financial statements in BDN #21472 and Nancy Laurence to LDB, August 20, 1912, BDN #20813; *Jewish Advocate*, April 5, 1912, pp. 2, 8. BD, esp. April 4, 5, 10, 26, and May 11, 1912; *Jewish Advocate*, May 31, 1912, p. 4.

92. One of the late expressions of Brandeis's earlier keen interest in Germany's social achievements is in a letter to Pierre Jay, January 4, 1909, *BL*, II, 215. Though he did not lose interest in Germany even after 1912, it seems that it was balanced by his growing interest in Britain and later in other countries, notably Denmark; for Denmark, ch. 1, note 65, *supra*.

93. Communication inviting LDB to a directors' meeting on December 27, 1906 in BDN #16123; invitation for the new Germanic Museum's occasion on June 8, 1912, and LDB's answer of May 14, 1912, in BDN #19844.

94. LDB to Robert La Follette, July 3, 1912, *BL*, II, 638; *Jewish Advocate*, July 12, 1912, p. 8; quot., October 4, 1912, p. 8; see also ibid., November 1, 1912, p. 8.

95. Fuchs, *Political Behavior*, pp. 57-62; *Jewish Advocate*, November 1, 1912, p. 8; ibid., November 8, 1912, p. 8; Link, *Wilson: the Road to the White House*, pp. 403, 422, 481.

96. LDB to Alfred Brandeis, October 25, 1912, LU, M-3.

97. LDB to Martha Silverman, November 12, 1912, BDN #20256; interview with Jacob Cohen.

98. De Haas in his *Brandeis*, pp. 51-53, merges his three meetings with Brandeis into the one that took place in "the early fall of 1910." This version is refuted by Brandeis's recollection as told by Mason, *Brandeis*, pp. 443, by BD, and by much indirect evidence. See also ch. 4, notes 17, 18, 64, *supra*. See note 38, *supra*; cf. Leo Shubow, "Jacob De Haas: Pioneer Editor and Zionist Trailblazer," paper presented at American Jewish Historical Society, April 22, 1963.

99. Quots., Ruth L. Deech, "Jacob De Haas: A Biography," in *Herzl Year Book* (New York, 1971), VII, 321 and *Jewish Advocate*, July 5, 1912, p. 8. The article, August 9, 1912, was in the series "In the Public Eye."

100. LDB to Eugene N. Foss, August 13, 1912, *BL*, II, 659; Mason, *Brandeis*, p. 443. *Jewish Advocate*, October 25, November 1, 1912, pp. 8, 6.

101. Quot., Link, *Wilson: The Road to the White House*, 338; for Elkus's letter see LDB to Eugene N. Foss, August 13, 1912, *BL*, II, 659.

102. For a critical comment on sources, see note 98, *supra*; De Haas, *Brandeis*, p. 52; Mason, *Brandeis*, p. 443.

103. De Haas, *Brandeis*, pp. 52-53; quots., ibid., p. 232 and front page; Mason, *Brandeis*, p. 443; Deech, "De Haas," pp. 322-327; Bernard Richards in *Jewish Advocate*, April 16, 1937, p. 9; quots., De Haas, *Brandeis*, p. 52 and LDB to Alfred Brandeis, August 14, 1912, *BL*, II, 660.

104. BD, March 13, 22, 1913; *New Century Club: A Brief History* (Boston, 1947), pp. 2-3; quots., De Haas, *Brandeis*, p. 54. See also Brandeis on Zionism in the Menorah address, this chapter and note 43, *supra*.

6. The Burden of His Jewishness

1. Quot., Arthur S. Link, *Wilson: The New Freedom* (Princeton, N.J., 1956), p. 11. Yonathan Shapiro, *Leadership of the American Zionist Organization, 1897-1936* (Urbana, Ill., 1971), p. 65; Henry Moskowitz to Norman Hapgood, February 11, 1913, quoted in Alpheus T. Mason, *Brandeis: A Free Man's Life* (New York, 1946), p. 388; Jacob Schiff to Max Mitchell, February 17, 1913, quoted in Shapiro, *American Zionist Organization*, p. 64; ibid., p. 64.

2. Mason, *Brandeis*, p. 385; LDB to Alfred Brandeis, March 2, 1913, *BL*, III, 37; for this conclusion and the following discussion, cf. Shapiro, *American Zionist Organization*, pp. 64-67. For Menorah see ch. 5, notes 48-50, *supra*. Bernard Richards to LDB, January 27, 1913, BDN #20204; LDB to B. Richards, January 28, 1913, *BL*, III, 22. For De Haas and FAZ see Shapiro, *American Zionist Organization*, p. 64.

3. For Max Mitchell, cf. Shapiro, *American Zionist Organization*, p. 64, and see BD, February 25, 1913 under heading "Insurgency." Quots., BD. Link, *Wilson: The New Freedom*, pp. 14-21; the cabinet list was published on March 4, Wilson's inauguration day, ibid., pp. 14-15.

4. Link, *Wilson: The New Freedom*, pp. 12-15; Woodrow Wilson to Cleveland H. Dodge, June 15, 1905; Wilson to Henry Lee Higginson, May 21, November 4, 1908, May 23, November 14, 1910; H. L. Higginson to Samuel Bowles, August 23, 1911; — in Henry Lee Higginson MSS, Harvard Business School Archives, Cambridge, Mass. Higginson's reluctant attitude toward Wilson is apparent not only from his relatively small contribution. On March 12, 1912, he gave five hundred dollars for Taft's campaign and on October 4, one thousand dollars to the Republican State Committee. See "Contributions," 1908-," Higginson MSS; Bliss Perry, *Life and Letters of Henry Lee Higginson* (Boston, 1921), pp. 432-433.

5. Arthur S. Link, *Wilson: The Road to the White House* (Princeton, N.J., 1947), p. 122. Higginson's editorial is quoted in *Boston News Bureau*, August 1, 1912, p. 6; Link, *Wilson: The New Freedom*, pp. 344, 472; Henry Lee Higginson to Woodrow Wilson, February 7, 27, 1913, Higginson MSS.

6. Henry Lee Higginson to Richard Olney, November 12, 1912, quoted in Link, *Wilson: The New Freedom*, p. 12; H. L. Higginson to Woodrow Wilson, October 11, 1912, February 27, 1913, in Higginson MSS.

7. For Higginson's influence in Doubleday Page and Co., see corresp. with F. N. Doubleday, years 1910-16, in Higginson MSS. Link, *Wilson: The Road to the White House*, pp. x, 313-318, and passim. See also Walter H. Page to Henry Lee Higginson, October 23, November 22, 1912, Higginson MSS.

8. Link, *Wilson: The Road to the White House*, pp. 336, 402-404, 485;

obit., *New York Times,* June 25, 1926, p. 1; *Boston News Bureau,* March 7, 1908, p. 5.

9. Cleveland H. Dodge to Henry Lee Higginson, October 23, November 22, 1912, Higginson MSS; James Kerney's *The Political Education of Woodrow Wilson* (New York, 1926) is a primary source for this topic, see ch. 19, esp. pp. 284-286; see also Link, *Wilson: The New Freedom,* p. 12 and Mason, *Brandeis,* p. 393. Cf. Irving Katz, "Henry Lee Higginson vs. Louis Dembitz Brandeis: A Collision between Tradition and Reform," *New England Quarterly,* 41 (March 1968), 67-78.

10. LDB to Alfred Brandeis, March 2, 1913, *BL,* III, 37; Barbara M. Solomon, *Ancestors and Immigrants: A Changing New England Tradition* (Chicago, 1956), pp. 123, 152-153, 173, 197; Joseph Lee to Henry Lee Higginson, March 9, 1909, November 29, 1910, February 27, 1912, January 1, 1913; H. L. Higginson to Franklin MacVeagh, January 2, 1913, and F. MacVeagh to H. L. Higginson, February 24, 1913; J. Lee to H. L. Higginson, March 12, 1913; — in Higginson MSS; Immigration Restriction League MSS at Houghton Library, Harvard University, Cambridge, Mass.

11. Quot., Solomon, *Ancestors and Immigrants,* p. 104; conclusions based on IRL MSS.

12. LDB to Prescott F. Hall, November 8, 1904, BDN #13258; Samuel D. Warren to LDB March 16, 1909, and LDB to S. D. Warren, March [17], 1909, BDN #17258; Paul Kellogg to LDB, February 1, 1911, and LDB to P. Kellogg, February 3, 1911, BDN #18930.

13. Houghton Mifflin Co. to LDB, April 1, 1912, and LDB to Houghton Mifflin Co., April 15, 1912, BDN #19844. Leon Sanders to LDB, March 26, 1913, LDB to L. Sanders, April 17, 1913, L. Sanders to LDB, April 25, 1913, and L. Sanders to LDB, May 21, 1913, BDN #20814.

14. Richard M. Abrams, *Conservatism in a Progressive Era: Massachusetts Politics, 1900-1912* (Cambridge, Mass., 1964), p. 143.

15. *Jewish Advocate,* January 7, 1910, p. 8, January 14, 1910, p. 8.

16. *Boston Herald,* February 12, 1916, p. 1; the list included Julian Codman, a leading liberal Democrat who had served as secretary and treasurer of Mass. Reform Club; also signing was Charles Francis Adams (1866-1954), treasurer of Harvard Corporation, whose name had appeared beside Brandeis's in the State's Gold Democrats manifesto, *Boston Herald,* August 1, 1896, pp. 1-2. For background, A. L. Todd, *Justice on Trial: The Case of Louis D. Brandeis* (Chicago, 1964), chs. 4, 5. For the role of Henry Lee Higginson and USM, ibid., pp. 89-95 and Albert Boyden, *Ropes-Gray, 1865-1940* (Boston, 1942), 110 and passim.

17. Solomon, *Ancestors and Immigrants,* pp. 204-205; Link, *Wilson: The New Freedom,* pp. 12-13; LDB to Mary P. Morgan, February 7, 1913, quoted in Mason, *Brandeis,* p. 391.

18. LDB to Norman Hapgood, July 9, 1913, *BL,* III, 129; Alex Kanter to LDB, December 22, 1912, and LDB to A. Kanter, December 31, 1912, BDN #20256; Aaron Horvitz to LDB, December 24, 1912, and LDB to A.

Horvitz, December 31, 1912, BDN #20204.

19. For the growth of nativism in America, 1910 to 1912, John Higham, *Strangers in the Land: Patterns of American Nativism, 1860-1925* (New York, 1971), pp. 176-178; in Massachusetts, Solomon, *Ancestors and Immigrants*, pp. 199-200. *New England Shoe and Leather Industry*, vols. of 1912-13; NACM, *Transactions of . . .* , 1912-13; quots., no. 94 (April 1913), p. 118; contributions to IRL in 1913, IRL MSS.

20. On the fading of the old stereotype, Solomon, *Ancestors and Immigrants*, pp. 167-174; conclusions as to the new stereotype of Jew as radical are mine; George Santayana, *The Last Puritan: A Memoir, in the Form of a Novel* (New York, 1936), pp. 424-425.

21. For USM's use of newspapers, *Boston American*, February 2, 3, 1912; Judson C. Welliver, "Sidney W. Winslow, Czar of Footwear," *Hampton's Magazine*, September 1910, pp. 326-339. On Brandeis's engagement in Washington, LDB to Alfred Brandeis, July 28, 1912, *BL*, II, 653; entries in BD, July 27, 28, 1912. *Washington Post*, July 26, 1912.

22. Clippings of *Washington Post* article in Brandeis's scrapbook, LU; LDB to Alfred Brandeis and to Robert La Follette, July 9, 1913, *BL*, III, 127-128, 129; all issues of *Truth* (Boston) are in Widener Library, Harvard University, Cambridge, Mass. LDB to R. La Follette, May 5, 1911, *BL*, II, 431; Benjamin A. Spence, "The National Career of John W. Weeks," Ph.D. diss. (University of Wisconsin, 1972), pp. 72-73, 167-189, 225-227; for USM's advertisement, *Truth*, 3, no. 12 (January 31, 1914) and following issues.

23. Henry L. Staples and Alpheus T. Mason, *The Fall of a Railroad Empire: Brandeis and the New Haven Merger Battle* (Syracuse, N.Y., 1947), ch. 8; quot., p. 98; *Boston Journal*, September 24, 1913, pp. 1, 3.

24. Obit. in the *New York Times*, November 18, 1927, p. 23; Staples and Mason, *Fall of a Railroad Empire*.

25. Donna Merwick, *Boston Priests, 1848-1910: A Study of Social and Intellectual Change* (Cambridge, Mass., 1973), p. 185.

26. Interview with Frank Buxton.

27. *Truth*, 1, no. 1 (November 16, 1912), 2, 3; quot., 3.

28. *Truth*, 1, no. 2 (November 23, 1912), 1, 10, 11; 1, no. 4 (December 7, 1912), 11; quot. about Brandeis and Untermyer, 1, no. 6 (December 21, 1912), 11.

29. Quots. from articles on LDB, ibid., 1, no. 4 (December 7, 1912), 8, and 1, no. 5 (December 14, 1912), 4-5; 1, no. 7 (December 28, 1912), 2, 6-7, 8.

30. Ibid., 1, no. 18 (March 15, 1913), 4, 8-9.

31. Notes 26, 27, *supra*; last issue of *Truth* appeared on November 19, 1914. Alpheus T. Mason to Gal, February 21, 1974.

32. *Jewish Advocate*, April 4, 1913, pp. 1, 8; Bernard A. Rosenblatt, *Two Generations of Zionism: Historical Recollections of an American Zionist* (New York, 1967), p. 56; *Jewish Advocate*, April 4, 1913, p. 8.

33. *Jewish Advocate*, April 4, 1913, p. 8.

34. Ibid., May 23, 1913, p. 1.

35. LDB to Alfred Brandeis, March 10, 1913, *BL*, III, 42; Link, *Wilson: The New Freedom*, p. 95.

36. Staples and Mason, *Fall of a Railroad Empire*, chs. 8-10; *New England Shoe and Leather Industry*, 10, no. 3 (March 1912), 8-9; Mason, *Brandeis*, p. 394.

37. *Jewish Advocate*, April 4, 1913, p. 1; LDB to Julius Meyer, April 17, 1913, *BL*, III, 65; LDB to Joseph Shohan, April 30, 1913, and ed. annotations, ibid., 77-78; Avyatar Friesel, *The Zionist Movement in the United States, 1897-1914* [in Hebrew] (Tel-Aviv, Israel, 1970), p. 174.

38. Jacob De Haas, *Louis D. Brandeis, A Biographical Sketch* . . . (New York, 1929), p. 53; LDB to Alice G. Brandeis, June 18, 1919 (on board R.M.S. *Mauretania*), *BL*, IV, 401; De Haas, *Brandeis*, p. 56. *Old Testament Apocrypha* . . . *Ben Sira*, interpreted with preface by E. S. Artom [in Hebrew] (Tel-Aviv, Israel, 1963).

39. *Jewish Advocate*, April 4, 1913, p. 8.

40. Henry F. May, *The End of American Innocence: A Study of the First Years of Our Own Time, 1912-1917* (New York, 1959), pp. 360-362; Melvin I. Urofsky, *American Zionism from Herzl to the Holocaust* (New York, 1975), pp. 118-127; quot., LDB to Zionists of America, August 31, 1914, *BL*, III, 291; LDB to Louis Marshall, August 31, 1914, ibid., 294.

41. Urofsky, *American Zionism*, pp. 120-121, 144-150; De Haas, *Brandeis*, pp. 56-61; Shapiro, *American Zionist Organization*, p. 77. Quots., LDB, "Acceptance of Chairmanship" (address given August 30, 1914), in Barbara A. Harris, "Zionist Speeches of Louis Dembitz Brandeis: A Critical Edition," Ph.D. diss. (University of California, 1967), p. 96.

Index